SPEAKING OUR MINDS

Speaking Our Minds

Why human communication is different, and how language evolved to make it special

Thomas C. Scott-Phillips

palgrave
macmillan

First published 2015 by
PALGRAVE MACMILLAN

Palgrave Macmillan in the UK is an imprint of Macmillan Publishers Limited, registered in England, company number 785998, of Houndmills, Basingstoke, Hampshire RG21 6XS.

Palgrave Macmillan in the US is a division of St Martin's Press LLC, 175 Fifth Avenue, New York, NY 10010.

Palgrave Macmillan is the global academic imprint of the above companies and has companies and representatives throughout the world.

Palgrave® and Macmillan® are registered trademarks in the United States, the United Kingdom, Europe and other countries

ISBN: 978–1–137–33457–2 hardback
ISBN: 978–1–137–33456–5 paperback

This book is printed on paper suitable for recycling and made from fully managed and sustained forest sources. Logging, pulping and manufacturing processes are expected to conform to the environmental regulations of the country of origin.

A catalogue record for this book is available from the British Library.

A catalog record for this book is available from the Library of Congress.

Printed in China

For my parents

Contents

Figures and Tables

Figures

Tables

Acknowledgements

I could of course not have written this book without the help of a great many people. I owe a particularly large intellectual debt to Dan Sperber and Deirdre Wilson, whose *Relevance Theory* provides a compelling paradigm for the study of human communication. I have also drawn heavily on Sperber's subsequent work on the evolution of communication. With the possible exception of Michael Tomasello, Sperber has more than anyone else to date been at pains to emphasize the importance of pragmatics for the origins of human communication and language, a point that I reiterate a number of times in this book. He also provided very valuable comments on an earlier draft of this work.

I was fortunate enough to, in 2009, spend some months in Tomasello's department at the Max Planck Institute for Evolutionary Anthropology in Leipzig. My time there, not only working with Tomasello but also interacting with the other members of his department, was critical for the development of the ideas in this book. Tomasello's influence is especially apparent through his many outstanding experimental studies on the communication and social cognition of human children and the non-human great apes.

My own intellectual development owes a great deal to my two former PhD supervisors, Jim Hurford and Simon Kirby, who introduced me to this topic, and mentored me through my early explorations. I have since learnt from many others too, but I would like to single out the effect that working with Stu West has had on my thinking and my writing, both of which are much sharper than they would otherwise have been.

I would also particularly like to thank Rachael Bailes, Max Burton-Chellew, Tom Dickins, Richard Moore, Cathleen O'Grady, and Andrew Smith, for the more than generous portions of their time they gave to comment on earlier drafts and discuss with me various aspects of this project in detail, and also Martin Edwardes, for his outstanding EAORC service, which keeps me abreast of new developments (look it up if you don't already know about it!). In addition I would like to thank Nicholas Allott, Jean-Baptiste André, Rob Barton, Nicolas Baumard, Tanya Behne, Richard Blythe, Holly Branigan, Erin Brown, Greg Bryant, Robyn Carston, Erica Cartmill, Coralie Chevallier, Nicolas Claidière, Hannah Cornish, Gergely Csibra, Robin Dunbar, Claire el Mouden, Julia Fischer, Jacob Foster, Andy Gardner, Alan Grafen, Gerlind Grosse, Dave Hawkey, Christophe Heintz,

Stefan Hoefler, Keith Jensen, Michael Lachmann, Bob Ladd, Heidi Lyn, Olivier Mascaro, Hugo Mercier, Olivier Morin, Daniel Nettle, Harriet Over, Martin Pickering, Drew Rendall, Graham Ritchie, Gareth Roberts, Sean Roberts, Barbora Skarabela, Katie Slocombe, Kenny Smith, Szabolcs Számadó, Monica Tamariz, Jamie Tehrani, Carrie Theisen-White, Daniel Wedgwood, and James Winters, all of whom have, at different times and in different ways, helped me develop the ideas in this book.

Finally, I would like to thank my parents, for their love and support, and Tamsin Saxton, who has provided me with both personal and professional support in far greater quantities than anybody has any right to expect.

Publisher's acknowledgements

The publisher and author would like to thank the organizations and people listed below for permission to reproduce material from their publications:

Figure 2.2 is reprinted from Scott-Phillips, T. C., & Kirby, S. (2013). Information, influence and inference in language evolution. In: U. E. Stegmann (Ed.), *Animal Communication Theory: Information and Influence* (pp. 421–442). Cambridge: Cambridge University Press. It is reprinted under a Creative Common license BY-NC-SA https://creativecommons.org/licenses/by-nc-sa/2.0/legalcode

Figure 3.1 is reprinted from GET FUZZY © 2009 Darby Conley. Used by permission of UNIVERSAL UCLICK for UFS. All rights reserved.

Figure 3.2 is reprinted from *Animal Behaviour*, *79*(1), Scott-Phillips, T., Animal communication: Insights from linguistic pragmatics, e1–e4, 2010, with permission from Elsevier.

Figure 5.1 is reprinted from *Cognitive Science*, *31*(6), Garrod, S., Fay, N., Lee, J., Oberlander, J., & MacLeod, T., Foundations of representation: Where might graphical symbol systems come from?, 961–987, 2007, with permission from John Wiley and Sons, copyright 2007 Cognitive Science Society, Inc.

Preface

This book is about the origins and evolution of human communication and language. This topic has at different times engaged a highly eclectic set of intellectuals including, to pick just the highest-profile examples, Jean-Jacques Rousseau, Charles Darwin, and Noam Chomsky. It is telling that each member of even this very short list is principally associated with a different academic discipline: philosophy, biology, and linguistics, respectively. A longer list of individuals would likely entail a longer list of traditional disciplines – because how and why humans, and only humans, came to have language are questions that span and are relevant to a heterogeneous collection of disciplines. In addition to the above three, it is also an important topic for anthropology, cognitive science, and primatology, among others. This broad relevance reflects the central role that language and communication play in human life.

This multidisciplinarity can be an obstacle to productive research. Contemporary academia is highly partitioned: each discipline and subdiscipline has its own specialized, often highly-concentrated body of knowledge, its own set of established problems, its own methods and methodological assumptions, and its own doyens and factions, many of which have deep sociological and historical roots. Such circumstances discourage attempts to relate the explanatory frameworks of one discipline to those of another. Instead, researchers are encouraged (sometimes explicitly, and sometimes more implicitly, by the way the profession is structured) to identify a particular niche in which they can become expert. The effect is that these niches become insulated from one another. Fields of specialist understanding develop, but bridges between those fields are left to decay, if they ever existed at all.

At least for the origins and evolution of language, this state of affairs is, fortunately, now changing. In the past two decades or so the topic has established itself as an area worthy of study in its own right, and new university courses dedicated to it spring up each year (my own introduction was through what was then a new MSc in the *Evolution of Language and Cognition*, at the University of Edinburgh). Many people now complete doctoral research in the area, and regular conferences and workshops allow researchers with different intellectual backgrounds to share knowledge and expertise. The first textbook was published in 2013 (McMahon

& McMahon). An interdisciplinary body of knowledge has now developed around the topic, and we are in a position to outline plausible accounts of the origins of human communication and language that are both theoretically and empirically grounded. This book is my own such outline.

My thesis is that the origin of language was the consequence of the creation of an evolutionarily novel form of communication, called *ostensive communication* (I will define ostensive communication in the first chapter; for now, think of it as 'intentionally overt' communication). Why did ostensive communication and hence language evolve in our species, and no other? The brief answer is that ostensive communication depends upon sophisticated forms of social cognition that are unique to humans, and which evolved in our species as a result of our über-social nature. Once this had emerged, we were able to begin to create shared, conventional codes which in turn, through interaction and usage, became ossified into words, grammar, and the other constituent parts of language.

As this brief summary suggests, *pragmatics* is central to my thesis. Pragmatics is typically thought of as a branch of linguistics. Its domain is not precisely defined, and it is often unfairly treated as peripheral to the mainstream of the discipline. One way to think of the province of pragmatics is to say that if semantics is the study of meaning in an idealized, isolated sense, then pragmatics is the study of meaning in context. It studies, for instance, how what is said is often quite different to what is meant. Understood broadly, this includes questions such as 'How is language used?' and 'What does it do?' Another way to think of pragmatics – and it is in this sense that I say that pragmatics is central to my thesis here – is to say that pragmatics is the study of the communicative basis of language use. A key question is: what cognitive processes are involved in the production and comprehension of linguistic utterances and other, related types of communicative stimuli? One of my central claims is that the evolution of these cognitive processes was a pre-requisite for the emergence of language.

Pragmatics has been too much neglected in language evolution research to date. By way of illustration, the index to *The Oxford Handbook of Language Evolution* lists only 8 pages under 'pragmatics', and none under 'ostension' (Tallerman & Gibson, 2012). In contrast, 213 pages are listed under 'syntax' and related terms, and 145 under 'meaning' and related terms. Others have noted this trend too: "those interested in the evolution of the biological pre-conditions for language have been looking in the wrong place: instead of looking at... the pragmatics of communicative exchange, they've been focussed on the syntax and combinatorics" (Evans & Levinson, 2009, p. 477). One of my main motivations in writing this book has been to correct this neglect, and hence to show how an appreciation of the ostensive nature of linguistic communication sheds light on all facets of the origins of language.

I have tried throughout to avoid specialist language and terminology, and to move through the ideas and arguments at a pace that is accessible to non-experts. As much as possible, I want linguists to understand the parts that are evolutionary biology, I want evolutionary biologists to understand the parts that are cognitive science, and so on. Consequently, readers may find the passages that draw on their own areas of expertise somewhat slow, while others are more challenging, but hopefully still comprehensible – and which sections this is true of will vary from reader to reader. This is probably somewhat inevitable, perhaps even desirable, in a genuinely multi-disciplinary project. Having said that, I see no conflict between making a topic accessible, and making a serious contribution to it. I aim to do both. As such, although the primary audience for this book are academics and students in any of the relevant fields, I have written it such that it should be accessible to anybody willing to make the effort.

You might also find that I do not much emphasize where and how my thesis links with recognizable schools of thought and traditional areas of enquiry within each of the relevant disciplines, or what implications it has for classic debates within those areas. Specialists in the relevant areas will probably be able to read my views between the lines, but I will not explicitly discuss how my thinking relates to, say, linguistic functionalism, or group selection, or the modularity of mind, or indeed any of the many other interesting but tangential topics. There are also a number of topics that are common points of interest and discussion within the literature on language origins, but which I discuss only very briefly, if at all. There are two main reasons for this. First, there are sufficiently many such topics, and links to other disciplines, that I simply do not have the space to deal with each properly. Second, this book is not assembled as a collection of chapters around a common theme, but rather as one extended argument – and as such I want to retain a focus on its central thread throughout. This will be harder to do if I pursue the various interesting asides that one would otherwise be tempted to.

For similar reasons, I have tried, as much as possible, to make my arguments positive ones, in favour of a particular view of the origins of language. I am of course critical of other perspectives where it is necessary or useful to be so, but in some cases I have avoided direct confrontation with some views that differ from my own, in order to maintain a focus on the positive case for my own views.

The book is organized as follows. In Chapter 1, I explain exactly what ostensive communication is, and how it differs from other communication systems. In Chapter 2, I argue that the emergence of anything even remotely like language depended on the prior existence of this ostensive communication. This means that in order to understand the origins of language, we must explain: (i) how ostensive-inferential communication works, and what cognitive abilities make it possible; (ii) how those cognitive abilities evolved; and (iii) how, once ostensive-inferential communication existed, the various communicative conventions (semantic, syntactic, phonological, etc.) that we call language might emerge. Chapters 3 to 5 address each of these points, in turn. In Chapter 6 I discuss questions of adaptation, function, and evolutionary stability in human communication. Finally, in the Epilogue, I summarize how my thesis addresses each of the major questions one might have about the origins and evolution of language. Each chapter ends with a brief summary, and a set of questions that the next chapter will seek to answer. I have also included a glossary of important terms. It is always important to be clear, particularly so with a multidisciplinary audience. Precision over terminology is part of that.

* * *

Chapter 1. *What is ostensive communication? How is it different to other forms of communication? How does linguistic communication relate to this distinction? Is the linguistic code different to the codes used in, say, animal communication, and if so how? What is meaning?*

Chapter 1

Two Approaches to Communication

1.1 "A good old fiddle"

The BBC radio series *The Ape That Got Lucky* was a series of spoof lectures on human evolution. The first episode concentrated on the origins of language and communication. One point made by the presenter, Chris Addison, is that context is critical to successful communication. He illustrates this with an example of a keen but shy violinist who, while at a party, says to you, "Wait until these people have all gone and I'll dig her out and have a good old fiddle". In the context his meaning seems clear but, Addison points out, the same sentence might be understood very differently if uttered at a funeral.

Jokes of this sort make use of the fact that context is critical to understanding what a speaker means. The example that the psycholinguist Steven Pinker uses to make this point comes from the 1960s American comedy *Get Smart*, in which the central character, Maxwell Smart, was assisted by a humanoid robot called Hymie. One of Hymie's most distinctive traits was that he interpreted commands in a highly literal way. The trademark case was "Give me a hand", in response to which Hymie would remove his own hand and pass it to Maxwell. Others included "Kill the light!" (Hymie uses his pistol to shoot the lightbulb), "Get hold of yourself!" (Hymie grasps each of his arms with the other), and "Knock that stuff off!" (Hymie knocks all the paper off the desk). There is a clear difference between Hymie's interpretation of the command and the meaning that Maxwell intended to communicate – and so when Hymie takes Maxwell's words literally, our expectations are violated in a humorous way.

What these and many other examples show is that there is sometimes a big difference between the *literal meaning* of what is said (sometimes called *sentence meaning* or *linguistic meaning* or *utterance meaning*), and the speaker's *intended meaning* (sometimes called *speaker meaning* or *utterer's meaning*). The literal meaning is the 'decoded' meaning, based upon the dictionary definitions of the words used, and the speaker meaning is the meaning that was actually intended. Sometimes the difference between these two is obvious and large, such as in sarcasm, and other times the difference is not so big – but it is always there to some degree. Even an utterance as apparently simple as "It's raining" can have multiple different intended meanings, such as 'I don't want to go out after all', or 'Get the umbrella'. In fact, "It's raining" does not even specify where or when there is rain, yet these facts are critical if the utterance is to be relevant. In short, even the most simple, straightforward utterance can be interpreted in different ways, depending on the context. The technical term for this is *underdeterminacy*: the literal meaning of an utterance underdetermines the speaker meaning (Carston, 2002a; Atlas, 2005). In other words, linguistic communication is never just literal meaning. Literal meaning helps us understand speaker meaning, but it is not the same thing.

My thesis in this book is that the origin of language was the consequence of the creation of an evolutionarily novel form of communication, in which underdeterminacy is an inherent and inevitable feature. Underdeterminacy is often seen as a defective quality for a communication system, one that creates ambiguity and misunderstanding. It is true that such vagaries do follow in its wake, but these characteristics are also assets, since they allow communication to be used in incredibly flexible, creative and indeed funny ways. It was, I will argue, the emergence of such a communication system that allowed our ancestors to create the expressively rich form of communication that we call language. This evolutionarily novel form of communication is called *ostensive-inferential communication*, or just *ostensive communication* for short.

In this opening chapter I will describe exactly what ostensive communication is, and how it differs from other types of communication. To do this, I will describe two different ways of thinking about the very possibility of communication. The first is called the *code model*. It is an intuitive way of thinking about communication, and it provides a good description of most and perhaps all animal communication. However, it is unable to handle the underdeterminacy that is inherent to human communication. In contrast, the second way of thinking about communication, called the *ostensive-inferential model* (or just *ostensive model*, for short), was developed to account for these realities. Having described these two approaches, I will then expand on several important preliminary issues, including the precise difference between code and ostension, how they interact with one another, the role of 'codes' in language, and the meaning of meaning, among others. These discussions will set the stage for my discussion, in Chapter 2, of exactly why the transition to ostensive communication was so revolutionary.

1.2 The code model

When presented with questions such as 'What is communication?' or 'How does communication work?', most people's intuitions are typically along the following lines: that communication involves the transmission of information, via some communication channel. Information is encoded into a signal, sent along this channel, and then decoded at the other end. If the algorithms for encoding and decoding are appropriately calibrated to one another, then what is encoded at one end is the same as what is decoded at the other end. The result is that information has been transferred, from the signaller to the receiver. This way of thinking about communication is called the *code model*.

The code model combines at least two metaphors of how communication works (Blackburn, 2007). The first is the idea that signals contain messages that are packaged up and sent along some channel, to be unwrapped at the other end. This metaphor is called the *conduit metaphor* (Reddy, 1979; Figure 1.1). (A conduit is a channel for conveying things from one location to another.) The power of this metaphor is illustrated by the degree to which it pervades our everyday language about communication: 'Get your message *across*'; 'His feelings *came through* clearly'; 'I couldn't *extract* the meaning from your writing'; 'I *gave* you that idea', and so on.

The second metaphor that contributes to the code model is the information-theoretic approach to communication developed by Claude Shannon (1948). Here, signals are seen as strings that are to be transmitted along a communication channel (Figure 1.2). The intellectual challenge comes from devising a way to do this that overcomes the presence of noise and error in the transmission process – particular problems for electrical engineering, telecommunications, and other areas that involve the transmission of digital information.

It is not difficult to see how the conduit metaphor and information theory combine to form the essence of the code model: 'information' is packaged up and then transmitted along a conduit, to be unwrapped at the other end. Having said that, the code model is not so much the precise summation of these two metaphors, but rather a general background assumption about how communication works that has been greatly influenced by them.

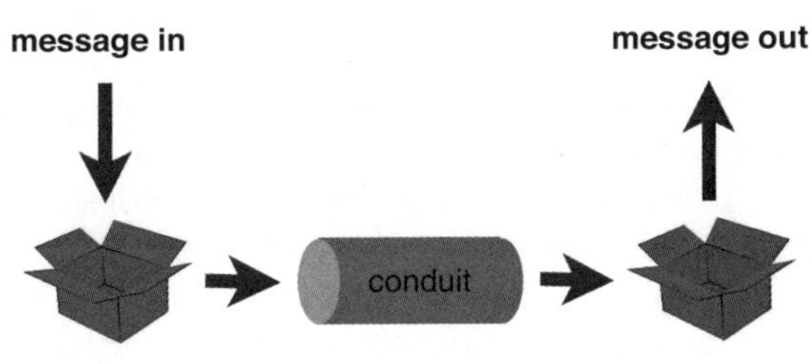

Figure 1.1 *The conduit metaphor.* In the conduit metaphor, communication involves the packaging of messages, which are then to be passed along a conduit, to be unwrapped at the other end.

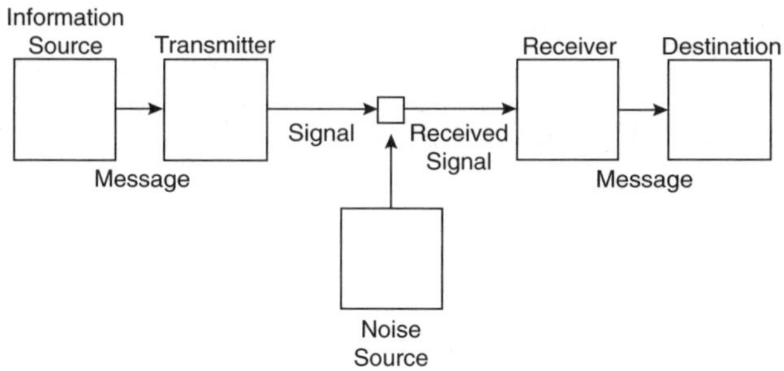

Figure 1.2 *The information-theoretic approach to communication.* Information is encoded, and then transmitted as a signal. During the transmission process, the signal may become distorted due to noise. The received signal is then decoded. Information theory provided a way for the processes of encoding and decoding to counteract the effect of the noise.

The code model has had impact on a great many researchers in a diverse range of disciplines. One particularly salient example is in the study of animal communication, where there are many examples of this way of thinking (Rendall et al., 2009). Here are three definitions of communication taken from that literature: "the provision of information from a sender to a receiver" (Bradbury & Vehrencamp, 1998, p. 2); "...the transmission of information from one animal to another. Information is encoded by one individual into a signal. When received by another animal, this information undergoes decoding..." (Green & Marler, 1979, p. 73); "the transfer of information via signals sent in a channel between a sender and a receiver" (Hailman, 1977, p. 52). And here is a definition of animal communication from a linguist: "One organism has a message in mind that he or she wants to communicate to another organism. He or she emits some behavior...that encodes that message. The other organism...perceives the behavior, identifies it in terms of the meaning encoded, and treats the result of that decoding as the meaning of the message" (Anderson, 2006, p. 17). There are many more definitions with a similar flavour.

The code model is highly intuitive, and can be used as a way to describe many instances of communication in a very simple and general way. As an example, consider bacterial communication. Many species of bacteria communicate by a process known as quorum sensing, in which individual bacterial cells produce small diffusible signal molecules in particular local environments (Schuster et al., 2003; Wagner et al., 2003). These molecules bind to cognate receptors on other bacteria, and in doing so effectively reveal the presence of the bacterium in the local environment. When the concentration of these molecules reaches a threshold level (the quorum), it triggers population-wide behaviour, such as gene regulation (Williams et al., 2007; Ng & Bassler, 2009). Such interactions are most easily described in terms of a code. The encoding algorithm is something like 'If in environment *X*, produce molecule *Y*', and the decoding algorithm something like 'If the concentration of molecule *Y* is above the threshold *t*, then perform behaviour *Z*'.

Following this logic, one student of animal communication once compiled a six-signal 'dictionary' for grasshoppers (Moles, 1963, pp. 125–126). It reads:

> Signal I: It is fine, life is good.
>
> Signal II: I would like to make love.
>
> Signal III: You are trespassing on my territory.
>
> Signal IV: She's mine.
>
> Signal V: Oh, how nice it would be to make love!
>
> Signal VI: How nice to have made love!

A dictionary like this is, in effect, a description of a code.

Communication of this sort depends upon mechanisms of association. In signallers, certain states of the world are associated with the production of particular signals; and in receivers, the reception of those same signals is associated with particular behaviours. In fact, this associativity is the defining feature of the code model. If communication is made possible by associations, it is, by definition, an instance of code model communication.

These associations can be more or less complex. For example, in many species signal production depends in part on whether an audience is around, and if so, what sort of audience that is. This is called *audience design* (see e.g. Gyger et al., 1986 for a review of audience design in chickens). Sensitivity to the existence and nature of the audience does not, however, imply that the system is not explicable in associative terms. It just means that the associations are nuanced to these environmental cues (i.e. the code might be 'if there is a leopard in the environment, and also members of my group/kin, then produce the relevant alarm call').

Some cases of human communication are explicable in the same associative terms. The ring of pigmented skin that surrounds nipples is called the areola. The areolar glands of new mothers secrete chemical compounds, which signal to newborns the location of the nipple, and hence of milk and its various nutrients (Doucet et al., 2009). In effect, this 'chemosignal' allows the mother's body to communicate with the infant's body. In terms of the code model, the encoding algorithm is 'if having just given birth, secrete chemical *X*', and the decoding algorithm is 'if *X* is detected, then move towards it'. Tears are also thought to contain a chemosignal, one that causes sympathy in others (Gelstein et al., 2011). It is likely that there are many more signals, chemical or otherwise, by which human bodies communicate with one another.

Another instance of code model communication in humans is involuntary laughter. Involuntary laughter is often called 'Duchenne' laughter, after the French physician who first distinguished the different muscles used in 'real' and 'faked' smiles. Several strands of research suggest that involuntary laughter serves a communicative function, namely to express social solidarity (Gervais & Wilson, 2005). Evidence also suggests that laughter in humans and laughter in the other great apes are evolutionary homologues of one another; that is, they both descended from the same common ancestral behaviour (van Hooff, 1972; Davila Ross et al., 2009; Bryant & Aktipis, 2014).

The same is likely to be true of several other behaviours such as snorting, smiling, frowning, sighing, pouting, and so on, which all occur in both humans and other animals, and have been hypothesized to serve a communicative function of some kind, typically one that involves managing social relations (Darwin, 1872; Owren & Bachorowski, 2003; Davila Ross et al., 2009). Monkey alarm calls fall into this box too: several lines of evidence, in particular common neural organization, suggest that these calls are homologous to spontaneous human emotional vocalizations, and not speech (Owren et al., 2011). The term 'gesture-calls' has been proposed as a label for the human forms of these behaviours, because of the evolutionary relationship that they share with the communicative gestures and calls of our primate cousins (Burling, 1993; 2005). The term has not caught on, but the idea that this class of behaviours should have an identifying label is correct. Regardless, the key point for the present purposes is that we communicate with these behaviours, and this communication is describable with the code model.

The point I am making is not that chemosignals and involuntary laughter operate by similar mechanisms. On the contrary, there are plainly many differences. The point I am making is instead that despite these differences, chemosignals and involuntary laughter (and grasshopper calls, and quorum sensing) do share one basic quality in common, which is that they depend upon *associations* of one sort or another, and are hence describable in the terms of the code model. This will be important shortly, when we come to contrast these examples with language and some other forms of human communication.

There are two final points that I should make about code model communication. The first is that it does not require that encoding and decoding be fully deterministic. Production and reception may be more flexible than this. For example, they could be used probabilistically instead. In this case, the code might read: if *X*, then do *Y* with a certain probability, and *Z* with some other probability (rather than simply 'if *X*, then do *Y*'). Computational models of the evolution of communication show that signalling systems can still emerge and be useful when these probabilistic codes are used (Vogt, 2002; Smith, 2005; Steels, 2011). Indeed, it seems likely to me that many cases of animal communication operate at least to some extent in this way.

Because they are not fully deterministic, such systems have been described as inferential (e.g. Smith, 2005). However they are still, strictly speaking, instances of the code model, because the basic paradigm remains one in which producers are prompted to transmit signals for particular meanings, which receivers then decode. Both production and reception are still associative, albeit in a probabilistic way.

The other point I want to make is that the competent use of code model communication systems is not necessarily a cognitively trivial task. For one thing, probabilistic codes can involve a great deal of complexity. But more than that, this type of communication can, in some cases, also involve a great deal of social intelligence. Of particular relevance to my concerns in this book is the possibility that code model communication systems can be used in an intentional way. I will discuss this possibility further in Chapter 4; here, I simply want to use it to make the point that just because a communication system may be predicated on associations, that does not, *a priori*, make it simple or unsophisticated.

From what I can gather, the label 'code model' appears to have been coined by the cognitive scientists Dan Sperber and Deirdre Wilson, in their seminal book *Relevance: Communication and Cognition* (1995). In that book, not to mention many further publications since, they contrasted the code model with an alternative way of thinking about communication. The next two sections present this alternative.

1.3 The expression and recognition of intentions

The code model depends upon associations, but there are some instances of communication that are simply not explicable in associative terms. For example, suppose that a couple have had a number of conversations about, say, a particular TV show, which many people think is brilliant, but which they both agree is terrible. Now suppose that they head to a party one evening, and a friend of theirs starts telling them how great he thinks the show is. The friend then leaves the conversation. One half of the couple wants to acknowledge to the other half that this is just the sort of thing they had been talking about. To do this, she can improvise and use an indefinite variety of behaviours: a raised eyebrow; puffed cheeks; a glance over the shoulder; sticking her tongue out; and many others. There is no code in operation here: none of these behaviours is conventionally associated with her intended meaning, even probabilistically. There is something else going on, something that requires an alternative to the code model. In this section I lay the foundations for the presentation, in the following section, of just such an alternative.

We all mentally represent the world in some way. For example, right now my mental representations include the knowledge that Durham is in England, the belief that tomorrow will be sunny, and my intention to write another 1,000 words before the end of the day. As this list of examples illustrates, mental representations can take several different forms: beliefs, assumptions, goals, knowledge, and so on. These representations can change, in particular when we are provided with new inputs that suggest we should change our existing representations in some way, or create new ones. For example, if I look up the weather forecast and it predicts rain tomorrow, I may, depending on how much I trust the forecast, update my belief about tomorrow's weather.

Often, we wish to change the mental representations of others. Right now, I wish and intend to change your mental representations about mental representations (or perhaps create new ones, if you have never thought about them before). When preparing dinner, I may wish and intend to create in my partner a belief that I need some help chopping the vegetables. To try and satisfy such intentions, we provide evidence for them, in the expectation that the audience will be able to infer what our intentions are, and act to satisfy them. Exactly what the evidence will consist of will depend both on the change the signaller is trying to cause, and the targeted individual's existing representations. In the case of the vegetables, one way to make my partner believe that I need help might be to push a large pile of unchopped vegetables, and a knife, in her general direction. Note that for this to work, she needs to already have a mental representation about how knives are used, and one that vegetables are normally chopped before cooking. Armed with these representations, and others, she is able to make appropriate inferences about what I intended by my actions. In this case, her representations (about whether I needed help) were easy to change, but in other cases (e.g. political views) they may not be.

An *informative intention* is a signaller's intention that the receiver change their representation of the world in response to the signaller's behaviour. I have an informative intention that my partner recognize that I need help chopping the vegetables. If you ask someone in the street for directions, you have an informative intention that the passer-by believe that you are lost, and need help. Here is a third example: I am in a coffee shop, I catch the eye of the waiter, and I tilt my coffee cup in a particular, somewhat stylized way. The waiter then comes over and refills my cup. Here, I have an informative intention that the waiter understands that I would like a refill. And so on. The content of an informative intention is, in colloquial terms, the information that it provides. More specifically, it is the changes that the signaller wants to make to the receiver's mental representations.

Informative intentions are not the only sort of intention involved in this sort of communication. The tilt of my coffee cup expresses my informative intention, but it also expresses something just as important: the very fact that I wish to communicate with the waiter at all. After all, I could be tilting the coffee cup incidentally. This is something that happens all the time, such as when chatting to friends. How does the tilt reveal to the waiter that it is a signal? In other words, how does it signal its own signalhood, and how does the waiter recognize as much (Scott-Phillips et al., 2009)? These questions highlight that in addition to an intention to make it clear to the waiter that she wants more coffee, I must also make it clear to the waiter that I am trying to communicate with him at all. My intention to do this – that is, my intention to create in my audience a representation of the fact that I have an informative intention – is called a *communicative intention*. This intention is expressed when I establish eye contact with the waiter and tilt my cup in a particular, *ostensive*, way.

If I did not make eye contact, and did not tilt my in an ostensive way, I would only be expressing an informative intention – and the waiter would likely never know that this is what I am doing. In short, if the expression of an informative intention is not accompanied by the expression of communicative intention too, then the intended audience would never know that they are the intended audience, and communication would not occur.

There are, then, two types of intention involved in this type of communication. One, the informative intention, is an intention that one's audience recognize *what* one is trying to communicate (for example, that I want more coffee). The other, the communicative intention, is an intention that one's audience recognizes *that* one is trying to communicate; in other words, that one has an informative intention. Another way to say this is to say that the content of a communicative intention is an informative intention. Signals that express communicative intentions, and hence informative intentions, are called *ostensive* signals.

Typically, both types of intention are expressed in one and the same behaviour, such as the tilt of the coffee cup. Here is another example (from Sperber, 2000). Mary is eating berries. She wants Peter to know that she thinks that the berries are very tasty, so she eats them in a somewhat exaggerated, stylized way, and pats her tummy as she does so. This reveals two things to Peter: (i) that Mary thinks the berries are tasty (this is the content of her informative intention); and (ii) that Mary wants to communicate this fact to Peter (this is the content of her communicative intention). If Mary simply ate the berries enthusiastically, but did not do so in any stylized or exaggerated way, Peter would still be able to infer that they are tasty, but not because Mary had expressed either an informative or a communicative intention. There would be no communication in that case. (I will define communication and other, related terms in the next chapter.)

Other cases illustrate that sometimes the content of the informative intention can be so transparent from the context that it does not need to be expressed by the signal itself. Then the signal has to do little more than make it apparent that communication is taking place i.e. it only has to express a communicative intention. The couple who communicate their views about a TV programme with a non-specific behaviour like puffed cheeks are an example. The puffed cheeks express the woman's communicative intention, but only very loosely express the content of her informative intention. This is because the context (the just concluded conversation, combined with the memory of the couple's previous private conversations) does so much work that explicit expression of the content of the informative intention is unnecessary.

In this respect, this example is different to, say, the coffee shop example. In that context, an ostensive signal directed at the waiter could potentially have one of several possible meanings (e.g. 'Can I have the bill?', 'I'd like an extra slice of carrot cake', and so on). Consequently the signal has to not only express a customer's communicative intention, but also specify the content of the informative intention. It is this latter concern that explains why it takes the particular form that it does. A different ostensive signal (e.g. a mime of signing a cheque) would express a different informative intention. In contrast, the puffed cheeks could have been replaced by one of several other possible behaviours, so long as the behaviour was produced ostensively, and the meaning would have remained more-or-less the same – because the content of the informative intention was mostly derived from the context.

A common response when presented with this account of what is involved in communication is to suggest that it is overblown, or over-theorized. It seems to be a complex description of something that is instinctively much simpler. In particular, the embedding of an informative intention inside a communicative intention might be seen as theoretically unnecessary, since on an intuitive level an informative intention alone seems sufficient. I will address these complaints in detail in Chapter 3, but let me here make one short point: that just because a formal description of a phenomenon is complex, this does not mean that we necessarily experience it as complex. A formal description of what is involved in, say, vision, is a mighty complex thing, but our conscious experience makes it seem far more straightforward than that. So there is no *a priori* reason to think that the fact that there is a disparity between our instinctive, everyday experience of communication and this formal description is problematic.

We are now ready and able to set out an alternative to the code model of communication. It is called the *ostensive-inferential model.*

1.4 The ostensive-inferential model

Ostensive-inferential communication is the expression and recognition of informative and communicative intentions (Sperber & Wilson, 1995). This expression and recognition is achieved by the appropriate use of evidence: signallers provide evidence for their intentions, and receivers interpret it (*ibid.*). This evidence can come in many forms, such as points, shrugs, vocalizations (including language) and indeed potentially any physical act that the signaller can perform. The receiver must then take this evidence and draw an inference about the signaller's informative and communicative intentions, and hence about the meaning the signaller intends to convey. Signallers and receivers thus perform distinct but complementary jobs in successful communication: the former provide evidence, and the latter interpret it. This is why the phrase 'ostensive-inferential' is double-barrelled: ostension is the provision of evidence; inference the interpretation. Nevertheless, 'ostensive-inferential' is a cumbersome term, and so from hereon I will often use the shortened terms *ostensive communication* and *ostensive model*, especially in later chapters.

This provision and interpretation of evidence contrasts with the associative processes of encoding and decoding employed in the code model. The puffed cheeks example illustrates the point most clearly. Suppose, quite reasonably, that the couple have never previously used that behaviour to communicate with one another – or even that they had never previously used it to communicate with anybody at all. If so, there is no way that it could be *associated* with the meaning the woman wishes to express. Furthermore, even if the puffed cheeks had become associated with something like lack of approval, this does not encode all that is relevant here: it does not, for one thing, encode what it is that is being disapproved. As such, the puffed cheeks cannot work as a piece of code model communication. Nevertheless, they could and indeed are likely to still be successful as a signal. This is because what such cases ultimately depend on is not the existence and use of any pre-existing associations, but rather the abilities of signallers and receivers to reason about each other's intentions and other mental states.

There is, then, a clear difference in the cognitive abilities required for ostensive-inferential communication, and those required for code model communication. The latter require the ability to form associations. This can be a simple task. Indeed, in its most basic form it is so simple that even bacteria can do it. Ostension and inference, on the other hand, are more complex. This is because the sort of evidence required for a particular intended meaning is specific to the current time, place, and intended audience, among other things (Sperber & Wilson, 1995). This means that to construct appropriate signals, signallers must take into account not just what it is they wish to communicate, but also their knowledge and beliefs about what their audience already knows or believes, given the current context. Receivers must do something similar, but in reverse: they must take into account not just the form that the signal takes, but also the context and their knowledge and beliefs about the signaller's general motivations and intentions (*ibid.*).

To illustrate, consider again the example of Mary eating berries in a way that makes it apparent to Peter that she thinks that the berries are tasty. Suppose now that Mary knows that Peter is curious about whether the berries are tasty or not, and Peter knows that Mary knows this. Now, Mary's intended meaning (that the berries are tasty) is the same as previously, but her knowledge of Peter's goals is different. Consequently, she produces a different behaviour: because she knows that Peter wants to know how the berries taste, all she does is nod approvingly; the exaggerated mime of pleasure that she performed in the previous scenario is unnecessary. As for Peter, he knows that Mary knows that he is curious about the tastiness of the berries, and so he is able to interpret her nodding correctly – *but he would not be able to do this if he did not have the knowledge that Mary knows about his curiosity*. What this shows (and many similar examples could be created or observed) is that exactly what sort of evidence is appropriate for a given intended meaning is not fixed, or even probabilistic; instead, it depends upon a range of contextual factors – and these include, in particular, the prospective signaller's beliefs and knowledge about the beliefs and knowledge of the intended conversation partner. The same is true of interpretation as well. As such, successful ostensive-inferential communication depends upon abilities to reason about others' minds, beliefs, knowledge, and so on. In short, it is inherently *metapsychological*: it is only possible between individuals able to think about each other's thoughts, to reason about each other's reasons, and so on.

This is, then, the crucial difference between ostensive-inferential communication and code model communication. They are made possible by different internal mechanisms. That is, *the mechanisms that are causally responsible for the existence of each type of communication are different in each case*: associations on the one hand, metapsychology on the other. Put in different but equivalent terms, the difference between these two types of communication is that in one, the signaller encodes the content, while in the other she provides evidence that she has a communicative intention to express some specific content.

Correspondingly, while the evolutionary function of both types of signal is to cause changes in the receiver's behaviour, the more immediate function is to do this in quite different ways: the production of ostensive stimuli is designed to change mental states, while the production of encoded stimuli is designed to trigger associative responses. (This difference between evolutionary and more immediate functions is typically called the ultimate/proximate distinction. I shall say more about it in §1.6.)

Another way to think about the difference between code and ostension is that it is analogous to the difference between mathematics and science. In mathematics, the correct answer to a question is determined using logical operators (e.g. +, −, ×, ÷, etc.), and as such when we use these operators we know, with certainty, that the answer arrived at is the correct answer to the question posed, so long as the inputs are correct and the operators have been correctly applied. In contrast, in science we can only amass evidence for the answer to a question, and so we can never *know*, with certainty, whether a proposed answer is correct. Instead we must make inferences about the most likely correct answer, given the evidence. Indeed, this is the very essence of what science is.

Similarly, because the code model is built on associations, then if a receiver assumes that these associations are correctly applied then she can fully (i.e. with 100 per cent certainty) determine what a particular signal means. (In the probabilistic cases, the receiver knows with certainty what the probability is that a particular signal has a particular meaning.) However in ostensive-inferential communication the audience is only ever supplied with evidence for an intended meaning, and so the best she can do is make inferences based upon that evidence – and to make these inferences, she must reason, just as the scientist must, about both the data she receives (the form the signal takes), and the conditions under which it was observed (what she already knows about the signaller's intentions, beliefs, knowledge, and other mental states). Furthermore, the signaller must also create the right sort of evidence, and this too requires reasoning about the other party's mental states. As such, these acts of ostension and inference are analogous to, respectively, the production and interpretation of scientific data.

Is there a third type of communication, with a different foundation still? None presently exists ("There just is not to this day... a third type of explanation of the very possibility of communication" (Origgi & Sperber, 2000, p. 149)). Unless and until philosophical research is able to generate a third account of how communication can even exist, these are our only two options. This is, incidentally, not an empirical question, but a conceptual/philosophical one. The question is: how is communication even possible? The code model and the ostensive-inferential model provide two possible answers to this question. No other answers presently exist.

1.5 Natural codes and conventional codes

Where does linguistic communication fit in to this distinction between these two different models of communication? The typical intuition is that it operates according to the code model. After all, there are clearly reliable associations between linguistic signals and their meanings: the word 'cat' is reliably associated with feline animals, for example. Many linguists consider this characterization at least sufficiently accurate to operate as a background assumption to their research (Reddy, 1979; Blackburn, 2007). Yet it is clearly not the whole story. We have already observed, in the opening passages to this chapter, how language is replete with metaphors, allusions and other figurative expressions that express far more than the literal, 'decoded' meanings of what is said. Furthermore, language is not the only piece of evidence that helps listeners determine a speaker's intended meaning. Other aspects of production, such as intonation and body language, are important too. For example, even an utterance as simple as "I'll see you later" can have a wide range of quite different speaker meanings, depending on the manner of its delivery, which could express, say, conviviality (such as from one friend to another, for example), a threatening attitude (from a bully to a victim), a prediction (from one work colleague to another), a request (from a suitor to his beau), or any one of numerous other dispositions. To determine between these readings, and indeed to use them appropriately, we must reason about our conversational partner's mental states. Linguistic communication clearly involves some use of ostension and inference, in addition to the linguistic code.

There is, then, a question about the relationship between the linguistic code on the one hand, and the role of ostension and inference, and pragmatics more generally, on the other. One way to conceive of this relationship is as follows: the development of widely shared associations between signals and meanings – codes – is what makes language possible, and the human capacity for ostension and inference then makes it especially powerful i.e. able to express an extremely wide range of propositions. This conception of the role of pragmatics in communication is the dominant one in mainstream, contemporary linguistics, although it is rarely if ever stated quite so explicitly. It is reflected in, for example, the textbooks, encyclopaedia entries and other material designed to provide a basic statement of the discipline's domain of enquiry: in the vast majority of cases, those aspects of language that involve the code (in particular, but not only, syntax and semantics) are presented as the central, core concerns, while pragmatics and other phenomena that are not easily accountable in terms of a code are presented as peripheral topics. The implicit assumption is that languages are, when stripped to their most basic features, extremely rich coding schemes. Thus, the code lies at the heart of the standard conception of language. Ostension and inference are bonus add-ons.

Evolutionary approaches have, for the most part, also adopted this assumption, although here too it is almost never expressed explicitly. Instead, it is a background assumption, of which we can observe only the surface manifestations (Scott-Phillips & Kirby, 2013). One such manifestation is the language used to describe linguistic communication. Let me quote a passage from a seminal paper in the field. It is littered with the terminology of the code model in general, and information theory in particular: "the vocal-auditory *channel* has some desirable features as a medium of communication: it has a *high bandwidth*... however it is essentially a *serial interface*... the basic tools of a *coding scheme* employing it are an *inventory* of distinguishable symbols and their *concatenation*" (Pinker & Bloom, 1990, p. 713, italics added).

A second manifestation of the assumption that languages are at their core very rich coding schemes is the research techniques used, and the questions that are pursued. For instance, there is a small industry of mathematical and computational models of the origins and evolution of signalling systems, which frequently extend their methods and claims to encompass language. Indeed, such models comprise a significant proportion of all research that purports to study language origins (see Kirby, 2002; Steels, 2011 for reviews of the computational models; and Skyrms, 2010 for detailed discussion of mathematical models). It is worthwhile to enter into a short discussion of these models to illustrate the general approach employed here.

A typical model frames communication as follows. There is a pre-defined set of possible states of the world. Which one actually applies at any given time is determined at random. This state then triggers the production of one member of a similarly pre-defined set of signals, which in turn triggers the production of one of a set of responses, also pre-defined. As such, the signaller's strategy is a set of mappings, from the states of the world to the signals they produce in each case; and the receiver's strategy a set of mappings from signals to responses.

The simplest possible model of this sort has two states (*A* and *B*), two signals (1 and 2), and two responses (*a* and *b*), with payoffs that are maximized if and only if state *A* leads to response *a* and state *B* to response *b*. If we then assume, for simplicity, that signallers will produce different signals for different states, and that receivers will produce different reactions for each different signal, then there are just two possible strategies for each player:

signaller strategy 1 (S1): state *A* ⟶ signal 1
state *B* ⟶ signal 2
signaller strategy 2 (S2): state *A* ⟶ signal 2
state *B* ⟶ signal 1
receiver strategy 1 (R1): signal 1 ⟶ response *a*
signal 2 ⟶ response *b*
receiver strategy 2 (R2): signal 1 ⟶ response *b*
signal 2 ⟶ response *a*

It is not hard to see that in such a game, the pairs <S1, R1> and <S2, R2> are equilibria. In these cases, state *A* leads to response *a*, and state *B* to response *b*, and hence payoffs are maximized. That is not the case with the pairs <S1, R2> and <S2, R1>. As such, if this set of strategies is subject to natural selection, one or the other of <S1, R1> and <S2, R2> will be the outcome (Skyrms, 2010). This basic game can be made more complex in numerous different ways, most obviously by manipulating the number of possible states, or signals, the probabilities of the different states, the payoffs associated with each outcome, and other component parts.

However, we need not enter into such details, because this basic sketch is sufficient to make the following, important point: that such models operate according to the code model. We know this because the associations that exist between states and signals, and between signals and responses, are associations that make communication *possible*; remove either of them, and there is no communication. This is the very definition of the code model. A great deal of research in language origins uses such models, to address topics such as the conditions under which shared codes can emerge. I am thinking here not only of mathematical models like the one above, but also the many computational models that have for a long time been a staple of the discipline (see Kirby, 2002; Steels, 2011 for reviews).

Yet any assumption that codes are what make linguistic communication possible in the first place, and ostension and inference are what make it powerful, is wrong. It is upside down. Instead, ostension and inference make communication possible, and the development of widely shared associations between signals and meanings is what makes it linguistic, and hence expressively powerful (Sperber & Wilson, 1995; Origgi & Sperber, 2000). We know this because if we consider what is actually entailed by these two alternative accounts of how linguistic communication works, it soon becomes apparent that only the ostension-makes-it-possible-and-codes-make-it-powerful account is plausible. The codes-make-it-possible-and-ostension-makes-it-powerful account is not.

To see why, recall the notion of underdeterminacy: the fact that linguistic meaning underdetermines speaker meaning (Carston, 2002a; Atlas, 2005). The existence of underdeterminacy is widely acknowledged. The most obvious examples are referring expression (e.g. pronouns, demonstratives), and figurative uses of language, such as sarcasm and irony, but there are a great many others, such as understatement, similes, and indirectness, and I gave some examples of these in the opening to this chapter. What is less appreciated is how far this underdeterminacy extends. We have already seen how even an apparently transparent utterance such as "I'll see you later" can have multiple different interpretations, and further examples are not difficult to provide. "Higher!", "It's raining", "Yes, please": all are open to multiple interpretations, depending on context. In other words, the literal meaning of each of these is more-or-less clear, but this is insufficient to determine the speaker's intended meaning. In fact, when we begin to study linguistic communication in this light, what we see is that there is underdeterminacy in *any and every* utterance you care to produce (Carston, 2002a; Atlas, 2005).

The problem is not the tractable one that literal meanings may correspond to more than one of a still finite number of speaker meanings, and that we must choose between them. It is far more serious than that. For any literal meaning, there is an *infinite* range of possible speaker meanings. To illustrate, consider again "It's raining". Two possible speaker meanings are, as I mentioned earlier, 'I don't want to go out after all' and 'Get the umbrella'. But here is a third: 'Even the weather can't lighten my mood'. And a fourth: 'I told you so!' I could go on, and that is the point. Here, then, is the challenge for the skeptic who doubts the ubiquity of underdeterminacy: describe an utterance and a corresponding list of possible speaker meanings that is *wholly* exhaustive, in the sense that there are no other possible speaker meanings whatsoever. This task is, I submit, impossible: given an utterance with literal meaning, and a list of possible speaker meanings that the literal meaning might be used to express, it is *always* possible to add another possible speaker meaning to the list.

One consequence of this fact is that the linguistic code cannot make linguistic communication possible. The existence and ubiquity of underdeterminacy means that the meaning that a speaker intends when they produce an utterance cannot ever be determined by analysis of the literal meaning of the utterance alone. In short: linguistic utterances are, on their own, unable to specify speaker meaning, and hence they logically cannot make any sort of communication possible.

To put the point another way: *as codes*, languages are very defective indeed. In fact, they are wholly ineffectual (Origgi & Sperber, 2000). Here is a simple illustration. Consider the following dialogue:

MARY: Would you like to join us for dinner?

PETER: I ate earlier.

The important thing to notice about Peter's response is that it does not, *on its own*, tell Mary anything at all that is relevant to her enquiry. It is only with the addition of context and shared knowledge (for instance, the knowledge that people do not eat two meals in one evening) that Peter's meaning becomes clear. The linguistic code is insufficient for communication to take place, but communication will still succeed – so it cannot be the linguistic code that makes linguistic communication possible. If Hymie the humanoid robot really could only process literal meaning, then it would not be only metaphors and similes that caused him problems. Every utterance would.

On the other hand, ostension and inference do make possible a form of communication onto which we can add linguistic codes, and in doing so provide our ostensive communication with a great deal of expressive power. We have already seen several examples of how ostension and inference can be used to communicate without language. All could be augmented by the use of sounds and/or gestures that are reliably, typically associated with certain referents. The phrase 'More coffee, please' could be said as I tilt my coffee cup; the word 'Idiot!' could be added to the puffed cheeks; Mary could say 'Yum!' to emphasize how tasty the berries are. These codes provide a way for us to say what we would otherwise have to show, and the consequence is that ostensive-inferential communication can be used far more precisely, and more expressively, than it otherwise would be (Wharton, 2003b). In this sense, linguistic communication is simply a very important special case of ostensive communication, one in which that ostensive communication is augmented by the linguistic code. In other words, ostension and inference are logically prior to the linguistic code.

In fact, the ambiguity that makes languages such ineffectual codes here becomes a huge asset, because it makes it possible for individual words to be efficiently used to express a diverse – in fact infinite – range of meanings, and in an efficient way too (Piantadosi et al., 2012). There is, then, a critical difference between the codes used in code model communication, and the codes used in language. The former makes a type of communication *possible*, albeit one that is restricted to a finite set of more-or-less fixed meanings. Consequently, whatever ambiguity there is in the system is limited to a finite set of alternatives, some of which will be more probable than others. Linguistic codes, however, are quite different. They do not make communication possible – because on their own, they have an unlimited range of things they might refer to, and hence they create unresolvable ambiguities. Instead, they are added to a foundation of ostension and inference, and in doing so they make that type of communication incredibly *powerful*. I can nonverbally but ostensively point to any of the objects in this room, but with language I can refer to any object in the world. I can make a request of others by pushing unchopped vegetables in their direction, but with language I can make requests about things remote in time and space. Languages make ostensive communication special.

In short, there is a qualitative difference between the codes used in the code model, and the linguistic code. Put simply, one makes a type of communication possible, the other makes a different type of communication expressively powerful. (In philosophical terms, they have different ontologies.) This difference is widely unappreciated, not only in evolutionary approaches to language, but in fact in the study of language and communication more generally.

Consequently, we invite misunderstanding if we use the same term, 'code', to describe both the linguistic code, which forms part of an ostensive-inferential communication system, and the code used in communication that is based upon the code model. To call both simply 'code' invites the misplaced assumption that these are two instances of the same sort of communication, which differ only in their degree of complexity. Instead, our terminology should recognize the qualitative difference between them.

Evolution is one area in which a failure to make this distinction can have serious consequences. An important evolutionary question is the extent to which various instances of animal communication are similar, or not, to linguistic communication, but we risk inadvertently pre-judging the matter if we use the same label to describe both. This is not to say that no other species communicates in an ostensive way. Whether they do or not is an empirical question, to which I will turn in Chapter 4. The point is instead that we should not pre-judge the matter by using the same term ('code') to describe both animal and linguistic communication. A failure to do this can lead, in turn, to a presumption that it is parsimonious to assume that the two types of code are evolutionarily related to one another: "we may see in [monkey] alarm calls a skeletal version of our own shared codes" (Hurford, 2007, p. 260). Now, this claim may or may not be true. I shall argue in later chapters that it probably is not, but that is not the point here. Instead, what I want to emphasize is that we cannot simply assume that the essential difference between the linguistic code and the code used in non-human primate communication is a difference of degree, even a large degree. It may instead be a difference of *kind*. And besides, there is certainly a difference of kind somewhere: much non-human communication, such as bacterial quorum sensing, does operate according to the code model, whereas linguistic communication does not. Our terminology should reflect this difference.

I will do this with the labels *natural codes* and *conventional codes* (adopted and partially adapted from Wharton, 2003a). Natural codes are those we observe in systems that operate according to the code model itself. Bacterial quorum sensing, mother-infant chemosignals, grasshopper sounds, gesture-calls, and the various other examples I discussed in §1.2 are all natural codes. In short, natural codes make code model communication possible. In contrast, conventional codes are those codes that enhance and make more expressive and precise an already existing system of ostensive-inferential communication. Languages are conventional codes, but there are other conventional codes too, such as Morse code. I will often simply use the term *conventions* as shorthand for conventional codes. The question for comparative research is: are the codes used in non-human communication natural codes, or conventional codes?

In the UK, one convention is that we drive on the left hand side of the road. We could in principle change this to the right side of the road, if we so wished, so long as we *all* changed our driving behaviour, and at the same time as each other. (Both Sweden, in 1967, and Iceland, in 1968, have done this, changing all the road signs over during the middle of one night.) In the specific context of communication, a conventional code is a reliable association between signal and meaning that holds by virtue of the fact that every member of the community agrees that it holds, and not because of any intrinsic association between the word and the meaning (Lewis, 1969; Clark, 1996). For example, 'dog' refers to canine animals (and not, say, feline ones) only because we all agree that it does. We could in principle all agree to change the word for 'cat' to something else, such as 'tac' (the same sounds, in reverse), and in theory this would not cause any confusion – so long as we all did this, and at the same time as one another.

Conventional codes exist at all levels of linguistic analysis: semantic (the meaning of words), syntactic (the grammar of a language); phonological (the organization of sounds in a language), phonetic (the sounds that are used in a language), and even pragmatic (e.g. in British English, the politeness convention to use indirect requests such as 'Would you mind...', rather than direct requests, wherever possible). It is not hard to see how the expressive potential of ostensive communication explodes with the development of these conventional codes.

Ask 100 linguists what a language is and you'll get 120 different answers. Depending on factors such as their theoretical persuasions, their subdisciplinary background, and their specific areas of interest, they will emphasize or downplay different aspects of it, such as universal properties of languages, the cognitive and psychological foundations of language, its role in thought, its use as a means of communication, and so on. My answer is this: a language is the rich, structured collection of conventional codes that augment ostensive-inferential communication within a given community. Tilting your coffee cup is ostensive but not linguistic, since the tilt does not (really) have a conventionalized meaning, but the words 'Can I have some more coffee please?', and the gestures used in sign languages, both do have conventionalized meanings, and as such are both linguistic. This view of a language as a set of conventional codes that augments ostensive communication recognizes both the pragmatic foundations of linguistic behaviour, and the importance and nature of the conventions that make languages different to other, simpler cases of ostensive-inferential communication, such as points, non-linguistic vocalizations, nods of the head, and so on.

I do not want to enter into a lengthy review of the similarities and differences between this and other views of what a language is, but it is worthwhile to briefly contrast my view with views that focus on structural features. By way of illustration, consider the controversy around Pirahã, a language spoken by an indigenous tribe of hunter-gatherers in the Amazon basin. Some researchers have claimed that Pirahã does not possess *recursion*, a property that other researchers have suggested is critical to language (Everett, 2005). (A language is recursive if some of its linguistic objects are embedded inside versions of the same type. For example, *I like the woman with the hat* has one noun phrase (*the hat*) embedded inside a larger noun phrase (*the woman with the hat*).) Others dispute the claim that Pirahã lacks recursion (e.g. Nevins et al., 2009). What I want to bring attention to is that whichever way this debate is resolved, nobody claims or will claim that Pirahã is not a language. In other words, even if it does lack recursion, that would not be enough, on anybody's terms, to conclude that Pirahã is not a language. Thus, recursion cannot be what makes a language a language. The same goes for all the various structural properties that languages possess: none of them define what a language is, because if we found a language that lacked them, we would not conclude that the observed language is not a language. Indeed, on some analyses there are *no* structural properties that are universal to all languages (Evans & Levinson, 2009). In that case, any attempt to define what a language is by reference to such properties is doomed. What *is* universal, however, is the fact that languages are rich, more-or-less stable collections of conventional codes that are used to augment ostensive-inferential communication.

Languages are not, however, the only way in which ostension and code can interact with one another. There are other ways too. In production, we can use natural codes in an ostensive way. An example is voluntary laughter. As discussed above, involuntary laughter is a natural code, but we can also exercise voluntary control over laughter (called non-Duchenne laughter), and we often do so in an ostensive way. One way of expressing sarcasm, for example, would be to laugh at a friend's supposedly funny joke in a highly- and possibly overly-stylized way that mimics genuine laughter, but which at the same time is obviously not genuine laughter. Such behaviour is ostensive: it expresses my intention that my friend knows that I do not think his joke was funny. The other gesture-calls provide similar examples: snorts, smiles, frowns, sighs, pouts and others can all be used in an ostensive way, in addition to the roles they play as natural codes (Wharton, 2003a).

What examples like this show is that, from an evolutionary perspective, the difference between natural codes and conventional codes is critical. What happens when we combine pragmatics and natural codes is quite different to what happens when we combine pragmatics and conventional codes. In the former case we get the use of natural codes, such as laughter, grunts, and so on, in ostensive ways; in the latter case, we get language.

This difference has a number of important implications for the study of the origins of language. The first is that it simply makes clear exactly what it is that we must explain, namely the origins and evolution of the capacity for ostensive communication, and the emergence and continued use of stable, conventional codes. The second implication is that research into the origins and evolution of codes is only of direct relevance to the origins and evolution of language to the extent that those codes being studied are indeed conventional codes, and not natural codes. Since language is a conventional code, then to study the evolution of natural codes and to use the results of that research to draw direct conclusions about the evolution of conventional codes is a category error. One area where this has occurred is comparative research on the communication systems of at least some non-human primates. I will discuss this research, and the important question of whether non-human primate communication is ostensive or not, in Chapter 4.

If there is one point that underpins everything else in this book, it is the one I have made in this section, namely that the common assumption that the linguistic code makes linguistic communication possible is simply false. Instead, linguistic communication is a type of ostensive-inferential communication, made possible by metapsychology. What the linguistic code does is make it expressively powerful. This insight is certainly not original to me. It has been most clearly developed by Sperber and Wilson, but versions of it run through the whole history of the philosophy of language. What I will do in the rest of this book is to describe the implications that it has for the origins and evolution of human communication and language.

1.6 Two meanings of meaning

There is one final preliminary topic that must be addressed before we proceed. It is the thorny matter of *meaning*, something that is legendarily the stuff of abstruse philosophical enquiry. It is a central concept for communication, yet its connotations differ depending on whether it is used within the context of the code model or the ostensive-inferential model of communication. In this section I describe and defend two ways in which the term can be coherently used. One, with its roots in pragmatics, applies to the ostensive-inferential model. The other, with its roots in evolutionary biology, applies to the code model. We shall see that despite several differences, there are also key features that these two approaches to meaning have in common, and these tell us something important about the nature of communication itself.

Let me start with meaning in pragmatics. One of the founding documents of pragmatics as a discipline is an essay, entitled simply 'Meaning', by the philosopher of language Paul Grice (1957). In it, Grice distinguished between natural and non-natural meaning. He did not give formal definitions of these two terms; rather, he illustrated them by way of examples. *Natural meaning* is meaning that derives from a reliable relationship between one thing in the world and another: those clouds 'mean' rain; those spots 'mean' measles. In contrast, *non-natural meaning* is, roughly, the meaning that we have so far referred to as speaker meaning or intended meaning: Mary 'means' that the berries are tasty; I 'mean' that I would like more coffee. It was this idea of non-natural meaning that Grice developed further; he said little more about natural meaning. Incidentally, the terminological link between natural meaning and natural codes is not coincidental: natural codes are what we get when things with natural meaning are used in code model communication (Wharton, 2003a).

Grice's elaboration of non-natural meaning proceeds in three stages. The first is to note that for me to mean something in this sense I must intend to manipulate or add to my audience's mental representations in some way. For example, perhaps I intend to create in my audience the representation that I would like more wine, or that these vegetables need chopping. The second stage is to note that my audience must recognize that I have these intentions. Suppose that I ask my friend to pour me another glass of wine and that, as I expected, he obliges. I expected this not simply because I had asked for more wine, but in fact because, as a result of my asking, my friend *understood* that I wanted another glass of wine. In other words, my request was directed towards the manipulation of my friend's mental states, and he poured me another glass of wine because he recognized this. If I had requested more wine and my friend had not heard me, but poured the wine anyway, simply because he is a good host, then my intentions would *not* have been satisfied.

These two conditions might seem sufficient to say that I 'meant' for my friend to pour me some wine, but, Grice argued, it is not. To see why, suppose that, instead of asking for more directly, I simply move my empty wine glass to a location where it is likely to be noticed by my friend, but I do not bring attention to the fact that the glass is empty in any way. Instead, I simply leave it there. Nevertheless, my friend sees that I have done this, and understands why I did so. Here, the same two facts as above apply – I still intended that my friend believes that I would like more wine, and my friend still recognized this – but Grice was not willing to grant that there is non-natural meaning in such cases. He argued, and I agree, that "deliberately and openly letting someone know", or "getting someone to think" is not quite enough for (non-natural) meaning (all quotes p. 382). However if, on the other hand, I had made eye contact with my host and simultaneously tilted my wine glass, or expressed my intentions in some other conspicuous way, then we would certainly say that I 'meant' that I would like more wine. The difference between these two cases is this: only in the latter do I *show* the fact that I intended that my friend believes that I would like more wine. Then, *as a result of this showing*, my friend understands what I meant. This is the third stage, and it is the heart of Grice's account of meaning: to mean something, I should intend that my audience believes it, *and they should believe it at least in part because they recognize that this was my very intention*. This is the meaning of (Gricean, non-natural) meaning. It is also the reason why ostensive-inferential communication can be glossed as *intentionally overt* communication.

This account has been much discussed, and in some cases reformulated (e.g. Strawson, 1964; Schiffer, 1972; Neale, 1992). However, in all reformulations one fact remains central, namely the auto-deictic character of the Gricean account; in other words, the fact that ostensive stimuli are effectively pointers to the very intentions that triggered their production in the first place. Indeed, this is arguably what makes an analysis 'Gricean' in the first place: analyses that include this quality are Gricean in spirit, even if they are not in letter; and those that leave it out are less reformulations of Grice, and more fundamental revisions. Perhaps appropriately, given its philosophical origins, this pragmatic notion of meaning is clear and well-developed.

In contrast, in evolutionary biology, and specifically in animal signalling theory, the term 'meaning' has been used in a more casual way, not subject to the detailed analysis that the Gricean notion has been. Instead, it has mostly been used in a colloquial, mostly anthropomorphic way i.e. *as if* animals have the same intentions as humans do. A related fact is that the vast majority of research on animal communication (perhaps all of it) implicitly adopts a code model of communication – not because there has been extensive consideration of whether the code model or the ostensive-inferential model is more appropriate, but rather because the model is very intuitive, and works well as a description of most (and perhaps all) animal communication. Indeed, I suspect that many animal communication researchers are not aware of the fact that they have adopted this model, or that there is an alternative.

The set of background assumptions that are embedded into the code model are rarely problematic for the study of non-human communication. However, they can become so when we wish to view human communication, which does not operate according to the code model (§1.5), through the lens of evolutionary biology, as we do when studying language origins. There is here the potential for misunderstanding and confusion. In order to avoid this outcome, some researchers think that we should avoid the term 'meaning' altogether, unless we do explicitly want to invoke the Gricean sense described above (e.g. Rendall et al., 2009). While sympathetic to the agenda behind this suggestion, I think it is too restrictive. Here I will try to explain how meaning can be profitably used within the code model. I will then discuss how that usage relates to the Gricean idea of (non-natural) meaning discussed above.

The first thing we must do is recognize an important distinction, central to evolutionary theory, between what are called ultimate and proximate explanations of biological phenomena (Scott-Phillips et al., 2011). Biological evolution is change in gene frequencies (Futuyma, 2005). There are two classes of question we can ask about these changes: why do they occur?; and what do the genes that do exist actually do (i.e. what proteins and hence organs do they create, how do those organs work, what behaviours do they lead to, etc.)? Answers to the first question are called ultimate explanations; answers to the second question, proximate explanations. In short, ultimate explanations are concerned with why a behaviour exists, and are correspondingly expressed in terms of the function of the behaviour in question (or the lack of any function); proximate explanations are concerned with how it works, and are correspondingly expressed in terms of the various causal mechanisms (be they physical, physiological, psychological, social, chemical, etc.) involved (Mayr, 1961; Scott-Phillips et al., 2011).

For example, an ultimate explanation of infant crying is that it elicits care and defence from mothers and other caregivers – this is the function of infant crying. Proximate explanations include the external triggers of crying, such as physical separation from the caregiver, cold, or a lack of food, and also the internal mechanisms, such as the limbic system and the endogenous opioids involved in the cessation of crying. As this example makes clear, these two different types of explanation are distinct and complementary, and neither is more important than the other. (As such, the term 'ultimate' may be unfortunate, since it might suggest that this type of explanation is the more important of the two. This is not the case, but the term is well-established, and as such it would be counter-productive to suggest an alternative.) The ultimate/proximate distinction is central to any evolutionary analysis of behaviour (Davies et al., 2012). This is because it is not simply a heuristic that researchers can choose to adopt, or not, as a way to organize their enquiries, but instead a logical consequence of the very definition of biological evolution (see above).

The headline point about meaning and animal communication is that here, 'meaning' is an ultimate level explanation of the signalling behaviour, applicable across all different types of communication system. In other words, when we talk about the meaning of an animal signal, we are making a statement about its ultimate function (Krebs & Dawkins, 1984; Scott-Phillips, 2008a). (In contrast, the Gricean account is a proximate explanation, applicable only to systems that operate with the mechanisms of metapsychology described above.) For example, the function of mating calls is to cause in others a willingness to mate, the function of marking territory is to cause others to not encroach upon that territory, and so on and so on. As such, when animal communication researchers use the term 'meaning', they typically do so to describe the command that would trigger these effects, *as if* this were an instance of linguistic communication. In other words, mating calls 'mean' 'come and mate with me', territory marking 'means' 'do not encroach upon this territory', and so on. This is not so much a theoretically developed notion of meaning, but rather a description of how the term seems to be used in practice.

However, when such research is conducted or interpreted through the lens of comparison with human language, the danger of misunderstanding is significant. This is not only due to the fact, already mentioned, that the evolutionary approach to meaning differs from the pragmatic one described above. It is also possible because with such interdisciplinary research a significant proportion of the intended audience is likely more familiar with other approaches to meaning (in particular the Gricean approach discussed above), and may hence interpret claims about the meanings of animal signals in terms quite differently to those intended. For example, when a researcher states that, say, a monkey call 'means' 'eagle!', she may only have in mind the idea that the ultimate function of the call is to elicit a response that is appropriate for the presence of eagles. She may not mean to suggest that monkey communication is ostensive, and hence that the monkey in some sense intends to change the mental representations of other monkeys, but there is however a danger that some audiences will interpret her comments in this way. Equally, it is also possible that she *does* think that monkey vocal calls are Gricean, but this too may not be clear. In short, there is significant potential for ambiguity and misunderstanding here. At the same time, both the Gricean approach to meaning, and this more intuitive, coded sense of the term, are coherent and useful. As such, I will employ them both, and where there is any ambiguity about which is being used, I will state which I have in mind.

These two approaches to meaning have at least one important feature in common, which is this: that both are, at bottom, about how signals *do* things to an audience, and indeed how they are *designed* to do so (Scott-Phillips, 2010a). In one case, what signals do is change behaviour, and the design comes by virtue of natural selection, which produces organisms that behave in goal-directed ways (Dennett, 1995; Gardner, 2009). In the other case, what signals do is change mental states, and the design comes by virtue of human intentions (notwithstanding the fact that the capacity for this is of course itself a product of natural selection). Indeed, one of the seminal texts in the history of pragmatics is entitled *How to Do Things with Words*, with the emphasis very much on the *Do* (Austin, 1955). In sum, then, 'meaning', in either sense of the word, is about doing things to others in a designed way. Of course, the broader idea that meaning derives ultimately from how it is used in the world has a long philosophical history that pre-dates pragmatics, most famously in the work of Ludwig Wittgenstein (1953). In the next chapter we shall see how the fact that the function of signals is to do things to others has profound consequences for how communication systems emerge in the first place.

* * *

Chapter 1. *There are two models of the very possibility of communication: the code model and the ostensive-inferential model. The former is built upon mechanisms of association; the latter upon mechanisms of metapsychology. Most and perhaps all animal communication can be described with the code model. It is commonly assumed that linguistic communication operates according to the code model, but it does not. It is instead an instance of ostensive-inferential communication that is augmented by a set of shared communicative conventions. For this reason, it is important to distinguish between these conventional codes, which augment ostensive-inferential communication, and natural codes, which make code model communication possible. The notion of meaning plays out differently in each of the two models of communication, but in both cases it is about doing things to others in a functional, designed way.*

Chapter 2. *What does animal communication theory tell us about how communication systems emerge? Do ostensive-inferential systems emerge any differently to code model systems? Why is human language the only communication system in the natural world that makes widespread use of meaningful combinatorial communication? Did ostensive-inferential communication evolve from coded communication, or from some other source?*

Chapter 2

The Emergence of Communication Systems

2.1 Combinatorial communication

Many people have noted the remarkable expressive power of language. As just one example, here is the opening passage of Steven Pinker's *The Language Instinct* (1994), probably the most widely read book about language and linguistics ever written: "As you are reading these words, you are taking part in one of the wonders of the natural world. For you and I belong to a species with a remarkable ability... Simply by making noises with our mouths, we can reliably cause precise new combinations of ideas to arise in each other's minds. The ability comes so naturally that we forget what a miracle it is" (p. 1). Like many before him, Pinker goes on to emphasize that a fundamental and crucial component of this expressive power is our capacity to combine together different linguistic elements (sounds, syllables, words) to construct larger entities with specific meanings.

This is *combinatorial communication*. In its most basic form, combinatorial communication involves two signals with distinct meanings, and a third signal whose form is the combination of the other two signals, but whose meaning is not the sum of the meanings of the two component parts (Figure 2.1). From this simple starting point, we can generate further signals of increasing combinatorial complexity. As I highlighted at the beginning of the previous chapter, languages are richly combinatorial. However, for the arguments I wish to make in this chapter, it will be sufficient to consider only this very simple form of combinatorial communication. We call the individual signals *holistic* signals, and their combination a *composite* signal.

Some animal communication systems satisfy some of the criteria for combinatorial communication, but not all. Birdsong, for example, involves the combination, in moderately complex ways, of many smaller, component elements (Berwick et al., 2011a). Whale song does too (Payne & McVay, 1971). However, these combinations do not change the meaning of the songs. Birdsong is used only to defend territory or attract mates, and the complexity of the song indicates the bird's ability to do this. In this respect, the combinatorial complexity of birdsong functions in a way that

form		***meaning***
A	$\rightarrow$	X
B	$\rightarrow$	Y
$A + B$	$\rightarrow$	$Z \neq X + Y$

Figure 2.1 *A simple form of combinatorial communication.* Two individual signals have two distinct meanings (responses), and their combination has a third meaning, which is not simply the combination of the meanings of the two individual signals. The first two signals are called holistic signals; the third a composite signal.

is analogous to pitch in human language. For instance, men with deeper voices are perceived by others as more dominant and more attractive than those with higher pitched voices, even though the meaning of what they say does not change with these changes in pitch (Puts, 2005; Puts et al., 2006). In the same way, birds with more syntactically complex songs are more dominant and more attractive than those with simple songs, but the meaning of the song does not change. Another way to make this point is to say that in birdsong, the useful information is not in the meaning of the song itself, but in how it is produced: the complexity of the song is itself the message.

The 'waggle dance', which honeybees use to indicate the location of sources of nectar, also involves the combination of distinct elements (Dyer, 2002). The direction that the bee faces during the main part of the dance indicates direction, and the duration of the dance indicates distance. However, the meaning of the composite signal is not different to the combination of the meanings of the two individual signals. In the terms of Figure 2.1, $A + B \rightarrow Z = X + Y$. It is hence not combinatorial in the sense I am using the term here, which would require that $Z \neq X + Y$.

There is however at least one animal species in which the system described in Figure 2.1 has been reported. Putty-nosed monkeys appear to have two distinct alarm calls, one for each of two predators, leopards (a 'pyow' sound) and eagles (a 'hack' sound). When one or the other of these calls is produced on its own, the monkeys urgently take appropriate evasive action: climbing trees for leopards; hiding in bushes for eagles. However when these two calls are produced together ('pyow-hack'), the effect is *not* simply the combination of these i.e. the monkeys do not behave as if avoiding both types of predator. Instead, the call seems to presage the movement of the group to a new location, and this movement does not occur with any urgency (Arnold & Zuberbühler, 2006; 2008). Other combinatorial systems of slightly increased complexity have been documented in some other non-human primates (Zuberbühler, 2002; Ouattara et al., 2009). Of course, the complexity of those combinations is dwarfed by the combinatorial complexity of language (Hurford, 2011).

The difference between human language and these more syntactically simple systems is not just quantitative. There is also a qualitative difference.

Unlike these other systems, the expressive scope of language is *unlimited*. Pinker again: “By the same logic that shows that there are an infinite number of integers – if you ever think you have the largest integer, just add 1 to it and you will have another – there must be an infinite number of sentences” (1994, p. 82). Pinker illustrates this by adding to the beginning of an existing sentence the phrase “Pinker wrote that…”. But he then trumps that with a new sentence, “Who cares that Pinker wrote that…?”, and so on and so on. We can freely add on new constructions like this, with the result that the range of propositions we can express is literally infinite. This aspect of language is often described with a soundbite from the 18th- and 19th-century linguist Wilhelm von Humboldt: ‘language makes infinite use of finite media’. In contrast, all other natural communication systems make only finite use of their media – and in comparatively limited ways too. In other words, the difference between language and other communication systems in the natural world is not simply large. It is unbounded.

The question, then, is why? Why does language have not just a complex form of combinatorial communication, but a system so rich that it can be used to express a literally infinite number of different propositions? And why does no other natural communication system do the same? These are among the defining questions of language evolution research, and in this chapter I will address them both.

My argument, in brief, will be this. When we study exactly how communication systems emerge, it becomes clear that without ostensive communication even the most simple forms of combinatorial communication, such as the one described in Figure 2.1, are generally unlikely to emerge, and that anything with the combinatorial complexity of languages vanishingly so. However once ostensive communication is available, these problems vanish, because ostension and inference allow us to create new signals in an evolutionarily novel way, that bypasses the constraints faced by other systems. In short, the emergence of ostensive-inferential communication made unbounded communicative complexity, which was previously impossible, possible. I will develop this argument from first principles – beginning, now, with a precise definition of communication.

2.2 The functional interdependence of signals and responses

In recent years a vibrant discussion has taken place in the animal signalling literature around a set of general conceptual questions about the nature of communication, such as: what is communication?; what do animal signals mean?; what role does information play in communication?; and so on (Rendall et al., 2009; Seyfarth et al., 2010; Stegmann, 2013). My main contribution to this discussion has been to articulate and justify some definitions of the most basic terms, in particular *signal*, *response*, *communication*, *cue*, and *coercion* (Scott-Phillips, 2008a; Scott-Phillips & Kirby, 2013). These definitions will be the starting point for my analysis of how communication systems emerge.

Communication occurs when an action (a signal) produced by an individual organism causes a change (a reaction) in another organism, where both the signal and the reaction have been designed for these purposes (Maynard Smith & Harper, 2003; Scott-Phillips, 2008a; Table 2.1). If the action has been designed for these purposes, but the reaction has not, then the interaction is *coercive*; and if the reaction has been designed for these purposes but the action has not, then the interaction is a *cue*. Cues have also been called *public information*, a label that usefully describes their essential property (Danchin et al., 2004). These definitions work across a range of *prima facie* cases, in the sense that they correspond to our intuitions about what is and is not a signal, a cue, and a coercive behaviour (Scott-Phillips, 2008a; 2010a; 2010b).

Before we look at some examples, I should clarify that the use of 'design' as a diagnostic principle could be supplanted with 'function': the two notions are equivalent for my purposes here. An item's *function* is the task that is historically responsible for the reproduction of the item in question (Millikan, 1984). Hearts, for example, make noise, contribute to body weight, and pump blood, among other things. Yet it is only the last of these that explains why hearts are reproduced from one generation to the next. Hence, this is their function. An item is designed if it has such a function. Consequently, to define signals and responses as those actions and reactions that are designed to fulfil mutually complementary roles in communication, as I have done, is to say that signals and responses have as their functions those mutually complementary roles.

Now, onto the examples. Red deer roar, and these roars are used to attract mates and defend territory (Reby & McComb, 2003). The mechanisms that produce these roars have been designed by the process of natural selection. At the same time, red deer also have mechanisms to respond to roars in adaptive ways, and these too are designed (Reby et al., 2005). And

Table 2.1 *Definitions of key terms in communication.* If an action causes a reaction, and both are designed for the purposes of playing that role in the interaction, then we can term the action a signal, the reaction a response, and the overall interaction communicative. If, however, one half or the other was not designed for these purposes, then the action is either a cue or a coercive behaviour.

	Action designed?	Reaction designed?
Signal/Response	Yes	Yes
Cue	No	Yes
Coercion	Yes	No
Accident	No	No

so here both production and reception are designed to play those roles in the interaction. Hence, the roars are signals. An example of a cue is a predator that has appeared on the horizon and hence been seen by its prospective prey. The prey might now make use of this observation to move to a different location. Assuming that the capacity to change behaviour in this way has evolved by natural selection, then the reaction is designed, but the 'action' (the predator being present at a particular location) was not. Finally, an example of coercion is camouflage (Maynard Smith & Harper, 2003). Camouflage affects the behaviour of another organism (predators are less likely to eat camouflaged prey), and camouflage evolved for that reason. However there is no evolved response. The predator is coerced to not pursue the prey. This example shows that 'coercion' is not always the most intuitive label, but it is moderately well-established in the relevant literature, and the alternatives (e.g. 'manipulation') all have their own, different drawbacks (*ibid.*).

Here is a set of examples of a different type (Scott-Phillips & Kirby, 2013). Figure 2.2 shows a male office worker engaged in three different interactions with three different colleagues: one that he is pushing to the floor, one that he is trying to entertain by doing so, and one (his boss) who, unbeknownst to the man, can see what is going on. With regards to the seated woman that he is pushing to the floor, his action (the push) is

Figure 2.2 *Examples of a signal, a cue, and coercion in human intentional behaviour (Scott-Phillips & Kirby, 2013).* This illustration shows one man (in the centre of the image) in three different interactions, each of which is of a different type *vis-à-vis* communication. In one, he is pushing a colleague from her chair. This is **coercion**. In another, he is seen pushing his colleague by a second colleague (on the right of the image), and he intended for this to be the case. This is **communication**; the push is a signal, and the laugh of his colleague is a response. In a third interaction, his boss (on the left of the image) has also seen him pushing his colleague, but this was not the man's intention; indeed, he does not know that his boss has seen him. The pushing is a **cue** for the boss; it guides the boss's future action, but this was not the function of the push.

designed for this purpose, but her 'reaction' (the fall) is not – and so this is coercion. With regards to the boss, the push causes him to view the man as unprofessional. This is a deliberate (i.e. designed) reaction to the scene, but the push itself was certainly not designed to cause this reaction – and so for the boss the push is a cue. Finally, with regards to the woman that the man wishes to entertain, the behaviour is a signal, designed to inform her that he is a playful and fun guy.

This second set of examples highlights that the same behaviour can have different statuses with regards to communication (i.e. signal, cue, coercion), depending on the identity of the receiver. This is because communication is an interactive phenomenon: to observe it, we must not look at individuals (either signallers or receivers), but rather at the interaction between them (Krebs & Dawkins, 1984; di Paolo, 1997; Maynard Smith & Harper, 2003). In this example there are three interactions, and each is different.

Several points about these definitions should be clarified. First, note that the source of design is irrelevant: what matters is only *that* behaviours are designed, not who or what designed them. The source of design in the first set of examples is natural selection, whereas in the second set it is human intentionality (which is, of course, in turn the product of natural selection). A further example is computer–computer communication, in which the design comes from the mind of the software engineer that built the program(s) being used. What this shows is that although design is a necessary part of communication, it can arise from a range of different sources. The second point to clarify is that it is possible for signals and coercive behaviours to fail to achieve the effects they are designed to, for example in particularly noisy environments. This does not stop them being signals or coercive behaviours; what matters for the definitions is whether they are designed to achieve effects, not whether they actually do have effects. Third, the definitions say nothing about whether the interaction is beneficial for either party. In particular, and perhaps somewhat contrary to its everyday usage, the term *coercion* does not imply that the interaction is against the reacting organism's interests; all that it implies is that the reaction is not designed to play that role in the interaction. Fourth and finally, note that although these definitions talk about signals, responses and so on as actions and reactions, and hence seem to imply behaviour, they should be understood more broadly. For example, signals and reactions can also be, say, structures on an organism's body, such as the bright colours that many organisms use to attract mates, or the camouflage example above. They can also be traces of behaviour e.g. dogs' urine to mark their territory, and written words. For convenience's sake I will from hereon usually only refer to behaviours, but this usage should be understood in a broad sense.

It is moderately common for communication to be defined not in terms of design but in terms of information transfer, from one individual to another (see e.g. the quotes in §1.2). However, this approach fails for one simple reason: it cannot distinguish between cues and communication (Scott-

Phillips, 2008; 2010a). The red deer roar and the appearance of a predator on the horizon both transfer information, but only the roar do we want to call a signal. I do not deny that it is possible to discuss communication in terms of information, or even that it is sometimes useful to do so (see e.g. Seyfarth et al., 2010). However, information transfer is a *consequence* of communication, not a definition of it (Scott-Phillips, 2010a).

Instead, what makes an interaction communicative is that it involves two behaviours, a signal and a response, which both possess two particular qualities. The first is interdependence: as I have emphasized, signals require responses, and responses require signals. The second is design: the two behaviours must be designed to interact with one another. In sum, then, communication is a matter of *designed* (or *functional*) *interdependence*. This quality is the essence of communication, and I will now use it to explain how communication systems emerge.

2.3 A chicken-and-egg problem

Here is a passage from *The Story of Dr. Dolittle*, the first of Hugh Lofting's Dr. Dolittle books, in which the eponymous character learns to converse with animals:

> At tea-time, when the dog, Jip, came in, the parrot said to the Doctor, "See, he's talking to you."
>
> "Looks to me as though he were scratching his ear," said the Doctor.
>
> "But animals don't always speak with their mouths," said the parrot in a high voice, raising her eyebrows. "They talk with their ears, with their feet, with their tails – with everything. Sometimes they don't want to make a noise. Do you see now the way he's twitching up one side of his nose?"
>
> "What's that mean?" asked the Doctor.
>
> "That means, 'Can't you see that it has stopped raining?' " Polynesia answered.

The Doctor faces two problems here. There is the obvious one that he just doesn't know *what* the different animal signals mean. But this passage also illustrates a second and deeper problem: in some cases, the Doctor doesn't even know *that* the animals are trying to communicate (' "Looks to me as though he were scratching his ear," said the Doctor'). This is a problem of signalhood: how do you even know when somebody else is trying to communicate with you?

This problem of signalhood is the consequence of the interdependence of signals and responses. Signals and responses depend upon one another to explain their very existence. One without the other is pointless. Why signal if the intended audience does not know that this is what you are doing, and hence will not respond? And why have a mechanism that determines responses, if the signals will never come? In sum: if signals and responses depend upon one another to explain their adaptive value, then how does the interaction emerge in the first place? We shall see in this section that the answers to these chicken-and-egg questions (which came first?) contain some very important implications for how communication systems emerge (Scott-Phillips et al., 2012; Scott-Phillips & Blythe, 2013).

A pair of solutions to the chicken-and-egg problem present themselves more-or-less immediately: one half of the interaction (i.e. either cues or coercive behaviours) evolves first for reasons independent of communication, and this then provides a selection pressure for the other half of the interaction to evolve (Figure 2.3). Both of these processes are well-established and observed in the empirical literature (Bradbury & Vehrencamp, 1998; Maynard Smith & Harper, 2003). The cue-first process is called *ritualization*; the coercion-first process, *sensory manipulation*.

Let's consider a couple of examples, one of each route. Urine is often used as a signal of territorial boundaries. How did this evolve? Various strands of research point to the following story (Maynard Smith & Harper, 2003). The urine was originally produced by the organism (let's say it's a dog) as a fear response, which was triggered by reaching the edge of the area in which it felt safe. This urine is then a cue for other organisms, in particular for other dogs, who may benefit from information about what is familiar territory for the focal dog (the dog that has urinated). If so, it will guide their future behaviour. They may, for example, initiate conflict only when the focal dog is outside this area. This may, in turn, have fitness consequences for the focal dog, and if so, then it will be selected to produce more or less urine, perhaps in the same or in different places, if doing so

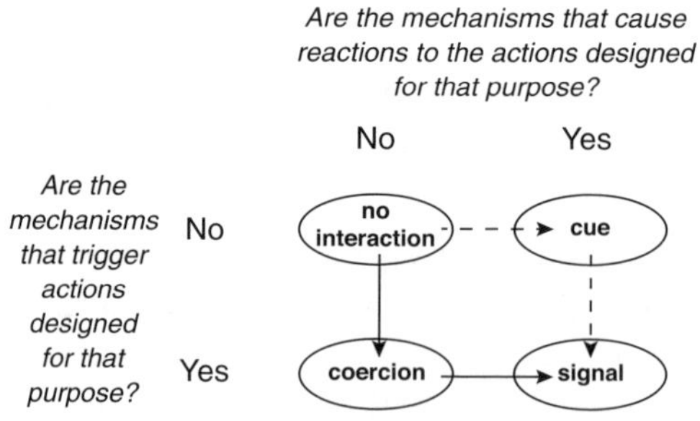

Figure 2.3 *Two routes to communication.* Communication involves a pair of interdependent behaviours, and so to reach this state from an initial state of no communication, one half or the other must evolve first for reasons independent of communication, and this may then provide a selection pressure for the other half of the interaction to evolve. In one direction this is called **ritualization** (dashed line); in the other, **sensory manipulation** (filled line).

improves those fitness consequences. Once that has occurred, then both action (urination) and reaction (initiating conflict only outside the territory) will have undergone selection, and hence have been designed to perform this role in the interaction. Communication has emerged.

In this urination example, the cue evolved first. This makes it an instance of *ritualization*, and animal communication research has described many further examples. It is a two-stage process: (i) an action (any action) is initially produced incidentally, and because of pre-existing mechanisms for reactions to events in the world, this action provides a reliable cue which others make use of; and then (ii) the (prospective) signallers had something to gain from the production of the cue, and hence evolved to do so. The cue thus becomes a signal. The consensus view is that "most animal signals probably evolved by ... ritualisation" (Maynard Smith & Harper, 2003, p. 68).

Let's now consider the other route: coercion first. A nice example is the offering of nuptial gifts, from males to females, that occurs in many insect species (Vahed, 1998). A specific case is the scorpionfly *Bittacus apicalis*, where males capture large prey and then offer them to females who feed on them during copulation (Thornhill, 1976). The conjectured evolutionary story is that the behaviour of offering prey initially evolved in the male because the female had a pre-existing mechanism that prioritized the opportunity to feed on large prey, and so the presentation of food gave the male an opportunity to mate. At this point, the presentation of the prey is coercive. However there was then later positive selection on the female to accept the prey in exchange for copulation. The offering is now a signal (Maynard Smith & Harper, 2003). This process is called *sensory manipulation*. Like ritualization, it has two stages: (i) there is a pre-existing mechanism for actions that cause effects in others; and (ii) the (prospective) receiver has something to gain from these effects, and so evolves to be receptive to the signal.

So far I have discussed both ritualization and sensory manipulation exclusively in terms of phylogenetic evolution by natural selection, but they can also occur ontogenetically i.e. within the lifetimes of individual organisms. The specific steps are these:

(i) Individual A performs behaviour *X*
(ii) Individual B reacts consistently with behaviour *Y*
(iii) If (i) and (ii) recur sufficiently often, then when A begins to perform *X*, B anticipates A's performance of *X* and hence performs *Y*
(iv) A anticipates B's anticipation of *X* and hence produces *X* in ritualized form so as to elicit *Y*

This process is much studied within primatology, as a way by which non-human primate signals might have emerged. An example is the chimpanzee 'nursing poke', in which an infant, held by his mother, pokes the mother's arm so as to indicate a desire to feed at her breast (Tomasello et al., 1985;

1997b; Call & Tomasello, 2007). It emerges in the following way. The infant initially attempts to move the mother's arm (step (i)). Once the mother has detected that this is what he wants she raises her arm voluntarily (step (ii)). As this process recurs over time, she comes to move her arm as soon as he begins to attempt to move it himself (step (iii)). Eventually the infant only need poke the mother's arm for her to react (step (iv)). In its general form this is exactly the same process as described above for ritualization, only here it occurs through repeated interactions, rather than repeated instances of natural selection: ontogenetic rather than phylogenetic ritualization (see Scott-Phillips, 2010b for further discussion).

Whether ontogenetic or phylogenetic, the processes by which communication systems emerge impose significant constraints on the creation of new signals, and these constraints impact on both signal form and signal meaning. Signals are ultimately descended from prior cues (in ritualization) or coercive behaviours (in sensory manipulation). This means that signal form is constrained by the set of cues and coercive behaviours that actually exist. If a particular form does not exist as either a cue or a coercive behaviour, it cannot become a signal, regardless of how useful it might be (Scott-Phillips et al., 2012). Similarly, signal meaning is constrained by the set of things in the world (events, objects, etc.) whose presence correlates with the prior cues/coercive behaviours. If these correlations do not exist, then this set of things cannot be referred to by any future signal. This suggests that if some forms or meanings are uncommon, this may simply be because the required prior states occur too rarely, or not at all. This point is important for the questions to which I will now turn: how can combinatorial communication emerge, and why is it so rare in nature?

2.4 The improbability of combinatorial communication

In its simplest form, combinatorial communication involves two holistic signals and one composite one (Figure 2.1). In this section I focus on the evolution of the composite signal. I begin my discussion by walking through one plausible story of how this might happen, using the reported putty-nosed monkey system as an example, for the sake of concreteness (see §2.1). Here, using the symbols from Figure 2.1, signal *A* is 'pyow' and signal *B* is 'hack' (so *X* is 'leopard!' and *Y* is 'eagle!'). Our question is: how can the signal $C = A + B$ ('pyow-hack') emerge, where the meaning of C is to move to a new location? I will now offer one possible answer to this question. It is important to note that it does not matter whether the specifics of this particular story are correct or not, since I am not making any claim about how the putty-nosed monkey system did actually evolve (although the story below does strike me as plausible). Rather, this story is a tool to help us understand the general process by which a combinatorial system might emerge.

The first thing to say is that the only reason *A* and *B* would typically be produced together would be if both a leopard and an eagle were attacking at the same time. What would be the monkeys' reaction to this? After a 'pyow', the monkeys climb trees – since this is the best way to evade the predation of the leopard; and after a 'hack', the monkeys head towards lower ground, to hide in dense bushes that eagles cannot easily attack. The best response to the situation is to move neither up into the canopy, nor down into the bushes, but rather sideways, to a different location. Under the circumstances, the safest place is, quite simply, anywhere but here. So if this scenario (leopards and eagles at the same time) occurs sufficiently often, then we should expect the monkeys to evolve the reaction of moving elsewhere if the two existing signals are produced together.

At this point, 'pyow' and 'hack' are both signals, but their coproduction is only a cue: it is informative about the fact that the group is likely to move to a new location. It is not a signal, since informing others about forthcoming movement is not the function of the coproduction of the two signals (this is why I am at this stage only calling it coproduction, and not a combinatorial signal). But now suppose that it would occasionally be useful for the monkeys to have a call that did inform the group of forthcoming movement to a new location. If so, then the monkeys will be selected to produce the two calls together when this need arises, since it will have the desired effect. Now it is the case that the coproduction of the two signals does have the function of informing others. This is now a new signal, and the system is now the one described in Figure 2.1. The composite signal has emerged by the cue-first process of ritualization. Because this signals' new meaning is not as urgent as the signals from which it was formed, subsequent evolution will likely lead to the loss of emotional intensity in the signal.

A plausible account of how the same system might emerge by sensory manipulation could also be developed, although it is less intuitive. It is also unnecessary for our purposes here. Indeed it does not matter, as I mentioned above, whether this particular story is true or not. Its purpose is only to serve as an example that allows us to describe the general steps necessary for the emergence of a composite signal. These steps will be very similar for sensory manipulation, since it is in large part a mirror image of the process of ritualization (§2.3).

Having walked through an example, let's now review the process by which a new, composite signal can emerge: (a) the two basic signals, *A* and *B*, were incidentally produced together, and this provided a reliable cue of some fact about the world, over and above the particular meanings of *A* and *B*, which others made use of; and (b) the (prospective) signallers had something to gain from communicating that fact, and hence were selected to do so. Compare these with the general conditions for the emergence of a new, non-composite signal, derived in §2.3: (i) an action (any action) is initially produced incidentally, and this provides a reliable cue of some fact about the world, which others make use of; and (ii) the (prospective) signallers had something to gain from communicating that fact, and hence evolved to do so. The key difference is this: while in the general case *any* behaviour can form the initial cue, in the combinatorial case it is a *specific* pair of behaviours that must form the initial cue (Figure 2.4).

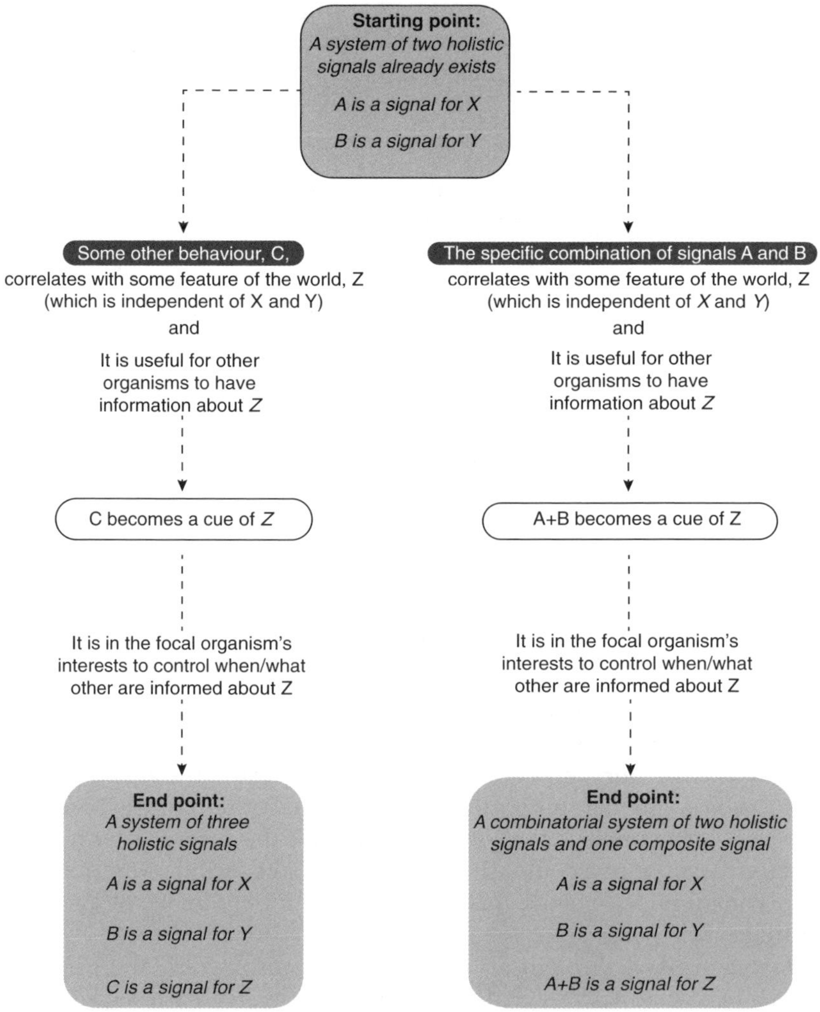

Figure 2.4 *Holistic signals are more likely than composite ones.* From an initial state of two holistic signals (*A* and *B*), a new third signal can be either holistic (*C*), or composite (*A+B*). Either way, it must emerge via either a cue-first or coercion-first process (see Figure 2.3). This figure illustrates the former; but the same argument applies to the latter as well. The key point is that C can be any behaviour the organism performs, but *A+B* is a *specific* behaviour, namely the combination of the two already existing signals (contrast the dark boxes in the figure). Consequently, there are many ways that a holistic signal can emerge, but only one way in which a composite signal can emerge – and so the former is far more likely than the latter.

This means that if a third signal is to emerge, there is only one way in which it might be composite, but many different ways in which it might be holistic. Consequently, it is overwhelmingly likely that new signals will be holistic, and composite signals should be far less common than holistic signals in the natural world. The same point applies to each subsequent change to the system, and so even if a small number of composite signals do emerge within one communication system, entire systems that make widespread use of combinatoriality are very unlikely to develop. This is not to say that composite signals will never emerge, only that they will be rare – which is exactly what the empirical data suggest is the case (Hurford, 2011). In collaboration with the theoretical physicist Richard Blythe, I have recently developed a mathematical model that fleshes out the details of this analysis, and it works very much as described here (Scott-Phillips & Blythe, 2013).

Previous models of the emergence of combinatorial communication did not reach the same conclusion (Nowak & Krakauer, 1999; Lachmann & Bergstrom, 2004; Nowak et al., 1999; 2000). It is instructive to consider why. These previous models asked the following question: under what conditions are composite signals advantageous, in comparison with holistic signals? The answers to this question are then used to explain why combinatorial communication appears to be rare. For example, one set of papers showed that in terms of information processing, combinatorial communication is not efficient, in comparison to entirely holistic systems, until the quantity of signals in the system exceeds a threshold (Nowak & Krakauer, 1999; Nowak et al., 2000). This threshold is higher than the number of signals observed in most natural communication systems and so, it is claimed, this explains why most natural communication systems are not combinatorial. Subsequent empirical data have contradicted these predictions: the putty-nosed monkey system has fewer signals than this threshold level, but is reported to be combinatorial nevertheless; and several systems have many more signals than the threshold level, but still do not combine them (non-human primate gestural communication, for example).

These previous models are representative of a common mistake, which is to treat communication systems as if they were part of an organism's phenotype, and hence to assume that if it would be adaptive for individuals to possess a particular signal, then natural selection will react to that. But if that is the case, then why do animal communication systems not have more signals? It would surely be useful for many organisms to communicate about all manner of topics, but they do not do so. The mistake is that communication systems are not part of any organism's phenotype. They are rather systems shared by groups of individuals; they are something that emerges out of the interaction of signals and responses. As such, they are subject to the constraints of interdependence described above – and previous models did not take these constraints into consideration. It is thus not a surprise that their predictions do not match the empirical data.

Another reason why previous models of the emergence of communication did not reach this conclusion is that they did not explicitly consider the possibility that no communication might take place. Instead, they build the fact of communication directly into the models themselves. Specifically, they pre-define at least one (and often two or even all three) of the following: the communication channel; the roles of signaller and receiver; or the forms that signals and/or responses can take. This approach means that the question these models ask is not how communication can emerge from non-communication, but rather how an already existing system will evolve, under various conditions of interest. In order to model the *origins* of communication, we should instead pre-define none of these aspects of communication, nor any other. Rather, we should define only the agents' possible actions, and allow the use of these actions for communication to be something that evolves. When we do this, we find that we are able to explain why combinatorial communication is rare in nature (Scott-Phillips & Blythe, 2013).

2.5 Ostension and inference: a third route to communication

The above arguments are all well and good but there is, of course, an elephant in the room. The prediction that combinatorial communication systems should be rare in nature, and that where they do exist they should be simple in form, is consistent with all that we know about natural communication systems – with one single, glaring exception. Human language is so embarrassingly combinatorial that it cannot be treated simply as a freakish outlier to the framework described above. A proper explanation of why language is so different is required. In this and the following sections I will argue that the key to this anomaly lies in the ostensive nature of human communication.

So far, we have seen that there are two routes to communication: ritualization and sensory manipulation. There is also a third way in which communication systems can emerge. I call this the *direct route*, since unlike the other two, it does not depend upon the prior emergence of cues or coercion, or indeed anything at all. Instead, communication emerges directly. Under what circumstances is this possible? It requires that an interdependent pair of behaviours (a signal and a corresponding response) come into existence *simultaneously*. This is possible only if signallers are able to make it apparent to their intended audience not only *what* it is that they wish to communicate, but also the very fact *that* they are attempting to communicate in the first place.

In Chapter 1, I discussed at some length the fact that humans can do this, and provided several examples: one where I tilt my coffee cup in a particular way to indicate to a waiter that I would like more coffee; another where Mary eats berries in a way that indicates to Peter that she thinks the berries are tasty; and a third where puffed cheeks were used to reference a previous conversation. In all these cases there is no cue or coercive behaviour on the road to communication. Instead, the signal is created *de novo*, and recognized as such by the receiver. Put another way: these behaviours signal their own signalhood. Their respective audiences grasp this, and so the signal and its response appear together.

Experimental studies of the emergence of communication systems provide a particularly clear demonstration of this process in action (Scott-Phillips et al., 2009; de Ruiter et al., 2010; Stolk et al., 2013). In these studies, pairs of human participants, who do not meet in real life, play simple computer games in which they control characters and shapes in very simple artificial environments. The challenge the participants face is to coordinate their behaviour with one another. To do this, they need to communicate, but they are not given any pre-existing signals, nor any dedicated communication channel. Indeed, the whole point is that there is no *a priori* difference between communicative and non-communicative behaviour. Consequently, participants must make their characters and shapes behave ostensively, so that their communicative intent is made manifest to their partner. These challenges prove difficult, but participants are able to overcome them, and in doing so they demonstrate that humans are able to establish a communication system directly, without going via cues and coercive behaviours. We know for certain that these other routes are not used, because the way in which the games are set up means that it is not even possible for cues and coercive behaviours to exist (Scott-Phillips, 2010b). Thus, if communication does emerge in these games (and it does), then it must, logically, be via this direct route.

How are we able to succeed at such tasks, and more generally to create new signals that reveal the fact that we wish to communicate? I hope that it is by now apparent that the answer to this question is our capacity for ostensive-inferential communication. By producing signals ostensively, we reveal to our intended audience not only the content of our informative intentions (for example: that I want more coffee; that Mary thinks the berries are tasty; that the woman despairs of humanity's taste in TV programmes) but also, crucially, and by definition, the content of our communicative intentions too i.e. the fact that we are trying to communicate at all. And inference allows the audience to grasp all of this. In sum: ostensive-inferential communication allows its users to create signals in a direct way, and in doing so bypass the chicken-and-egg problem analysed above (Table 2.2).

An important point to note about this direct route to communication is that, unlike signals that emerge by either of the other two routes, there are no constraints on either signal form or signal meaning. A signal is free to take any form the signaller wishes it to, so long as (i) the signal is produced in an ostensive way, so that its communicative function is inferable by the

Table 2.2 *The three routes to the emergence of new signals.* The first two might, in principle, apply to any communication system that emerges by a dynamic process – natural selection being the obvious example. The third, direct route is more restrictive: it will only be observed if (prospective) signallers have the social cognitive capacities necessary to make their intentions manifest, and the intended audience has the capacities necessary to recognize this. Exactly what these capacities are is discussed in Chapter 3.

Route	Description	Example
Ritualization	A cued reaction evolves first, for reasons independent of communication, and this then provides the selection pressure for the signal to evolve; once it has done, the cued reaction can be called a response	Urination as a marker of territory
Sensory manipulation	A coercive action evolves first, for reasons independent of communication, and this then provides the selection pressure for the response to evolve; once it has done, the coercive action can be called a signal	The offering of nuptial gifts in insects
Direct	Signaller produces behaviour that makes manifest to the intended audience not only what is being communicated, but that something is being communicated at all	Tilting a coffee cup to indicate to the waiter that you would like more coffee

intended audience, and (ii) the combination of signal form and contextual information is sufficient to make the content of the informative intention similarly inferable. Outside these two requirements, the signal can be of any form at all. This is nicely illustrated by the example of the puffed cheeks. This was a new signal, created in the moment (i.e. directly), and it could have taken one of many forms (throwing one's arms up in the air; a roll of the eyes; and so on). Certainly, it was not constrained by the process by which it emerged, in the way that signals that have emerged by ritualization or sensory manipulation necessarily are. In the next section, we will see how the removal of these constraints allows the transition to a combinatorial communication system to take place.

2.6 The creation of combinatorial communication

By now the main argument I want to make should be apparent. We have seen that combinatorial communication is unlikely to emerge by either ritualization or sensory manipulation, because of a chicken-and-egg problem – but this leaves language unexplained. We have also seen that ostension allows its users to create new signals directly, without constraints on signal form and signal meaning. These two facts together explain how ostensive communication allows widespread combinatorial communication to emerge.

A good real-world illustration of this process is the creation of homesign. Homesigners are deaf children born and raised by hearing parents. Lacking the input of a conventional sign language, they must create new communication systems themselves. The psychologist Susan Goldin-Meadow has spent many years documenting and studying homesigners, and what she has found is that the systems they create have all of the most fundamental properties of more established languages (2005). One of these properties is combinations of existing signals.

Here is one simple example. The child, Karen, is already familiar with pointing, and also with a 'twist' gesture that means 'open'. She then spontaneously uses these two behaviours together: she points to a jar of soap bubbles and then, without pausing, produces an iconic 'twist' action with her hands. In doing so, she indicates to the adult that she would like her to open the jar. At first blush, this seems unremarkable, but that is only because, as fully competent users of ostensive communication, you are fully accustomed to such acts of creation as an everyday occurrence. The point here is not simply that we can combine things together – there is no particular reason to think that combining existing signals is in any way cognitively challenging. (If you do not already believe this, then the experiment I will describe at the end of this chapter should convince you otherwise.) It is rather that, because she has the required metapsychological abilities, it is possible for Karen to provide just the right sort of evidence for whatever her intended meaning might be, and that in this case that right sort of evidence happens to involve the combination of two existing signals.

Note that in a different context, the meaning of Karen's behaviour could be very different indeed. Suppose, for example, that the adult had just tried to open the jar by twisting it, but had failed, and that this had amused Karen. Now Karen could use the same combined signal to make a humorous reference to this past event. This flexibility is possible only because both Karen and the adult have the metapsychological abilities required to engage in ostensive communication (I shall discuss these abilities in more depth in the next two chapters). On the ostensive side, Karen produced the signals in such a way that it was apparent that they are in fact one signal, comprised of two parts; this is why she does not pause between the two. On the inferential side, the adult must assess what Karen's intended meaning was, given her knowledge of the context, and of the meanings of the two component parts.

This same observation also makes it clear that the meaning of Karen's signal is not simply the sum of the meanings of the two component parts, which are 'open' and 'look at that'. There is nothing in the composition of these two signals that the thing to open and the thing to look at should be the same: that aspect of the situation is additional. Yet this fact poses no problems: this new, composite signal is used spontaneously and successfully, and there is no interruption of the normal flow of communication. This is a clear exception to the general constraints described above, in which a new composite signal had to emerge by either ritualization or sensory manipulation (Scott-Phillips & Blythe, 2013). In short, the existence of ostensive communication makes it possible for a species to overcome the constraints, described above, that otherwise make the emergence of combinatorial communication unlikely.

Here is a second example of how ostension and inference allow humans to overcome the constraints that the interdependence of signal and response places on the emergence of combinatorial signals. It is from an experimental study on the creation of graphical communication systems (Theisen et al., 2010). Pairs of participants played a game much like the party game Pictionary. In the experiment, one player draws a concept from a pre-specified list, and the other player must guess what it is, but without using conventional signs like letters and punctuation. The pairs worked through the list several times, taking turns to draw and to guess. Crucially, all the concepts on the list were conceptually related to other items on the list, in a systematic way. For example, the list included: *teacher*, *school*, and *school bus*; *doctor, hospital*, and *ambulance; farmer*, *barn*, and *tractor*. What often happened was that signs that were associated with one aspect of a concept were used, spontaneously, to refer to the same aspect of another concept. For example, a drawing of a tree, which had been used as part of *barn*, and a drawing of a generic vehicle, which had been used as part of *school bus*, were drawn together to refer to *tractor*. On another occasion, the generic vehicle was drawn alongside a stethoscope, which had itself previously been used to refer to *doctor*. The intended meaning was *ambulance*. Just as with Karen, what we see here is that existing signals are combined in such a way that the meaning of the composite signal is a function of the meanings of the component parts *and* the context (the game), all in conjunction with one another.

A final example is spoken language. Let's return to the point made by Steven Pinker with which I began this chapter: that we can extend any existing sentence by simply adding an additional expression to it, such as "Pinker wrote that…". Here, the two existing signals are: (i) the existing sentence; and (ii) the expression "Pinker wrote that". When we combine these, we create a new sentence. Importantly, the meaning of this new sentence is not simply the combination of the meanings of the two individual signals. It also depends on the way they are combined. Suppose that the existing sentence is "I didn't know that". Then the meaning of the new sentence would depend on the order in which this was combined with the new expression "Pinker wrote that": the two possible orders produce very different (literal) meanings.

Of course, all of these examples involve already fluent users of language – a richly combinatorial system of communication. This makes the whole process seem straightforward; so much so, in fact, that it is easy to miss what is important about this. However among groups in which ostensive-inferential communication has only just developed, the combining of existing signals would have been an ingenious step, and the meaning of these composite signals may not have been immediately or obviously apparent. On the contrary, the whole process was probably rather haphazard and painstaking at first. I will discuss what this early ostensive communication might have looked like in Chapter 5.

2.7 Continuity and discontinuity in the origins of language

We are now ready to consider the different ways in which linguistic communication could have emerged. The starting point is a coded communication system, with a fixed and limited set of signals, and the end point is a system of ostensive-inferential communication, made powerful by a large set of conventional codes. The question is: how do we get from A to B? (Whether the starting point preceded or followed the split of our lineage from that of other primates is irrelevant to the immediate question of how we get from code to ostension. If this change preceded the split from the last common ancestor, then there may be evidence of ostension in the communication systems of our closest primate relatives. If on the other hand it followed the split, then there should be no such evidence. I will discuss whether such evidence exists, and more generally whether non-human primate communication is ostensive, in Chapter 4.)

The most basic distinction to make with regards to different approaches to this problem is whether there is continuity or discontinuity between the two end points. An assumption of continuity appears to be an implicit, background assumption of much research on the origins of language. Here are two examples: "It seems quite plausible that the early pre-cursors of language were much more, perhaps almost entirely, coding-decoding in nature. The contexts in which signals were given would have been so limited and so stereotyped that little or no contextual inference would have been necessary. There are degrees of 'coding-decodingness'" (Hurford, 2011, p. 572); "it seems perfectly possible...that our ancestors were able to get on their way to linguistic communication as know it, *without* first becoming proficient mind-readers" (Bar-On, 2013, p. 348, italics in original). Imagine a continuum between, at one end, a system entirely predicated upon codes, and at the other, a system in which codes are augmented by ostension, inference and other pragmatic phenomena. For defenders of the continuity hypothesis, the origins of language involve a transition from one end of this continuum to the other. This transition is assumed to happen in conjunction with the evolution of ever-greater pragmatic capability.

This assumption of continuity between a fully coded communication system at one end, and language at the other, is simply not justified. Let me reiterate a key point from the previous chapter (§1.5): that languages are not sets of codes that are augmented by ostension and inference. The reality is, in an important sense, the very opposite of this: linguistic communication is ostensive-inferential communication augmented by the linguistic code. As such, it's not even clear what continuity could even mean here, and there is certainly no reason to assume that one grew out of the other.

To these problems we can now add the following fact, which follows from my analysis in this chapter of how communication systems emerge: in a system without ostension and inference, the historical pathways along which communication systems must proceed mean that anything more complex than the most simple forms of combinatorial communication is vanishingly unlikely to emerge. In other words, it is not at all "perfectly possible" that some sort of early linguistic state could have emerged prior to ostension and inference. On the contrary, it is all but *im*possible. The arguments I have developed in this chapter and the previous one show that in fact, nothing that looks even remotely like language can emerge prior to the evolution of ostensive-inferential communication.

Even worse, we have already seen what happens when ostension and inference are added to an existing system of coded communication, and the result is not language (§1.5). In the last chapter I discussed how a class of human behaviours that includes laughs, snorts, smiles, frowns, sighs, pouts and so on are probably evolutionary homologues of similar behaviours in our primate cousins (Burling, 2005; Davila Ross et al., 2009; Fitch & Zuberbühler, 2013). All are produced instinctively, as reactions to social events, and are likely all natural codes. I also discussed how we can additionally use these behaviours in a voluntary way, as ostensive signals. I can, for example, voluntarily frown or sigh in an ostensive manner, as a reaction to my friend's suggestion about where we should go for dinner. We can do this because we have added the capacity for ostensive communication to a basic, coded communication system that we share with other primates. This, then, is what happens when ostension is added to an existing system of coded communication. The result is not language, but a set of universal expressive behaviours that can be used flexibly to imply a range of social dispositions, attitudes, inclinations and the like.

Furthermore, I know of no detailed account of what a supposed transition from natural codes to conventional codes might look like. One tentative suggestion is that 'expressive communication' (examples given include teeth-baring, tail-wagging, head tilts, and so on) may form a bridge between animal communication and human language (Bar-On, 2013). However, how this proposal addresses the problems I have raised in this chapter is not clear, and I see no reasons to think that such solutions will be forthcoming. Indeed, expressive communication appears to be a class of code model communication, and is hence subject to the very problems I have highlighted here.

For all these reasons, the assumption of continuity between natural codes and conventional, linguistic codes is not viable. Many important components of the story are missing. For instance, exactly what the required "degrees of coding-decodingness" might look like is nowhere stated. Formal analysis suggests that even the first steps on the path to a richly combinatorial system are all but impossible without ostension and inference. And we already know that when ostension and inference are added to coded communication, language is not the result. In sum, it is, contrary to the quotes above, not at all plausible that "the early pre-cursors of language were much more, perhaps almost entirely, coding-decoding in nature".

Other researchers have arrived at much the same set of conclusions from different lines of argument. Many linguists, for example, have emphasized how several of the most important differences between language and other communication systems in nature are qualitative rather than quantitative (e.g. Bickerton, 1990). In particular, human language is infinite in scope, whereas other systems are limited to a finite range of topics – and since you can't get to an infinite range by simply increasing the current range again and again, then there must be a discontinuity of some sort.

A different route to language immediately makes itself apparent, if only we drop the assumption of continuity. It is this: the cognitive mechanisms that make ostensive-inferential communication possible evolved first for reasons unconnected with communication, but once sufficiently advanced they made ostensive communication possible. The creation of conventional codes then followed, as a way to make this new form of communication expressively powerful. It follows from this that in order to explain the origins of language, what we must understand is: (i) exactly what cognitive abilities make ostension and inference possible; and (ii) how they evolved. Then, armed with this knowledge, we can ask (iii) how, once ostensive-inferential communication exists, it is used to create the various communicative conventions (semantic, syntactic, phonological, etc.) that we call language. The next three chapters will address points (i)–(iii), in turn.

Defenders of the continuity hypothesis make at least two distinct errors. The first is to take the Darwinian lesson that biological form changes gradually, and assume that it also applies to function: animal codes and linguistic codes are both used for communication, and hence, the continuity assumption goes, it is parsimonious to assume that one grew out of the other. But this is wrong. Seeds and semen are both used for reproduction, but we would not assume that one evolved from the other. Similarly, wings and legs are both used for locomotion, but one did not evolve from the other. Biological *form* changes gradually, but *functions* can be discontinuous. Bird wings, for example, originally evolved as heat-regulation devices. Here, a continuous, quantitative change in form (the growth of appendages) resulted in a discontinuous, qualitative change in function (from heat-regulation to flight).

The second error is to assume that linguistic communication is made possible by the existence of codes (i.e. it operates according to the code model) and, hence, that ostension and inference, and indeed pragmatics in general, augment the linguistic code. This assumption is widespread, but wrong. In the previous chapter I both explained why it is wrong, and gave examples of its pervasiveness in language evolution research (see especially §1.5). Nevertheless, if a researcher does hold this assumption, and many do (often unknowingly), then continuity from other systems that are also assumed to operate according to the code model makes intuitive sense. Too many language evolution researchers have simply not thought about the distinction between natural codes and conventional codes in enough depth.

Together, these two mistakes lead to an assumption that there is a Darwinian story that involves a transition from a system of very limited expressivity to a system of vast (in fact infinite) expressivity. This is akin to an assumption that, since flying covers a greater area far more quickly than does, say, walking, and since these are both forms of locomotion, the former must have evolved out of the latter. Clearly this is not the case, and the same is true with regards communication. Ostensive communication is far more expressive than coded communication, but that is no argument in favour of continuity. To argue otherwise, or to argue that this is at least a parsimonious position, is to also argue that it is parsimonious to assume that flying evolved from walking.

This is not to say that there are no specifically linguistic adaptations; that is, adaptations that make the acquisition and use of communicative conventions run more easily and smoothly. On the contrary, it is entirely plausible that such adaptations exist (see Chapter 6). However, the evolution of these traits must have occurred after the initial evolution of ostensive communication itself, because before then there would have been no selective pressure to cause their evolution. Why would any species evolve the capacity to make something run efficiently before the thing itself even exists? Natural selection has no foresight (Dawkins, 1986). Instead, the picture must be this: ostensive communication evolved first, this led to the development of conventional codes – languages – and this change would have provided the selection pressure for the evolution of language-specific adaptations.

Before we move on, I want to briefly mention a recent experiment of mine that encapsulates one of the headline messages of this chapter. It was motivated by the playback experiments used to show that some non-human primates do seem to use a system that is combinatorial, at least in the sense set out in Figure 2.1. In playback experiments, the stimuli of interest are recorded and then played back to the organisms, and their reactions recorded. In the case of non-human primate alarm calls, these playbacks are produced by speakers hidden in bushes and elsewhere. The stimuli are either the natural noises of the predators (if we want to see what alarm calls are made in response to these) or the alarm calls themselves (if we want to see the reactions to these alarm calls). In the experiment with the putty-nosed monkeys, the 'pyow', 'hack', and 'pyow-hack' calls were used as stimuli, and the monkeys were observed to react differently in each case, and the response to the 'pyow-hack' calls was different to the sum of the reactions to the other two calls (Arnold & Zuberbühler, 2008). As we have seen, these findings have led some researchers to suggest that the system described in putty-nosed monkeys is in some sense an evolutionary pre-cursor of human language: the very smallest beginnings of syntax (Zuberbühler, 2002; Hurford, 2011). On this view, an important difference between humans and primates lies in their ability to process signal combinations.

Not so fast. There is a hidden assumption in this conclusion, namely that differences in communication systems reflect differences in species' cognitive abilities to process pairs of jointly produced signals; in other words, that combinatorial communication is in some sense cognitively demanding, and hence only possible in a cognitively sophisticated species. However, the analysis presented in this chapter suggests otherwise. The arguments I have presented lead to the conclusion that combinatorial systems are rare simply because of a chicken-and-egg problem in the creation of composite signals. The prediction that follows from this is that although combinatorial communication will be rare in nature, there is no reason to think that it will be exclusive to the primate lineage. Thus, there may be species that are totally unrelated to humans, and which have totally different cognitive abilities to us (or indeed, no cognitive abilities), but who also use combinatorial communication.

I have tested this prediction in collaboration with teams of microbiologists at the universities of Nottingham and Edinburgh. We conducted a playback experiment on a species totally unrelated to humans, and with no higher cognition: the bacterium *Pseudomonas aeruginosa*. As I outlined in Chapter 1, many species of bacteria communicate by a process known as quorum sensing, in which individual cells produce and react to small diffusible signal molecules, whose density reveals the presence or absence of other bacteria. Just as with the putty-nosed monkey experiments, we exposed *Pseudomonas aeruginosa* to four experimental conditions: two with separate signal molecules, one with the combination of the same two molecules, and a baseline condition of neither signal. We then compared the responses, and found the same general pattern of results as the putty-nosed monkeys system: the effect of the combined signal differs both from the effects of each signal individually, and from the composite effect of the two individual signals (Scott-Phillips et al., 2014; Cornforth et al., 2014).

What does this tell us? Clearly relative levels of cognitive sophistication cannot explain the distribution of combinatorial communication in the natural world. I do not think this should be a surprise: there is no *a priori* reason to think that combinatorial signals will be difficult to process. However, the main point I want to emphasize here is a more subtle one: communication systems, being *systems*, are not themselves biological traits subject to natural selection. They are instead the product of two interacting traits, namely mechanisms for production and mechanisms for reception. What I have sought to show in this chapter is that this interdependence has serious implications for how we think about the evolution of communication. One of these implications is that we cannot simply assume that if we find combinatorial communication in another species, then it is an evolutionary pre-cursor of language.

It is instructive to compare this case with, say, the twist signal given by the homesigning child, Karen (§2.6). There is a sense in which natural codes like this bacterial one are not really combinatorial at all. After all, there is no 'combining' going on. There is really just a third holistic signal, that happens to be comprised of the same pieces as other existing holistic signals. The same seems to be true of the putty-nosed monkey calls: the most recent experimental results suggest that the putty-nosed monkeys interpret the 'combinatorial' pyow-hack calls in exactly this idiomatic way, rather than as the product of two component parts of meaning (Arnold & Zuberbühler, 2012). In contrast, the ostensive creation of new composite signals is clearly combinatorial: although the meaning of the composite signal is not the exact sum of the meanings of the component parts, it is in part a function of those meanings (and the context).

The rarity of combinatorial communication in the natural world cannot be explained by cognitive differences between species, since bacteria have a very different 'cognitive' system to our own, yet they seem to have a communication system that, in terms of its combinatorial complexity, is as close to human language as any other. An alternative explanation must be found, and in this chapter I have sought to provide one. The headline conclusion is that the transition to language followed the emergence of an evolutionarily novel form of communication: ostensive-inferential communication. The next questions to ask, then, are: how does this type of communication work, what cognitive mechanisms make it possible, and how might those mechanisms have evolved? These are the topics of the next two chapters.

* * *

Chapter 2. *In general, animal communication systems emerge in one of two ways: ritualization or sensory manipulation. These processes constrain the form that animal signals can take, and these constraints in turn explain why combinatorial communication is rare in nature. However, they can be overcome if a species has the ability to communicate ostensively. This suggests that the origin of language, which is massively combinatorial, depended on the prior evolution of ostensive communication.*

Chapter 3. *How does ostensive communication work? What are its governing principles? What cognitive mechanisms make it possible? What role does theory-of-mind play? What do the data from children tell us about cognition and communication? Is communication cooperative?*

Chapter 3

Cognition and Communication

3.1 Pragmatic competence

At one point in Lewis Carroll's novel *Through the Looking Glass, and What Alice Found There*, Alice encounters Humpty Dumpty, a large talking egg perched atop a wall. In the conversation that follows, Humpty Dumpty hectors Alice for her innocent understanding of the world of words and their meanings. In so doing, he introduces several problems of meaning and interpretation better than do many of the standard textbooks on semantics and pragmatics. In Carroll's hands, the inherent ambiguity of words and sentences is made animate. In one passage, Humpty Dumpty slyly demonstrates to Alice that listeners often read more into sentences than was literally said:

> "How old did you say you were?"
>
> Alice made a short calculation, and said "Seven years and six months."
>
> "Wrong!" Humpty Dumpty exclaimed triumphantly. "You never said a word like it!"
>
> "I thought you meant 'How old *are* you?'" Alice explained.
>
> "If I'd meant that, I'd have said it," said Humpty Dumpty.

(Humpty Dumpty's point here is so trivial that readers often do not even notice it on a first reading. He had asked "How old *did you say* you were?" and not "How old *are* you?") Then in a later passage Humpty Dumpty does the converse, and insists that Alice should read much more into his use of a word than that word's usual, literal meaning. He concludes an argument he is making by saying "There's glory for you!" The story continues:

> "I don't know what you mean by 'glory'," Alice said.
>
> Humpty Dumpty smiled contemptuously. "Of course you don't – till I tell you. I meant 'There's a nice knock-down argument for you!'"
>
> "But 'glory' doesn't mean 'a nice knock-down argument'," Alice objected.

> "When I use a word," Humpty Dumpty said, in rather a scornful tone, "it means just what I choose it to mean – neither more nor less."
>
> "The question is," said Alice, "whether you *can* make words mean so many different things."

Humpty Dumpty is haughty and grumpy, but the thing is: he is also right. You *can* make words mean many different things. Indeed, you can make them mean pretty much anything at all, if you have the right context. As I explained in Chapter 1, this is a distinctive and inevitable feature of a communication system built upon ostension, because in such systems, meaning is not encoded, but instead evidence is provided for it – and the same piece of evidence can imply many different things, depending on the context in which it is found. Furthermore, it was the transition to this type of communication system that made the emergence of language possible (Chapter 2). These facts raise the following interesting question: how do we do this? That is: how, as signallers, do we know what sort of evidence to provide for a given meaning?; and how, as listeners, do we make the right sort of inferences about that evidence?

I call the ability to perform these tasks *pragmatic competence*. The idea of pragmatic competence can be fleshed out by a comparison with the idea of fluency. Fluency in a language is the mastery of its particular conventions (words, grammar, sounds, etc.). As a native speaker of English I have, by definition, mastery of the conventional codes of English. At the same time, I have an only rudimentary grasp of the set of conventions of Spanish. The idea of fluency is made coherent by the existence of variation; that is, people who are not fluent: if everybody on the planet were native speakers of the same language, the notion of fluency would cease to be meaningful. This is why fluency is something we normally associate with syntax and semantics, phonology and phonetics: all vary between native and non-native speakers of the same language. For the same reason, we do not typically associate the idea of fluency with pragmatic ability, since it does not, for the most part, vary between individuals, or across languages (and where it does vary, we call it a disorder, not disfluency). Whatever language we speak, we are able to use words and phrases to express our intended meaning, and to take context into account in our comprehension of others' utterances. When speakers of two mutually incomprehensible languages attempt to communicate, any failure to do so is not normally due to any pragmatic incompetence on either part, but instead due to the lack of a conventional code over which they both have some command.

In the rare cases where we deliberately choose to override our pragmatic competence, communication breaks down. The cognitive scientist Jean-Louis Dessalles often starts his presentations by emphasizing how unusual it would be if any of us did start to behave in a pragmatically unusual way. In his book *Why We Talk* he says "I sometimes make students do a simple experiment that consists of saying something irrelevant when among their friends or in their family circle" (2007, p. 282). He goes on to give some examples. Here is one:

> Context: Two people walking along a street, past a bin.
>
> A: The bin's green.
>
> B: What are you on about?!

A's comment is true and comprehensible, but irrelevant to anything at hand, and as such was pragmatically *in*competent – hence B's baffled response. Humpty Dumpty did similarly, when he started to use words in any way he pleased, regardless of whether or not Alice was familiar with those usages. His use of 'glory' to mean 'a nice knock-down argument' might have worked with a different speaker, but Alice is young and not used to highly abstract metaphors. Like Dessalles' student, his wilful use of such language, when he would have known Alice would likely struggle with it, was pragmatically incompetent. The predictable result was a failure in communication.

Pragmatic competence makes ostensive communication possible. In the previous two chapters I argued that, evolutionarily, it was the origins of this ability that enabled language to emerge. The next question to ask, then, is how humans are able to do this. That is: what principles best describe and govern ostensive communication, and what cognitive mechanisms make it possible? The classic starting point for these questions comes from the philosopher Paul Grice, whose work on meaning we discussed in Chapter 1. The next section outlines the Gricean approach. However, Grice's proposals are problematic in several respects, not least that they are cognitively implausible. Several alternatives have been proposed, some of which seek only to adjust and modify Grice's original ideas, and others that propose more radical change. The most influential of these approaches has been Relevance Theory, which provides a powerful and empirically testable and tested framework. In §3.3 I will describe its central ideas. This will then form the background for my discussion, in the remainder of this chapter, of the cognitive mechanisms that make it possible for us to engage in pragmatically competent ostensive communication.

3.2 The maxims of conversation

It is easy to lose sight of what pragmatic competence actually consists of. Indeed, while the notion of fluency is recognized by anybody who has ever come into contact with speakers of a different language, the role that pragmatic competence plays in language was not properly articulated until the work of a group of philosophers of language in the middle of the 20th century, the most influential of which was Paul Grice (see Grice, 1989 for a collection of his work on this topic). Grice was the first to provide a detailed exposition of exactly what ostensive communication consists of (i.e. the expression and recognition of intentions; see Chapter 1), and also the first to provide an account, based on what he called the *Cooperative Principle*, of how speakers and listeners might actually do this.

The Cooperative Principle is: 'Make your contribution such as it is required, at the stage at which it occurs, by the accepted purpose or direction of the talk exchange in which you are engaged'. This is normally done by obeying four *maxims of conversation*: Quality (tell the truth), Quantity (do not say too much or too little), Relation (be relevant), and Manner (be clear and concise). The idea is that speakers choose, in most cases, to adhere to these maxims, and this adherence provides a sufficient basis for listeners to infer the speaker's intended meaning (Grice, 1975). To illustrate how the maxims are supposed to operate, consider the following exchange (from Levinson, 1983):

A: Where's Bill?

B: There's a yellow VW outside Sue's house.

Taken literally, B's utterance fails to address A's question. It appears to violate the maxims of Quantity (the presence of the yellow VW is more information than was requested) and Relation (what has the yellow VW to do with where Bill is?). There is, then, an apparent failure of cooperation. However, rather than draw the conclusion that B is uncooperative, A assumes that this is not what has occurred and instead searches for implicatures that can enrich his interpretation, such that B's utterance does satisfy the four maxims. This course of reasoning leads him to conclude that Bill owns a yellow VW, and so may be in Sue's house at the moment, and that this was A's intended meaning.

Numerous objections can be and have been lodged against this basic picture, and the goal of much research in pragmatics has been to alter, refine, and otherwise fine-tune the Gricean analysis in response to these problems (e.g. Levinson, 1983; Horn, 1984). The result is that (neo-)Gricean pragmatics resembles "an untidy collection of usage principles, accrued over decades of careful observation, which together give some substantial account of uncoded utterance meaning. It may be a bit ramshackle, but it delivers the goods; and new developments help to remedy deficiencies" (Levinson, 1989, p. 469). Although these observations were made more than 20 years ago, they remain a reasonable description of much of the discipline today.

However, it is not at all clear how this "untidy collection of usage principles" is instantiated in the mind (Sperber & Wilson, 1995; Wilson, 2000). In fact, while the Cooperative Principle and its subsequent refinements address the philosophical concerns raised by Grice and his contemporaries, they lack psychological and empirical plausibility. This can be seen most clearly when we consider how communication guided by the Cooperative Principle might actually work (the argument below follows Sperber, 2000, and Sperber & Wilson, 2002). Consider a dialogue as simple as:

ANN: Can we trust John to do as we tell him and defend the interests of the Linguistics Department in the University Council?

BOB: John is a soldier!

How can Bob's utterance, which is metaphorical, be interpreted in a sensible way? Below is a possible course of reasoning that Ann might pursue, based on the idea that what listeners do in interpretation is to first search for interpretations that are consistent with the Cooperative Principle, and consider alternatives only if this strategy fails:

i. Bob seems to have said that John is a soldier.
ii. Bob does not believe that John is a soldier, and he knows that I know that he does not believe that John is a soldier.
iii. Yet Bob is respecting the Cooperative Principle, and in particular, the maxim of Quality (be truthful).
iv. (ii) and (iii) together imply that Bob cannot mean that John is a soldier.
v. Bob must be trying to convey a closely related meaning, one that is compatible with the presumption that the speaker is cooperative.
vi. By inference to the best available explanation, Bob means that John is like a soldier: he is devoted to his duty, obedient to orders, etc.

The distinctive feature of this approach is that the initial, non-metaphorical interpretation (that John is literally a soldier) is considered and rejected before any metaphorical interpretation. If this is indeed how comprehension works, then metaphorical utterances, along with irony, indirect speech, implicature and other non-literal uses of language, should take longer to process, and be more prone to error, than literal language use. A large literature of psycholinguistic evidence shows that this is simply not the case (Gibbs, 1994; Gibbs & Tendahl, 2006). Further problems with the Cooperative Principle, which I will not exhaustively survey here, include, among others, the fact that several of its key concepts (e.g. Relation) are only vaguely defined, its predictions are almost entirely *ex post facto*, and several important aspects of how it is supposed to work are not fleshed out (Wilson & Sperber, 1981; Sperber & Wilson, 1995). In particular: how does the listener even know that a maxim is being violated, and hence that they should search for some non-literal interpretation? In sum, the Gricean approach to pragmatics, and consequently some of the neo-Gricean approaches that build upon it, exhibits several problems that render it psychologically and empirically implausible.

This state of affairs led the anthropologist Dan Sperber and the linguist Deirdre Wilson to develop an alternative, post-Gricean approach to pragmatics. On the one hand, they took inspiration from Grice's attempt to address serious conceptual issues about communication including, most importantly, the inability of the code model to handle a number of cases of everyday language use (Grice, 1957, 1969). On the other hand, they wished to develop an account of human communication that was cognitively plausible and empirically testable. The result was *Relevance Theory* (Sperber & Wilson, 1995).

3.3 A paradigm for pragmatics

For many years pragmatics was seen, and in some quarters still is seen, as a topic of only peripheral relevance to the study of language. This is quite natural if one thinks (falsely) that linguistic communication operates according to the code model, whereby the linguistic code makes communication possible. On this view, pragmatic abilities make it unnecessary for speakers to fully encode one's meaning, although one could have done so, if required. Pragmatic abilities are simply a bonus that makes life easier. If this is your view, then it follows that the code should be the primary, central object of study for linguistics, and indeed that is the case for much of the discipline. From here, it is easy and natural to treat pragmatics as a file drawer into which are thrown those awkward aspects of language that do not fit so straightforwardly into a code model. The result is that many analyses of language "force a clearly pragmatic matter into a syntactico-semantic straitjacket" (Bar-Hillel, 1971, p. 401). This is plainly unsatisfactory, and there is now increasing recognition that it is more accurate and more useful to see pragmatics as the study of a capacity of mind, namely the capacity for pragmatic competence (Sperber & Wilson, 1995; Carston, 2002a). Relevance Theory has been at the forefront of this change.

Relevance Theory accepts and builds upon some of Grice's insights; most importantly, that human communication involves the expression and recognition of intentions. At the same time, it rejects others, such as the need for the Cooperative Principle described above. Because of this partial rejection of Gricean theory, Relevance Theory is often presented as a *post-*Gricean theory, to be contrasted with the more traditional neo-Gricean accounts that constitute the "ramshackle" edifice built more-or-less atop the Gricean foundation. It has had a profound and substantial impact in both pragmatics and cognitive science. In this section I outline the central ideas of Relevance Theory, as important background to the subsequent discussion of the cognitive mechanisms involved in communication (for further background see e.g. Wilson & Sperber, 2012).

As its name suggests, at the heart of Relevance Theory is the notion of *relevance*. The relevance of a stimulus is defined as a trade-off between, on the one hand, the extent of worthwhile changes that the stimulus has on one's mental representations (called *positive cognitive effects*), and, on the other, the *processing effort* required to achieve them. As an example, consider again Humpty Dumpty and Alice. He asks her how old she is. She could truthfully say any of the following:

(a) Under 18 years.
(b) Seven years and six months.
(c) Either I am seven years and six months, or 2,368,956 divided by 4 is not 592,239.

All of these are relevant to Humpty Dumpty, to some degree. That is: all contain information that will change his mental representations in a worthwhile way. After all, they all provide information about Alice's age, as requested. In fact, (b) and (c) change his mental representations in the same way: both contain the information that Alice is seven years and six months. However, (b) requires less processing effort than does (c) – and hence is the more relevant of the two. (b) is also more relevant than (a), but for a different reason. (a) and (b) require more-or-less the same degree of processing effort, and both have worthwhile information, but (b) has *more* worthwhile information, since it more directly answers Humpty Dumpty's question. Thus, (b) has more worthwhile effects than (c), but for the same processing effort, and so is the more relevant of the two. Relevance is, in sum, the trade-off between positive cognitive effects, and processing effort.

The relevance of an ostensive stimulus is always dependent on the specifics. The two qualities on which it depends, cognitive effects and processing effort, both vary according to the situation in which the stimulus is produced: who the listener is, what they already know, what information is already contained in the present communicative context, and so on. As such, there is no such thing as the relevance of an utterance, or indeed of any ostensive stimulus, independent of listener or context. What is relevant to me, now, may not be relevant to you, nor to my future or past self.

Relevance Theory makes two headline claims about relevance, and the role it plays in ostensive communication. These two *Principles of Relevance* are the centrepieces of the theory.

The first principle is the *Cognitive Principle*. It states that *human cognition tends to be geared towards the maximization of relevance*. In other words, our cognitive systems are such that both our decisions about what stimuli to attend to (ostensive or otherwise), and our interpretations of those stimuli, tend to maximize the relevance of the stimuli.

In her book *On Looking: Eleven Walks with Expert Eyes*, the cognitive scientist Alexandra Horowitz reports on eleven walks she took around the same New York City block, each with a different companion, all of whom attended to and pointed out different things in that environment. The book's opening passage elegantly illustrates how our decisions about what to attend to affect, in the most fundamental way, how we understand the world: "You missed that. Right now, you are missing the vast majority of what is happening around you. You are missing the events unfolding in your body, in the distance, and right in front of you ... This ignorance is useful: indeed, we compliment it and call it concentration ... [and] we tend to bring this focus to every activity we do – not just the most complicated but also the most quotidian" (2013, pp. 1–2). Horowitz does not mention the Cognitive Principle of Relevance, but her research nevertheless converges on a crucial aspect of it: "Attention is an intentional, unapologetic discriminator. It asks what is relevant right now, and gears us up to notice only that" (*ibid.*, p. 12). And then, once we have decided what stimuli to attend to, we must interpret them, and what the Cognitive Principle claims is that, of the many possible interpretations, the ones we choose tend to be those that are most relevant for us.

The Cognitive Principle is, in effect, a claim about the efficiency of the human mind, specifically that it is well-designed to interpret the world around it – which, from an evolutionary perspective, is precisely what we should expect to be the case. It does not claim that human cognition always or necessarily converges on the most relevant interpretation of incoming stimuli, nor that there are no individual differences in this respect; it claims only that, on average, human cognition tends in the direction of maximal relevance. In other words, it tends towards optimal performance, just as any trait that is important for an organism's survival and prosperity should do.

To illustrate how this Cognitive Principle works in the context of ostensive communication, let's revisit an example exchange from earlier in the chapter:

A: Where's Bill?

B: There's a yellow VW outside Sue's house.

Previously, we explained this in terms of the Gricean maxims: B's utterance violates the maxims of both Quantity and Relation, and so A was forced to search for an alternative interpretation. Relevance Theory explains it as follows. In order to interpret B's utterance, A searches for an interpretation that optimizes relevance i.e. one that maximizes the positive cognitive effects, and minimizes the processing effort required. (Relevance Theory also describes how this search is performed, although I will not enter into those details here; see Girotto et al., 2001.) This optimization is achieved if we assume that Bill drives a yellow VW. Then, B's utterance achieves positive cognitive effects in A, and indeed achieves those effects in a way that requires less processing effort than any other stimulus would have done (e.g. 'There's a red Volvo and a yellow VW outside Sue's house'). Experimental studies support the claim that human cognition looks to maximize the relevance of stimuli it receives; in other words, that it attempts to achieve the greatest cognitive effects for the smallest amount of cognitive effort (van der Henst et al., 2002b).

The second principle of relevance is the *Communicative Principle*. It states that *every ostensive stimulus carries a presumption of its own optimal relevance*. What this means is that when signallers produce signals, they produce those signals that maximize the relevance of the stimulus to the audience, given both the signaller's goals and preferences, and what the signaller knows about the receiver's goals and preferences. In other words, they will produce the signal that, given their intended meaning, is the most relevant, in the technical sense described above. This fact thus motivates receivers to interpret the stimuli, and helps them make sensible inferences about the signaller's intended meaning.

Here is a simple, real-world example: when approached in the street and asked for the time by somebody who says they have an appointment soon, people will round their answer (e.g. to say "5 to 3" instead of "2:56", or "4 minutes to 3") if the appointment begins between 15 and 30 minutes' hence. If, however, the appointment is within the next 15 minutes, then they will not round their answer (van der Henst et al., 2002a; Gibbs & Bryant, 2008). This is because the precise, non-rounded answer requires more processing effort on the part of the listener, and so is used only if that effort is compensated by a corresponding cognitive effect – and this is only the case if there is not long until the appointment, since time is then of the essence. Similarly, we expect Alice to say that she is seven years and six months, and not either of the other two options, since these either achieve fewer cognitive effects (in (a)), or require more cognitive effort on the audience's part (in (c)), and would hence be less relevant.

In essence, the Communicative Principle of Relevance says that the very act of producing an ostensive stimulus is in effect a guarantee that it is worthwhile for the intended audience to pay attention to the stimulus itself – because doing so will lead to positive cognitive effects for them. What this means in practice is that the very production of an ostensive stimulus effectively says to the audience 'This signal is *for you* – you will find value in it'. Receivers then can then use this fact as a basic assumption in their inference of the signaller's meaning. Suppose that we are in a bar. My glass, which is visible to both of us, is empty. It is possible that I would like another drink, but unless I say or do something to indicate as much, you would not have any grounds to conclude that I *do* want a drink. If, however, I pick up my glass and wave it in front of you, then, by the Communicative

Principle of Relevance, I effectively announce that the emptiness of my glass has an interpretation that is relevant for you. Knowing this, you now have grounds to conclude that I do indeed want a further drink.

Here is another example. *Get Fuzzy* is a comic strip that appears in many newspapers worldwide. It features an advertising executive and his two anthropomorphized pets, one cat and one dog. The recurring joke is the stereotypical behaviour of the two animals, and specifically the self-centred cat's exploitation of the naïve, simple dog. In the strip in Figure 3.1, the banal conversation of Satchel (the dog) infuriates Bucky (the cat), because it seems to have no worthwhile cognitive effects, and is hence a distraction and waste of time. In other words, it fails to deliver the degree of relevance that was implicitly promised the moment Satchel opened his mouth. Irrelevance is in a sense a form of deceit, and Bucky reacts accordingly.

Sometimes people are very explicit about the fact that what they have to say is worth paying attention to. The 15th- and 16th-century philosopher Francis Bacon had his publisher print, on the front of one of his works, the following words: *Francis of Verulam reasoned thus with himself, and judged it to be for the interest of the present and future generations that they should be made acquainted with his thoughts.* To be so explicit about the fact that the audience should pay attention was perhaps somewhat immodest, but what Relevance Theory tells us is that we all do this, every time we speak.

At the same time, the signaller is not always correct that what they have to say is worthy of attention. Some people take many words to say very little (and so their signals demand more processing effort than is necessary), and others are bores, at least some of the time (and so what they say has insufficient cognitive effects for the receiver). We all know people like Satchel the dog. However, such variations around the optimum are tiny in comparison to the range of variation that is possible in principle, and which we simply do not see in those who are pragmatically competent – which is all typically developing humans.

Figure 3.1 *Expectations of relevance?* According to the Communicative Principle of Relevance, Satchel the dog's utterance carries a guarantee of relevance – but Bucky the cat does not see where that relevance might come from. GET FUZZY

The Principles of Relevance operate at a quite different level of analysis to the Gricean maxims. The maxims are a description of what speakers are simply thought to aim for, and which they can choose to violate, as a normal and legitimate means of communication, if they so wish. They are normative. That is: they describe a norm that individuals are, for the most part, expected to adhere to, but can choose not to. In contrast, the Principles of Relevance are fundamental facets of human communication. They are not something that speakers aim for: they are what pragmatically competent individuals *do*. We could not violate the Principles of Relevance even if we wished to. When Dessalles' students make irrelevant statements, their audiences do not assume that they have violated the Principles of Relevance. Instead, the audience is simply confused, because pragmatically competent individuals do not violate the Principles of Relevance, by definition. Indeed, if any of us did habitually produce irrelevant utterances, we would likely soon be seen as socially incompetent in one way or another. (In contrast, we violate the Gricean maxims all the time.) Furthermore, if the Principles did not hold, then communication as we know it simply would not be possible (see below). Unlike the Gricean maxims, it is at this most foundational level of analysis that the Principles of Relevance operate.

The two Principles of Relevance, Cognitive and Communicative, interact with one another to make ostensive communication possible. Without them, ambiguity and misunderstanding would be so widespread that communication would fail far more often than it succeeds. If the Communicative Principle did not hold, then receivers would not be able to assume that signals are more-or-less optimally relevant, and would consequently not be able to determine the speaker's intended meaning. And if the Cognitive Principle did not hold, listeners would not be able to interpret that evidence correctly. Here is a simple illustration (Wilson & Sperber, 2004):

> PETER: Did John pay back the money he owed you?
>
> MARY: No, he forgot to go to the bank.

To take just one aspect of this reply: how does Peter know that the 'bank' is the one on the high street, and not the one on the side of the river? The answer is that he does not and cannot know this, unless: (i) he assumes that Mary intends him to find her utterance relevant i.e. that the Communicative Principle holds; and (ii) he is able to determine with some degree of accuracy what the most relevant interpretation of Mary's utterance actually is i.e. that the Cognitive Principle holds. If either of these conditions did not hold, then he would not be able to determine which bank Mary was referring to, and consequently even an utterance as apparently straightforward as "No, he forgot to go to the bank" would be fatally ambiguous.

Rival frameworks for pragmatics exist, each with their own advocates and arguments (e.g. Horn, 1984; Levinson, 2000; Bara, 2010) – but none, in my view, has anything like the same appeal as Relevance Theory, either theoretically or empirically (see e.g. Origgi & Sperber, 2000; Carston, 2002b; Wharton, 2009; Wilson & Sperber, 2012 for defences of Relevance Theory). There are four main reasons for this. The first is that its predictions have stood up to a significant amount of empirical scrutiny, including a good number of controlled laboratory experiments (see van der Henst & Sperber, 2004 for a review of direct experimental tests of Relevance Theory; and Henderson et al., 2009 for a review of research that shows how considerations of relevance determine where we direct our attention). The second is that it has been successfully used to develop and test novel experimental predictions in several adjacent disciplines, for instance developmental psychology (e.g. Southgate et al., 2009) and language acquisition (e.g. Henderson et al., 2013), among others. The third reason is that it integrates with theoretical frameworks in many disciplines adjacent to pragmatics, including cognitive anthropology (e.g. Sperber, 1996), psycholinguistics (e.g. Noveck & Sperber, 2006), semantics (e.g. Carston, 2002a), evolutionary biology (e.g. Scott-Phillips, 2010c), and others.

Finally, I have already mentioned the fourth reason why Relevance Theory is to be preferred over the supposed alternatives: the *type* of explanation it provides. Whereas neo-Gricean accounts are post-hoc descriptions of what speakers aim for, Relevance Theory provides an explanation of the principles by which ostensive communication must work, given the different goals and abilities of speakers and listeners (Scott-Phillips, 2010c; see also §6.3). One review expressed dissatisfaction with this aspect of Relevance Theory, complaining that such generality is "too ambitious and globally reductive" (Levinson, 1989, p. 456; see also e.g. Cummings, 1998). The review concludes with a quotation from Abraham Lincoln: "People who like this sort of thing will find this the sort of thing they like" (*ibid.*, p. 470). Perhaps this is true, but I do not see it as a criticism. The people who like this sort of thing are lumpers (people who search for generality in their explanations; to be contrasted with splitters, who search for specificity) – and there is nothing wrong with lumping in science. On the contrary, it is how we develop our major theories and paradigms. Relevance Theory does this for ostensive-inferential communication, and hence for pragmatics.

3.4 Recursive mindreading and ostensive communication: the theory

In one episode of the US sitcom *Friends* ('The one where everybody finds out') the main characters divide into two factions engaged in an elaborate game of bluff and double bluff, where each side pretends that they don't know that the others know that they know what the others know. At one point Phoebe declares "They don't know that we know they know we know!", and Joey, in response, just shakes his head, baffled. Playing on the same theme, here is a passage from James Joyce's *Ulysses*: "What, reduced to their simplest reciprocal form, were Bloom's thoughts about Stephen's thoughts about Bloom and Bloom's thoughts about Stephen's thoughts about Bloom's thoughts about Stephen? He thought that he thought that he was a jew whereas he knew that he knew that he knew that he was not". In this section I will explain both how and why this sort of recursive mind-reading is critical for ostensive-inferential communication.

My question in this section is: what cognitive mechanisms make ostensive communication possible in the first place? I should immediately make it explicit that my goal is not to list all the mechanisms involved in ostensive communication. Plainly, many different aspects of human cognition contribute towards an explanation of why ostensive communication takes the form that it does (if, say, our memory were more or less powerful than it is, then perhaps our sentences would be longer or shorter than they are, and our conversations more or less haphazard). Instead, what I want to identify is those mechanisms without which there could be no ostensive communication at all. In short: my focus here is on what makes ostensive communication exist in the first place, not what makes it the way it is. What makes ostensive communication possible is a critical question to ask because, as we saw in the previous chapter, the transition to language became tenable only after the prior advent of ostensive communication. What made ostensive communication possible ultimately made language possible too.

The obvious starting point for any discussion of this sort is *theory-of-mind*: the ability to mentally represent the mental states of others (Premack & Woodruff, 1978; Apperly, 2011). I can think and reason about your thoughts, and you about mine, and as such we both have theory-of-mind. Theory-of-mind is the one trait that uncontroversially features in all discussions of the various social cognitive abilities necessary for ostensive communication, and hence for language (e.g. Hurford, 2003; Cheney & Seyfarth, 2005; Tomasello, 2008; Fitch et al., 2010). The general reasons why theory-of-mind is so widely accepted as critical are not difficult to see: when we communicate with others, we must know something about their minds in order to understand their intended meanings, and indeed to tailor our own utterances to them. Most evolutionary analyses of why theory-of-mind is necessary for ostensive communication stop here, and move on to the question of whether it is shared, in some way or another, by other species (e.g. Fitch et al., 2010). That question is of course critically important, and I will discuss it in the next chapter.

However, exactly how theory-of-mind contributes to pragmatic competence is rarely spelt out. I will do this here. What we shall see is that there are reasons why it is of critical importance to ostensive communication that are even more basic and fundamental than the general reasons given above. In particular, we shall see that the very act of ostensive communication, in both production and comprehension, is an exercise in reading others' minds. Moreover, it involves not just the mental representation of others' mental states, but the mental representation of others' mental representations of one's own mental states, and indeed several further levels of representation beyond these. I call the ability to entertain and process these multiply embedded levels *recursive mindreading*, or *mental metarepresentation*. (I use these terms because the phrase 'theory-of-mind' is used by a great many researchers in a great many subtly different ways, and I neither wish nor need to enter into any discussion of such minutiae; 'mindreading' comes with less baggage.) When discussing recursive mindreading, subscripts can be used to indicate each embedded level: I can think$_1$ about what you think$_2$ about what she thinks$_3$..., and so on. Phoebe's declaration was an announcement of a meta-meta-meta-representation: "They don't know$_1$ that we know$_2$ they know$_3$ we know$_4$!" The number of embedded representations involved is sometimes called the order of intentionality.

To begin, I would like to reiterate what ostensive communication is defined as: the expression and recognition of communicative intentions (and hence informative intentions too) (§1.4). Like all intentions, communicative intentions are mental states. What does it mean to express and recognize them? To answer this question, and hence show that ostensive communication involves high levels of recursive mindreading, I will walk through a series of scenarios, each with an additional level of mindreading, and spell out what is and is not entailed at each of these extra levels. These stages are not original with me; they are reconstructed versions of scenarios described elsewhere (in particular Sperber, 2000, but also Grice, 1982). We shall see that only once we have added several levels of mindreading does proper ostensive-inferential communication actually occur.

Scenario one. Mary is picking and eating berries. She does this because *the berries are edible.*

Scenario two. Mary is picking and eating berries. Peter is watching her, and hence forms a belief about the edibility of the berries. Here, *Peter believes*$_1$ *that the berries are edible* (because otherwise Mary would not be eating them). Note that Mary may or may not know that Peter is watching. Whether she does or not, it makes no difference to her intentions or behaviour.

Scenario three. Mary is picking and eating berries. Peter is watching her. Mary knows that Peter is watching her, and she wants him to believe that the berries are edible. So: *Mary intends*$_1$ *that Peter believes*$_2$ *that the berries are edible*. Here, note that Mary's behaviour here is identical to her behaviour in scenarios one and two. All that has changed is that in scenario two Mary informed Peter about the edibility of the berries only incidentally (indeed, she need not even have known that she was doing this), whereas here she does so intentionally – and she can satisfy this intention (that Peter believes that the berries are edible) simply by picking and eating berries. She need not and does not do anything more than this. Mary's intention is an informative intention.

Scenario four. Mary is picking and eating berries. Peter is watching her. Mary knows that Peter is watching her, and she wants him to believe that the berries are edible. Furthermore, Peter knows that Mary knows that he is watching her and, for whatever reason, he has reason to believe that she would like him to believe that the berries are edible. Correspondingly, *he believes*$_1$ *that she intends*$_2$ *that he believes*$_3$ *that the berries are edible*. Mary, however, does not know that Peter believes this. After all, she has not yet made her intention manifest to Peter. Indeed, Mary's physically observable behaviour is the same as it is in scenarios one, two, and three. As yet, she has not picked berries in a way that signals to Peter that her behaviour is intended to be informative. She has not yet signalled signalhood. All that is different between this and scenario three is that here Peter believes, correctly, that Mary has an informative intention.

Scenario five. Mary is picking and eating berries. Peter is watching her. Mary knows that Peter is watching her, and she wants him to know that the berries are edible. Furthermore, Peter knows that Mary knows that he is watching her, *and* Mary knows that Peter knows this. As such, when she eats the berries, *she intends*$_1$ *that he believes*$_2$ *that she intends*$_3$ *that he believes*$_4$ *that the berries are edible*. In this scenario, an important change occurs: Mary has reason to modify her behaviour. Previously, in scenarios three and four, she could satisfy the only intention she had in these scenarios simply by picking and eating berries. Here, however, she has two intentions. One of them (... *intends*$_3$ ...) is the informative intention discussed previously, and she satisfies it in the same way: by picking and eating berries. The other (... *intends*$_1$ ...) is, however, new to this scenario. It is a communicative intention, and it is not satisfied by simply picking and eating the berries. Its goal is to cause Peter to believe that Mary has an informative intention (... *intends*$_3$ ...), and so to satisfy this intention Mary picks and eats the berries in a particularly stylized, exaggerated manner. This reveals to Peter not only that the berries are edible, but also that she intends to reveal as much to him.

Scenario six. As per scenario five, including the fact that Mary picks and eats the berries in a particularly stylized, exaggerated manner. Because of this, Peter grasps both of Mary's intentions, informative and communicative, as laid out above. As such, *Peter believes*$_1$ *that Mary intends*$_2$ *that he believes*$_3$ *that she intends*$_4$ *that he believes*$_5$ *that the berries are edible*. This is ostensive-inferential communication proper.

Let me reiterate the crucial point here: it is only in scenario five that Mary has a communicative intention. This is why, in order to satisfy her intentions, she can and should do more than simply pick and eat the berries. Such behaviour was sufficient in scenario three, where her only intention was that Peter believe that the berries are edible. However in scenario five she has an additional intention, and this can only be satisfied by a behaviour that reveals that she intends that Peter believes that she intends that Peter believes that the berries are edible. This is why she picks and eats the berries in a stylized, rather than normal way. She could equally well have had another behaviour stand in place of this – she could have mimed eating the berries, for example – so long as the behaviour in question has no plausible explanation except as a way to make it apparent to Peter that she intends to make him believe that the berries are edible; in other words, that she *means* that the berries are edible (§1.6). Correspondingly, it is only in scenario six that Peter recognizes Mary's communicative intention. Once Mary's behaviour has no other plausible explanation, then, assuming that he has sufficient metarepresentational abilities, Peter has sufficient evidence to conclude not only that the berries are edible, but also that Mary intended him to believe that. This is what he does in scenario six.

Put another way, if we only have scenarios one to four, then we would live in a world where there would be no material difference between eating berries because you want to, and eating berries to let me know that they are edible. Nobody would signal signalhood. As potential 'signallers', we would try to influence others' behaviour, but would have no way to make it apparent to our audience that we were doing so, and hence why they should pay attention to us. As 'audiences', we would be able to interpret others' intentions, but we would have no way to know when others actually want us to, and hence no way to reliably determine when they actually mean something, and hence what they mean. This is clearly not what the real world is actually like – yet it is what we get if we stop at scenario four.

Correspondingly, it is only in scenario six that the interaction becomes an instance of communication. As discussed in Chapter 2, communication involves designed interdependence (§2.2): an action should cause a reaction, and both behaviours should be designed to fulfil their half of this interaction. In scenarios one to four, there is an action (Mary eats the berries) which causes a reaction (Peter creates a mental representation that the berries are edible), but they are not designed to be opposing halves of the same interaction: even in scenario four Peter does not know that Mary is trying to influence him, and hence does not know that there is any interaction that his behaviour can be half of. This is why 'signallers' and 'audiences' are in scare quotes in the paragraphs above: at this stage, these labels do not technically apply. In fact, these scenarios illustrate the role that interdependence plays in the definition of communication. In scenarios two to five Mary's behaviour is a cue for Peter, and in scenarios three to five Mary is coercing Peter. However, interdependence, and hence communication, does not arrive until scenario six, when Mary expresses and Peter recognizes her communicative intention. This makes their behaviours interdependent, and the interaction communicative.

These scenarios also, incidentally, reiterate that the content of a communicative intention is an informative intention. In other words, that to express a communicative intention *is* to make it apparent that one has an informative intention. As such, a communicative intention is not simply an intention to communicate. It is more specific and rich than that: it is an intention that the audience recognize that one has a particular informative intention. This is exactly what we have in scenario five: Mary expresses her communicative intention (that *she intends*$_1$ *that he believes*$_2$...) that Peter recognizes that she has an informative intention (...*that she intends*$_3$ *that he believes*$_4$ *that the berries are edible*). In scenario six, Peter recognizes that this is Mary's intention, and ostensive communication thus occurs.

Note that in addition to this role in the *creation* of ostensive communication, mindreading is also necessary for the competent *use* of ostensive communication. It is theoretically possible that ostensive communication could be used poorly. This would in particular be the case if speakers provided inappropriate evidence for their communicative intentions, and/or if listeners made inappropriate inferences based on the evidence provided to them. Crucial here is *common ground*: the information (the mental representations) that is known to two (or more) individuals, and which both of them know, or believe, that the other knows (see Clark, 1996 for extensive discussion). Without common ground, signallers would not know what sort of evidence would be the right sort of evidence to lead receivers to the signaller's intended meaning; and receivers, for their part, would not be able to make the right sort of inferences. In the terms of Relevance Theory: what is and is not common ground helps signallers establish what the optimally relevant stimulus will be, and it helps receivers establish the relevance of that stimulus. Of course, misunderstanding can still occur if either party is mistaken about what is or is not in the common ground. For example, when Americans and Brits converse, confusion and indeed embarrassment can easily arise if either side makes the mistaken assumption that there is common ground over the meanings of the words bun, faggot, fanny, pants, pissed, rubber, and shag, among others.

For the present purposes, the critical point to make is that, just as they were for the creation of ostensive communication, mindreading skills are essential here. The point is easily grasped: pragmatic competence requires that signallers provide the right sort of evidence *for this particular audience*, and the audience, for their part, must assume that the speaker has sought to provide the right evidence for them in order to interpret the utterance correctly. Both these tasks involve the representation of others' minds (Sperber & Wilson, 1995; Clark, 1996; Gibbs & Tendahl, 2006; Tomasello, 2008). Indeed, these are the reasons why mindreading (theory-of-mind) is almost always listed as a crucial pre-requisite for pragmatic competence. What is less appreciated, and what I have sought to bring attention to in this section, is that, in addition to this role in the execution of ostensive communication, mindreading is also critical to the creation of ostensive communication in the first place. Without it, there could be no ostensive communication, and hence no linguistic communication, and no languages.

3.5 Recursive mindreading and ostensive communication: the data

The hypothesis that ostensive communication is ultimately an exercise in recursive mindreading is often greeted with skepticism, for it seems to involve a complex description of something that is phenomenologically simple. Put simply, when we actually communicate, it feels like a cognitively straightforward activity, and not at all like the complex task described in the previous section. For instance, "The problem... [is] that intuitively we don't feel that in everyday communication we are engaging in such complex and recursive cognitive processes" (Gómez, 1994, p. 68). The literature on cognition and communication contains several sentiments of this sort (e.g. Glüer & Pagin, 2003; Breheny, 2006). These intuitions are often fleshed out with the observation that there are types of communicator that seem to falsify the recursive mindreading claim. Specifically, young children are pragmatically competent but, it is commonly assumed, likely do not have a good command of high-level recursive mindreading abilities. If this objection is correct, it would seriously undermine the analysis presented in the previous section. In this section I shall explain why the objection is misplaced.

The classic test of basic mindreading abilities is the *false-belief task* (first used in Wimmer & Perner, 1983). The idea is that the most robust demonstration that an individual is able to represent others' minds is when the content of those minds is different to what the focal individual knows to be the case (Dennett, 1978). The false-belief task is typically played out using toy dolls. One character (typically called Sally) puts an object (say, a ball) inside another (a metal box). Sally then exits the scene, and another character (typically called Ann) comes along. Ann moves the ball from the metal box and into a different, cardboard box. Ann then exits, and Sally returns. Then the experimental subject is asked the key question: where will Sally look for the ball? If the subject is able to represent Sally's mind, then s/he should say that Sally will look where Sally thinks the ball is, namely in the metal box – *even though s/he knows that the ball is elsewhere*. But if the subject is not able to represent Sally's mind, then s/he will not say this, and will either pick the cardboard box (where s/he knows the ball is), or pick at random.

Children under four years of age typically fail this task (Wellman et al., 2001). Success rates can be modified slightly by manipulating the contextual details of the task, and there is obviously some variation between individuals. Nevertheless, this basic finding has been consistently replicated in multiple different laboratories over many years. In short, children's failure in the classic false-belief task before the age of four is among the most robust results in all psychology.

Yet, at the same time, even young children are very adept communicators. This can be clearly seen both in experiments and in natural data. Here are just a few examples (see also §4.4). If an object that an adult wants falls from a shelf, the child will only point out its new location if the adult had not seen the object fall (O'Neill, 1996; Liszkowski et al., 2008). One-year-old children are able to take account of the social context, such as the signaller's motivations, or the child's past experiences with them, when comprehending a signaller's behaviour (Liebal et al., 2009). Analysis of children's natural language shows that their grammatical choices are sensitive to both what their conversational partner already knows, and what the conversational partner is currently attending to (see e.g. Skarabela, 2007; Skarabela et al., 2013; Hughes & Allen, in press).

These and many similar findings are hard to simultaneously reconcile both with results from the false-belief task, and with the recursive mindreading claim presented in the previous section (Breheny, 2006). Put simply, the headline result from decades of research with the classic false-belief task, and the fact that even young children are pragmatically competent, together seem to falsify the claim that ostensive communication involves recursive mindreading.

A similar dilemma arises with Autism Spectrum Disorder (ASD). As a spectrum disorder, ASD encompasses a wide range of symptoms, which can be more or less present in different individuals. As a result, there is a great deal of individual variation here, in terms of both pragmatic competence and performance on the false-belief. Many ASD patients fail the classic false-belief task; indeed, failure at the false-belief task has long been seen as a classic diagnostic of ASD (Baron-Cohen, 1995; Frith, 2003). Many also lack pragmatic competence, to at least some degree (Surian & Siegal, 2008). Nevertheless, at least some ASD patients are able to use ostensive communication, yet still fail the false-belief task. As with the child data, this pair of facts is hard to reconcile with the recursive mindreading claim (Glüer & Pagin, 2003).

At this point, there are two ways in which we can turn. Either we accept the recursive mindreading claim, and argue that, contrary to the pictures painted above, children and ASD patients in fact *do* possess high-level recursive mindreading abilities. Or we can reject the recursive mindreading claim, and look to develop some other, less demanding account of what cognitive mechanisms are necessary to engage in ostensive communication. Certainly, something has to give.

Among those researchers who have engaged with this dilemma, the second of these two strategies has been the more popular. That is to say, several researchers, in reaction to the above facts, have made tentative proposals about how an alternative, less demanding set of cognitive mechanisms could make ostensive communication possible (e.g. Gómez, 1994; Breheny, 2006; Moore, 2014). I do not think this approach will be fruitful. That is to say: I do not see how the analysis presented in the previous section can be simplified any further. I have not been persuaded by any of the above cited suggestions.

Instead, I think that the present dilemma can be resolved with the other, currently less popular strategy i.e. to argue, contrary to a commonly and easily made assumption, that pragmatically competent children and ASD patients plausibly *do* possess high-level recursive mindreading abilities.

In 2005 a new approach to the false-belief task was developed, different to the classic test in a subtle but important way. Whereas in the classic false-belief task, children are explicitly asked where they thought the character (Sally) would look for the object (the ball), in these newer tasks, children are not asked about the characters' mental states directly, but instead the child's behaviour is used to infer what the child understands about others' mental states. For example, in one study the infant is prompted to help an experimenter, effectively playing the role of Sally, to find a ball, which is in one of two boxes. If the experimenter tries to open the box where they believe the ball is, but the child knows that it is elsewhere, then when prompted to help the experimenter, a child able to represent the experimenter's mind should direct them to open the other box, where the ball is (Buttelmann et al., 2009). Other experiments, including the studies that pioneered the change from the classic task to these newer, less direct tests of mindreading, use the time a child or infant spends looking at different aspects of a scene as a measure of their expectation of what will happen, or of their surprise at what has happened, and use this to infer what the child does and does not know (Onishi & Baillargeon, 2005; Southgate et al., 2007; Surian et al., 2007).

The major difference in results between these newer studies and the classic false-belief tasks is the age at which children typically succeed: whereas the explicit task is not passed until around the fourth birthday, implicit tasks are passed within the first 18 months of life, and in many cases within the first 12 months (see Baillargeon et al., 2010 for a review). These results have been replicated cross-culturally, in infants from numerous non-Western societies and cultures (Barrett et al., 2013).

One way to understand this finding is by analogy with, say, an infant's knowledge of physics. After a certain age, a child will be able to tell you, explicitly, that when objects are released they will fall to the floor, that when propelled they will be subject to air resistance, and so on. Younger children, in contrast, cannot express these facts in this way, but they do manipulate objects in ways that depend upon having this knowledge: they *expect* that if they let go of a ball in mid-air, it will fall to the ground. In other words, even infants have a 'folk physics'. In the same way, the findings of these new false-belief tasks suggest that they also have a 'folk psychology': an implicit understanding that other people have minds and mental states of their own.

Perhaps unsurprisingly, the claim that even young infants are capable of mindreading has generated a great deal of discussion (e.g. Caron, 2009; Carruthers, 2013; see Hutto et al., 2011 and Low & Perner, 2012 for collections of views). Some of this discussion strikes a very skeptical tone (e.g.

Heyes, in press; see Scott & Baillargeon, in press for a compelling response). One explanation of the divergence in performance on implicit and explicit tasks is that there are two systems for mindreading: one that emerges early in life, and which is automatic, fast, and unconscious; and another, which emerges later, that is the opposite of this i.e. deliberate, slow, and amenable to conscious introspection (Apperly & Butterfill, 2009). Another suggestion, pertinent to the themes of this book, and which may be congruous rather than in opposition to the two-systems account, is that children's core mindreading abilities are overwhelmed when, in addition to tracking another individual's beliefs, they must also communicate with an experimenter, a task that also and independently involves mindreading (Helming et al., 2014). One finding consistent with this view is that while two-year-old children fail the false-belief task when directly asked what Sally will do, they pass it when the exact same question is not addressed to them directly, but is instead simply voiced aloud, as part of an adult's thinking process (He et al., 2012).

Unless one accepts the most skeptical arguments (and I do not), then the key point here is that the results of these new mindreading tasks seriously undermine the intuition that mindreading is or must be a cognitively demanding task. In particular, these and other findings suggest that mindreading is often less like thinking, and more like perception i.e. something that we do unconsciously, as part of the background cognition that manages much of our daily lives (Apperly, 2011). Certainly, many experiments have now shown that we track the beliefs of others automatically, as part of our intuitive monitoring of the world around us, and that like our perceptual experiences, these representations of others' mental states fade quickly if we do not focus on them (e.g. Cohen & German, 2009; Kovács et al., 2010; van der Wel et al., 2014). This insight explains why, although mindreading sounds difficult when we articulate what it involves (think of all those embedded intentions with Mary and Peter), that does not imply that it is in practice cognitively demanding. As I mentioned in Chapter 1, to formally describe how vision and other forms of perception work is an intellectually complex task, but that does not mean that the everyday task of seeing things is demanding. The same may be true of mindreading: it looks complex on paper, but that is no reason to assume that it places overwhelming or even significant demands on cognition.

I see no reason why this point should not also apply to recursive mindreading. There is certainly no *a priori* reason why embedding one thing inside another instance of itself should be cognitively demanding. Indeed, we entertain metarepresentations in other domains all the time: a spoken or written description of a painting, for instance, is a representation of a representation. Moreover, there are good reasons to think that mental metarepresentations are in fact *more* easily processed than these 'public' metarepresentations: when equivalent public and mental versions of the same metarepresentation are directly compared, it is the public version that is more slowly processed (Cohen & German, 2010). In sum, there are good reasons, both theoretical and empirical, to conclude that recursive mindreading is not cognitively demanding. More likely, it is, like simple mindreading, something that we do habitually and subconsciously, as part of our everyday, low-level perception of the world around us.

Numerous everyday behaviours make sense once we accept this conclusion. Suppose, for instance, that I drop a pen on the floor, and I think$_1$ it has landed over there, and so I look for it there. You, however, have seen that it actually landed somewhere else, and so you go to pick it up for me. In other words, you think$_1$ that I think$_2$ that the pen is over there (and actually you know otherwise). Now suppose that our friend observes this simple scene, and understands why you did what you did. In that case, the friend thinks$_1$ that you think$_2$ that I think$_3$ that the pen is over there. Already this is three levels of recursive mindreading, and this is a very simple, everyday occurrence. Similarly, the narratives of plays and soap operas often involve multiple levels of mindreading, and this does not pose a problem to comprehension. The scene at the end of Act II of Shakespeare's *Othello*, for example, includes the following state of affairs: Iago intends$_1$ that Cassio believes$_2$ that Iago intends$_3$ that Desdemona intends$_4$ that Othello considers$_5$ Cassio's rehabilitation (van Duijn, 2012). This play has been understood and enjoyed by literally millions of theatregoers, over hundreds of years.

In comparison to the huge literature on basic mindreading, there is a dearth of studies that empirically investigate recursive mindreading skills. Probably the most widely known finding from this small body of research is that adult performance on higher-order tasks appears to drop dramatically after the fifth level (Kinderman et al., 1998). However, detailed analysis of the methods used in this and, until recently, all other recursive mindreading studies, reveals a number of methodological problems that are serious enough to cast doubt on these conclusions (O'Grady et al., under review). Furthermore, these previous studies only tested mindreading abilities explicitly (by asking participants direct questions), and not implicitly (by using participants' reactions to specific events to gauge understanding) – yet as we have seen, the developmental literature shows that a difference in the mode of presentation can make a dramatic difference to performance in mindreading tasks.

In light of this, two MSc students of mine, Cathleen O'Grady and Christian Kliesch, conducted an experimental study of recursive mindreading, using both implicit and explicit measures. They wrote and directed a series of short films, during which characters discussed and found things out not only about one another, but also about what they thought others knew, and so on. In a typical scenario, a boy fancies a girl, but believes that she likes somebody else, whereas in fact she thinks that he wants to go out with her friend. And so on and so on. Having watched the films, participants were then presented with two scenes that each purported to depict what happened next. Only one of these was plausible given what had already occurred, and the participants were asked to choose which of these two scenes was the most likely outcome. These questions varied in the number of levels of mindreading required to process who knew or believed or understood who fancied whom, and hence to answer the questions correctly. We found that even at the highest level of metarepresentation that we prepared (the seventh level) participants performed significantly above chance levels (O'Grady et al., under review). This suggests, consistent with the arguments above, that recursive mindreading is simply not as difficult in reality as it seems on paper. Humans can entertain not only metarepresentations, but even meta-meta-meta-meta-meta-meta-meta-representations.

My suggestion, then, is that the way to resolve the apparent contradiction between children's performance on the traditional false-belief task, and their obvious competence with ostensive-inferential communication, is not, as others have suggested, to attempt to deflate the theoretically well-developed thesis about how ostensive communication involves recursive mindreading skills. For one thing, no compelling deflationary theory presently exists. Rather, we should deflate the assumption that recursive mindreading is cognitively demanding. Children pass implicit false-belief tasks at very young ages, and adults can entertain multiply embedded mental states. Further research is necessary here, especially on children's abilities with recursive mindreading. That literature is presently small and, more importantly, it has not yet made use of the implicit experimental designs that have so radically transformed the study of basic mindreading (see Miller, 2009 for a review). Nevertheless, the idea that both adults' and children's communication really does involve recursive mindreading is not only plausible, but is in fact the most parsimonious interpretation of the literature at the time of writing.

What about ASD patients, at least some of whom have a degree of pragmatic competence, but fail the false-belief task? Just as the development of implicit false-belief tasks has transformed our understanding of children's mindreading abilities, recent developments have also changed our understanding of ASD patients' mindreading abilities. In particular, many lines of evidence now point to the conclusion that the core deficit in ASD is not one of social cognition *per se*, as has long been thought, but rather of social *motivation* (Chevallier et al., 2012). The motivation to engage socially and share experiences with others is a key component of human psychology. This is diminished in ASD patients, with the result that performance on tasks that measure social cognition is impaired (*ibid.*). This explains why some ASD patients are able to communicate ostensively, yet simultaneously fail the false-belief task.

It is time to take stock. The previous section explained why ostensive communication involves high levels of recursive mindreading. This insight derives from a theoretical framework with a base that is both broad (i.e. widely influential) and deep (i.e. well-developed). Nevertheless, there are two commonly made objections to this account. The first is that both young children and some ASD patients can and do communicate in a pragmatically competent way, but they fail the classic test of basic mind-reading ability. The second is that the recursive mindreading account places cognitive demands on its users which are surely too great for a behaviour that we perform so easily. In both cases, I have surveyed data that suggest otherwise. In doing so I have undermined these objections, and hence nullified the supposed need to develop alternative accounts of how ostensive communication works.

Before continuing, it is worthwhile to reiterate why I have focused so much in this and the previous section on recursive mindreading abilities. It is *not* because I think or wish to suggest that these abilities are simply a magic bullet that explains everything we may wish to know about the origins of communication and language. On the contrary, there are clearly numerous other aspects of human psychology and biology involved. However, what recursive mindreading does is make ostensive communication possible in the first place. *That* is why I have focused on it. Without recursive mindreading there are no informative intentions, no communication intentions, and hence no ostensive communication. In short, recursive mindreading supplies the fundaments for how we communicate with one another. It is, in the unvarnished sense of the word, fundamental.

3.6 Cooperation and communication

To end this chapter, I want to change topic slightly and briefly discuss the role that cooperation plays in ostensive communication. Humans take part in a great deal of joint activity, in which two or more individuals work together towards some goal. For example, when I say "After three: one, two, three..." this tells you when to start lifting so that *we* can achieve our joint goal to lift a heavy box. This sort of collaborative activity is ubiquitous in human life. The ability and motivation to mentally represent and hence pursue joint goals in this way is called *shared intentionality* (sometimes called *'we'-intentionality*) (Searle, 1995; Tomasello et al., 2005). The behaviour of many species is functionally collaborative; that is, it achieves an outcome from which many individuals will benefit (ants building a nest, for example). However, in humans this collaboration is also instantiated at a cognitive level: when we take part in these joint activities, we mentally represent ourselves as part of a larger whole (an 'us'), which is more than the sum of its parts. Shared intentionality is uniquely human: Tomasello and his colleagues have conducted a great many experiments comparing the cognitive abilities of human children and great apes, and time and again chimpanzees simply fail to engage in even the most simple joint behaviour, either with human caregivers or with other chimpanzees, in both experimental and naturalistic conditions. This is in stark contrast to human infants, who routinely do (Tomasello et al., 2005).

Thinking about (ostensive) communication through the lens of shared intentionality has led the developmental and comparative psychologist

Michael Tomasello to develop the thesis of *cooperative communication*. The central claim here is that, at least in terms of how it is processed in the mind, ostensive communication is not so much a case of *me* talking to *you* and *you* talking to *me*, but rather a case of *us* communicating with one another (Tomasello et al., 2007; Tomasello, 2008). It is a joint, collaborative activity, something that *we* do together (Clark, 1996; Tomasello, 2008; Galantucci & Sebanz, 2009).

It is important to be clear about what sort of cooperation is involved here (Scott-Phillips, 2010a). There are three different ways in which we might say that a communicative interaction is cooperative, or not. For one thing, communication can be used deceitfully and dishonestly, but this is a quite different matter to how signallers and listeners are actually able to understand and be understood. This is the difference between *communicative* and *informative cooperation* (Figure 3.2). Communicative cooperation

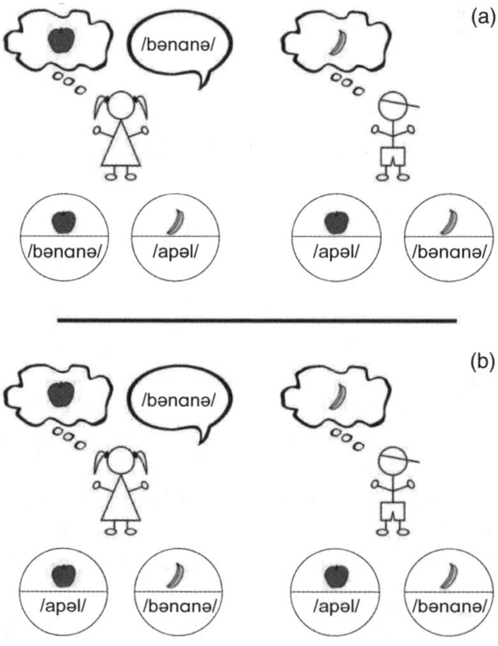

Figure 3.2 *Two types of cooperation in communication (Scott-Phillips, 2010a).* In both (a) and (b) the girl has said 'banana' having thought of an apple, and this fails to correspond to the boy's mapping of the sound (which is as per the convention in English). However, the reasons for this failure are different in each case. In (a) the girl has a different (in fact, the precise opposite) mapping from sounds to meaning than the boy. In (b) the girl has the same mappings as the boy but has, dishonestly, chosen to communicate a different meaning than the one she has thought of. In short, (a) depicts informative non-cooperation; (b) depicts communicative non-cooperation (see Scott-Phillips, 2010a for further discussion).

is about using the linguistic code in conventional ways, so that your audience can infer your intended meaning (this is what Paul Grice's Cooperative Principle (§3.2) is about); whereas informative cooperation is about whether what we mean is deceitful, or not. (I will examine the evolutionary issues around honesty and dishonesty in Chapter 6.)

A third type of cooperation, different to both of these, is *material cooperation*: the ends to which communication is used, either pro-social or not (Hurford, 2007). If I tell you that I think you're a bastard, it is possible that I'm being both communicatively cooperative (I'm using all the words and the grammar in that sentence in the conventional ways) and informatively cooperative (I really do think you're a bastard!), but I'm clearly being materially uncooperative. Unlike the other two types, material cooperation is not necessary for communication to take place. It just determines whether that communication takes place in a pro- or anti-social context.

Tomasello's thesis is about communicative cooperation, which he argues depends upon the human capacity for shared intentionality (the ability and motivation to represent and hence pursue joint goals). In other words: Tomasello's claim is that in order for ostensive communication to work at all, both speaker and listener must treat and pursue the act of communication as a *collaborative*, joint activity, in which speakers provide the right sort of evidence for their intended meaning, and the listener assumes that this is what speakers have done.

I am unconvinced that shared intentionality is *logically* necessary for ostensive communication. If this were true, then if we were to remove shared intentionality from the mix, there would be no ostensive communication at all – and I am not sure this is true. That shared intentionality helps to explain why ostensive communication is the way it is, rather than some other way, I do not doubt, but I do not see why speaker and listener *must* mentally represent themselves as an 'us' in order to be understood by one another. Unlike mental metarepresentation, shared intentionality does not seem to make ostensive communication *possible*. Rather, it helps to explain how and why we use it in the way that we do.

Having said that, thinking shared intentionality does highlight an important aspect of ostensive communication that might otherwise go unrecognized. Shared intentionality is not only the *ability* to represent and pursue joint goals, but also the *motivation* to do so (Tomasello et al., 2005). Several researchers have pointed out just how much we are motivated to communicate with one another, and how zoologically unusual this is (e.g. Dessalles, 2007; Fitch, 2010). Until recently, we did not, however, have a term to describe this compulsion. In an attempt to rectify this, the evolutionary biologist Tecumseh Fitch has suggested that we use the German word *Mitteilungsbedürfnis*, which he translates as "a drive or need to share thoughts and feelings" (2010, p. 140). *Mitteilungsbedürfnis* is one of our most distinctive characteristics. It is "as bizarre as our bipedality or hairlessness" (*ibid*., p. 201). It is also one of the first things that visitors from other galaxies notice about us: "One of the things Ford Prefect had always found hardest to understand about humans was their habit of continually stating and repeating the very very obvious, as in 'It's a nice day', or 'You're very tall', or 'Oh dear, you seem to have fallen down a thirty-foot well, are you alright?' " *The Hitchhiker's Guide to the Galaxy* is a comic novel, but this is a scientifically astute observation.

Is ostensive communication itself similarly distinctive of humans? It is that question, and related ones about the evolutionary environments in which ostensive communication is likely to have evolved, to which we shall now turn.

* * *

Chapter 3. *Ostensive communication is governed by the two Principles of Relevance: that human cognition tends to be geared towards the maximization of relevance (this is the Cognitive Principle); and that every ostensive stimulus carries a presumption of its own optimal relevance (this is the Communicative Principle). Both principles are supported by the empirical data. Ostensive communication involves high levels of recursive mindreading, but contrary to a common intuition, this recursive mindreading is likely not cognitively demanding. Human communication is cooperative in two distinct senses, and it is important to distinguish between these.*

Chapter 4. *What can comparisons with other species tell us about the origins of language? Is non-human primate communication ostensive? Many studies of non-human primate communication focus on intentional communication: is this the same thing as ostensive communication? If not, what is the difference? In what evolutionary environment(s) might the social cognition required for ostensive communication have evolved?*

Chapter 4

The Origins of Ostensive Communication

4.1 Communication and the comparative method

Arguably the most prominent linguist of Darwin's time was a gentleman named Max Müller. Müller was no Darwinian, and in fact used language as evidence against Darwin's ideas. As far as Müller was concerned, the origins of language simply could not be explained by the theory of natural selection (Müller, 1873). He hence concluded that natural selection, at least as applied to humans, could not be right. Presaging Chomsky, one of the observations Müller used to build his argument was that languages simply cannot be acquired by any other species. He thus proposed a thought experiment: even if raised among humans, no ape, argued Müller, would acquire human language. Although Müller was not a Darwinian, this thought experiment captures the essence of one of the key scientific tools that follows from Darwin's ideas: that we can learn a great deal about evolutionary history by way of *comparison* – in this case, a cross-species comparison of language acquisition abilities. Müller fully expected that such comparisons would highlight insurmountable differences between the proverbial man and brute.

Müller may not have expected anyone to actually take up his challenge to rear and train apes to speak language, but attempts to do this recurred throughout the 20th century. The first such experiment took place in the 1930s, when Luella and Winthrop Kellogg attempted to rear a chimpanzee, Gua, alongside their own son, Donald. However, rather than Gua acquiring language alongside Donald, if anything Gua's influence retarded Donald's development, and after nine months the experiment was abandoned (Kellogg & Kellogg, 1933). One of the reasons for Gua's failure to acquire language is simply that apes do not have the vocal apparatus to imitate human sounds (and so, it turns out, Müller's prediction was basically right, albeit for reasons different to the ones he gave). The ape-language experiments of the 1960s and 1970s, which are mostly known by the name of the apes involved (Washoe, Nim, Koko, Lana, Kanzi, Sarah, etc.), thus focused on other modalities, in particular either sign language, or artificial systems that use tokens or keyboards (see Anderson, 2006 for a review). This approach had some success, in the sense that at least some of the apes developed competent command of communication systems that have some, although certainly not all, of the distinctive features of natural human languages.

An even earlier pioneer of comparisons between the communication of humans and other primates was Richard Garner, a professor at the Smithsonian Institute in Washington, DC. Garner recorded the vocalizations of monkeys, and then played them back to other members of the same species, so that the effects, and hence the 'meaning' of the vocalizations, could be systematically studied (Garner, 1892). He did this first with captive monkeys in the US, but later travelled to the French Congo to conduct similar experiments in the field. Although they are now widely recognized as a highly productive approach to the study of animal communication, playback experiments of this sort actually fell out of favour shortly after Garner's work, and remained so for much of the 20th century (see Radick, 2007 for a history of the playback experiment).

The *comparative method*, of which both playback studies and ape-language experiments are examples, is an extremely powerful tool for evolutionary analysis (Harvey & Pagel, 1991). The basic idea goes all the way back to Darwin: take a family tree of different species, and compare, on the one hand, the extent to which the trait is present in each species, with, on the other, what differences there are in the species' ecologies, or how closely related the two species are. Correlations in these variables can then be used to either generate or test hypotheses about why and how the trait evolved.

Alternatives to the comparative method as a way to determine how a trait might have evolved are thin on the ground. One possibility is to study and date fossils. However, in the case of language, communication, and indeed behaviour in general, that option is simply not available. Another is genetics, but our knowledge of the genetic basis of communication and language is not sufficiently advanced for this to tell us much, at least for now. Consequently, comparisons with other species have been important for the study of language origins ever since Darwin (Darwin, 1872; Hockett, 1960; Hauser, 1996; Fitch, 2010).

Contemporary comparisons with language often adopt a multi-component perspective (Fitch, 2010). That is, the various component parts of language are identified, and cross-species comparisons are made for each. There are two reasons for this approach. The first is simply that if we treat language as a single entity, then the comparative method will, on its own, tell us nothing: humans have it, and other species do not, and there is not much more to say (Anderson, 2006; Hurford, 2011). The second reason is that language is not a single monolithic trait anyway (Hurford, 2003; Fitch, 2010). Instead, its biological foundations are many: speech production, speech perception, language processing, memory, imitation, and so on. The composite result of all these components – language – is uniquely human, but many (perhaps all?) of the individual parts are shared with various other species (Fitch, 2010). The idea, then, is that we should carve language at its joints, and compare each component part separately.

An example of this multi-component approach is research on vocalization and speech production (see Fitch, 2010 for the full details). In other primate species, and indeed in most mammals, the larynx, which houses the vocal folds that manipulate the pitch and volume of vocalizations, sits high in the throat. However in adult humans it is descended; it sits lower in the throat. For many years it was thought that this descended larynx was uniquely human. A descended larynx makes it possible for us to produce a far greater range of speech sounds than would otherwise be the case (Lieberman, 2007; Fitch, 2010). Many researchers had thus suggested that the larynx descended in humans in order to make speech possible, and that this outweighed the cost of a greater risk of choking. However, comparisons with other species have since shown otherwise: some other mammalian species, including red deer and dogs, to pick just two, also vocalize with a descended larynx (Fitch & Reby, 2001). Based on these and other comparative observations, the consensus view is now that the function of a descended larynx is to change the acoustic properties of vocalizations so as to exaggerate the animal's size (Fitch, 2000; Fitch & Reby, 2001). The fact that it increases the range of distinct vocalizations is likely simply a by-product of this. Either way, this is one area where the comparative method has informed our understanding of a component part of language. So far, so good.

However, we must be careful. There are two potential mistakes that are easy to make here. Neither applies to comparative work on the apparatus of speech (this is one reason why it is often held up as a paradigmatic example of how to do comparative research with language) but both apply to most other areas of language evolution. The first potential mistake is to not appreciate how the interdependency of signals and responses constrains the forms that signals and responses might take. This fact alone makes comparisons between different communication systems hazardous. (I made this point at length in Chapter 2. The crux of the matter is that communication systems, being *systems*, are not themselves biological traits subject to natural selection, but are instead the product of two interacting traits, namely mechanisms for production and mechanisms for reception. As such, it is not at all clear how comparisons between communication systems should be interpreted.) The second potential mistake is to assume that comparisons between language and the communication systems of other species are like-with-like comparisons – yet they may not be. In particular, comparisons between natural codes and conventional codes are certainly not like-with-like comparisons.

This latter point deserves expansion. The difference between conventional codes and natural codes is not like the difference between, say, the human eye and the octopus eye. There, the same sort of thing, that performs the same basic function, has evolved independently in two separate taxa.

Where they differ is in the mechanistic details. In contrast, conventional codes and natural codes are *not* the same sort of thing as one another, and do *not* have the same basic function. One makes a type of communication possible; the other makes a (different) type of communication expressively powerful (§1.6). The difference between them is not a matter of mechanistic details, as it is in the case of the eye, and as such, it is a category error to directly compare natural codes and conventional codes in the standard way (see Deacon, 1997 for related arguments). (This is not the old biology vs. culture argument. Linguistic conventions are part of, and not distinct from, the natural, biological world. The point I am making is that they are not the same sort of biological entity as animal signals. Whether any other species actually makes use of conventional codes, as humans do, is of course an empirical question, which I will address in this chapter.)

The case of *functional reference* illustrates how we can be led astray if we are not cognizant of these points. Vervet monkeys are reported to have three distinct alarm calls: one for leopards, one for eagles, and one for snakes (Seyfarth et al., 1980a). If one of these calls is produced, the other monkeys take action to avoid the predator in question. Acoustically, the calls do not resemble the sounds of the corresponding predator in any way. As such, they share two important properties with words: they identify specific things in the world, and their form is arbitrary. This is just as things are in language, where word form is unrestricted by meaning: we can refer to a canine pet as 'dog', 'perro', 'šuo', or indeed any other word. Consequently, the vervet alarm calls were, initially at least, interpreted as being meaningful in the same way that words are (Seyfarth et al., 1980b). The technical term is *reference*: the calls *refer* to things in the world. Using the logic of the comparative method, some researchers suggested that calls such as these are evolutionarily related to linguistic words; that is, that linguistic words descended directly from this sort of non-human primate vocal communication (e.g. Zuberbühler, 2005). This conclusion was criticized on the grounds that the calls may not be referential in the same way that words are, and so the term *functional reference* was adopted instead, as a way to have things both ways: to acknowledge the criticism that the calls are not strictly referential like words (hence why it is only 'functional' reference), but at the same time to bring attention to the claim that they still perform the same role that words do. This label kept such comparisons on the agenda with regards to comparisons with language. However, this approach still misses the key point that these may not be like-with-like comparisons. Specifically, if non-human primate alarm calls are natural codes (and I will argue below that they are), then they in fact do *not* function as words do. Natural codes make communication possible, but words do not. Words are instead parts of conventional codes, and they function to make ostensive communication powerful (§1.6). For these and other reasons, there are now calls to abandon the term 'functional reference' altogether (Rendall et al., 2009; Wheeler & Fischer, 2012; but see Scarantino, 2013 for a partial defence).

(Another example of why evolutionary analysis cannot directly compare the surface properties of different communication systems is combinatorial communication. I discussed the difficulties of direct evolutionary comparisons of combinatorial communication at some length in §2.7.)

None of this is to say that we should not study the communication systems of non-human primates, or indeed any other species, either for its own sake, or as a way to inform evolutionary analyses of language. That is not my point. However, when we do so we should keep clear what such comparisons can and cannot tell us. In particular, we should keep in mind the fact that, since communication systems are not themselves biological traits, some comparisons may be less informative than they first appear.

In Chapter 2 I established that the key comparative questions to ask with respect to language origins are *not* the commonly asked questions about the surface properties of communication systems, but rather those about ostensive-inferential communication, and the cognitive mechanisms that make it possible. This chapter addresses those questions. Specifically, I will ask whether great ape communication is ostensive, and whether any non-human primate species possess the cognitive mechanisms that make ostensive communication possible. For both these questions I will conclude in the negative. Much of my discussion will focus on chimpanzees, but only because they are, by some distance, the most studied of the great apes. There is no particular reason to think that the general conclusions I will draw would be different if we had greater knowledge of the abilities of any of the other great ape species (gorilla, orangutans, bonobos), although such data would of course be very welcome. I will also suggest possible ways in which ostensive communication might have emerged in humans, and highlight the selection pressures that might have led to this outcome.

4.2 The difference between intentional and ostensive communication

Anthropomorphism is easy to do, and doubly so with non-human primates. If you have spent anything more than just a few minutes observing the behaviour of our nearest relatives, you will understand why it is very easy to assume that they have the same sort of intentions, beliefs, desires and other mental states as we do. This is as true of their communication as it is of anything. It is thus important to develop criteria that allow us to distinguish between communicative behaviour that is driven by intentions and other mental states, and that which is not.

The principal theoretical construct used in this literature is *intentional communication*. Multiple different criteria are used to determine whether or not a signal has been used 'intentionally' (see Liebal et al., 2014 for a review). Exactly which criteria are actually used in any given experiment is subject to a fair degree of variation. All of the following are commonly used, although none of them are universal: (i) social use (sensitivity to the presence and composition of an audience); (ii) gaze alteration (the initiation and maintenance of eye contact during communication); (iii) sensitivity to attentional state (signal is adjusted depending on the attentional state of the audience); (iv) use of attention-getters (behaviours used to gain the attention of an audience); (v) persistence and elaboration (continued use of a behaviour until its objectives have been met, and the use of alternative or modified signals in case of failure); (vi) flexible use (use of the same signal for multiple ends, and/or multiple signals for the same ends; i.e. means–ends dissociation); and (vii) response-waiting (after signalling, waiting for a response). (Whether or not these are appropriate criteria for 'intentional communication' is a separate question, tangential to my concerns here.)

Any of these criteria might be indicative of intentionality, but at the same time it is always possible to provide alternative explanations in terms of lower-level cognitive mechanisms (Liebal et al., 2014). Take, for example, the criterion that if a signal is produced intentionally, then it should show sensitivity to the attentional state of the target recipient. Several primate species do this, in their interactions with both conspecifics and humans. However, these results can also be explained in terms of a simple behavioural rule to only produce the signal when the face of the targeted recipient is oriented towards the signaller. Such rules do not involve any intentionality. 'Killjoy' explanations of this sort are available for all the criteria proposed.

At the same time, however, the more criteria that are satisfied, the more parsimonious it becomes to reject the idea that the behaviour is best explained in terms of a suite of simple behavioural rules, and to conclude instead that the signals are under intentional control (Liebal et al., 2014). Consequently, while some of the above criteria are generally accepted to be stronger evidence for intentionality than others (for example, persistence and elaboration are better evidence than social use), the best evidence for intentionality is *convergent* evidence (Byrne & Bates, 2006). If all, or nearly all, of the above criteria can be satisfied, then the most likely explanation is that, yes, the signals are produced intentionally. On the other hand, if only, say, two or three of them are, then lower-level explanations remain a reasonable possibility.

Non-human primates communicate with both vocal calls and gestures, just as humans do. Using the criteria and approach described above, the majority view has for some years been that non-human primates' gestural communication is intentional, but that their vocal communication is not (Call & Tomasello, 2007; Pollick & de Waal, 2007). Advocates of this position argue that "on practically every dimension available, great apes display more sophisticated communicative skills in the gestural rather than in the vocal modality... [gestural communication, but not vocal communication] would seem to be a paradigmatic case of intentional action" (Tomasello, 2008, p. 33). Others disagree, and give three main reasons for doing so (see Slocombe et al., 2011 for discussion). The first is methodological inconsistency between studies that use the different modalities. (This is often for purely practical reasons: methods that are suitable for one domain are not so easily applied in other domains. The obvious example is the playback experiment, which is used productively in vocal studies, but does not easily translate into the gestural medium.) The second is that more recent studies describe data that suggest that great ape vocal communication may indeed be used intentionally, contrary to the above conclusion (e.g. Schel et al., 2013). The third is that intentional signals are often contrasted with more automatically-produced, emotional signals, but this may be a false dichotomy.

Regardless of how these debates play out, we must keep in mind that what we wish to investigate is ostensive communication, and the mechanisms that make it possible. How, then, does intentional communication relate to ostensive communication? These two theoretical notions are used in two different literatures, but are meant to speak to the same set of questions, about the cognitive basis of communication. Are intentional and ostensive communication the same thing as one another, just expressed in different terms? If not, how are they similar, and how are they different? To what extent is evidence of one evidence of the other?

To begin to answer these questions, recall the list of criteria used to identify intentional communication: social use; gaze alteration; sensitivity to attentional state; use of attention-getters; persistence and elaboration; flexible use; and response-waiting. These criteria are designed to investigate whether or not a signal is used in a goal-directed way – hence, 'intentionally'. As such, the intentionality studied in intentional communication research is, at least in practice, about *how* signals are used, and specifically, about whether the signals are used in the pursuit of a cognitively represented goal, or not. A typical question in this area is whether signals are 'under intentional control'. In contrast, the defining feature of ostensive communication is not any aspect of *how* signals are produced, but rather *what* the signal expresses. Specifically, ostensive signals are those signals that express a communicative intention (§1.4). Intentionality is one part of this, but it is not the same thing.

Correspondingly, it is possible for a signal to be intentional but not ostensive. To illustrate, let's return to Mary and Peter. As before (see §3.4), Mary is picking and eating the berries, so that Peter learns that the berries are edible. Here are seven particular facts that might be true of Mary's behaviour: (i) she only picks and eats the berries when Peter is around; (ii) as she eats the berries, she alternates her gaze between Peter and the berry bush; (iii) if Peter is not looking at her, she stops eating the berries, until he does look at her; (iv) if Peter is not looking, she sometimes coughs or does something else that might direct his attention towards her; (v) if Peter does not seem to grasp that the berries are edible, Mary repeats her behaviour, and perhaps performs it in a slightly different way; (vi) on other occasions

Mary has used similar behaviour in other communicative contexts e.g. when the berries are especially tasty; and (vii) after she has picked and eaten the berries, Mary waits to see how Peter behaves. As you will no doubt have noticed, these are the seven criteria commonly used by animal communication researchers to identify intentional communication (see above). If all of these are true, then Mary's behaviour is intentional by the terms of that field of study. Critically, however, *none of these aspects of Mary's behaviour make it ostensive*. That is not to say that her behaviour is not ostensive, only that nothing here necessarily makes it so. More precisely, none of these aspects of her behaviour necessarily expresses a communicative intention. That is what it means for something to be ostensive (§1.3), and there is nothing in any of these criteria that logically does this.

Another way to make this point is to say that behaviours (i)–(vii) may be intentional, but they are not *overtly* intentional. As such, they do not, in and of themselves, express the fact that Mary's behaviour is *for Peter*. Consequently, Peter has no reason to conclude that Mary has either a communicative or an informative intention. By way of illustration, consider again persistence and elaboration, which is arguably the criterion that is most superficially similar to ostensive behaviour: even here, there is nothing that requires Mary's behaviour to be overtly directed towards Peter, or in any other way to be manifestly different to eating berries normally. As such, behaviours that satisfy this criterion do not need to be ostensive.

In sum, ostensive communication is not simply a fancy philosophical term for what primatologists have studied under the banner of intentional communication. These two types of communication are related but distinct. Specifically, while ostensive communication is necessarily intentional, intentional communication need not be ostensive. Over the next two sections I will make the argument that intentional but not ostensive communication is what is going on in much great ape communication (Scott-Phillips, in press). Instead, what is intentionally produced is a natural code.

4.3 Do great apes communicate with ostension and inference?

How can we analyse whether a communication system is ostensive, or not? By definition, for a type of communication to qualify as ostensive communication it must involve the expression and recognition of both communicative and informative intentions (§1.3 and §1.4). As such, there are four things that must be shown:

- the expression of informative intentions
- the recognition of informative intentions
- the recognition of communicative intentions
- the expression of communicative intentions

Do any species other than humans engage in these four behaviours? In particular, do chimpanzees? And, by way of comparison, do human children? This section addresses these questions. Before I begin, I should note that strictly speaking it is not strictly correct to split things up in this way. Informative intentions are embedded within communicative intentions (§1.3), and so to express and recognize a communicative intention is, by extension, to express and recognize an informative intention. However, for empirical purposes it is helpful to make this distinction as a useful way to organize our analysis, so long as we do not lose sight of this fact when we draw our conclusions.

First up is the expression of informative intentions i.e. the production of behaviour that is designed to affect the audience's mental state. Experimental evidence shows that when they communicate, children do indeed intend to change their audience's mental states. Specifically, if they make a request for an adult to pass them, say, a ball, but that request is satisfied only fortuitously (i.e. if the adult misunderstood, but the child coincidentally obtained the ball anyway), then the children will correct the adult's misunderstanding nevertheless (Grosse et al., 2010). This shows that their intention is not simply to affect the adult's behaviour (i.e. to get the ball), but rather to change mental states, which will affect behaviour in turn. To my knowledge, no similar experiment with chimpanzees has been conducted.

Next, the recognition of informative intentions. Here, the precise experiment that would most directly address this question has not been conducted with either children or great apes. The critical test for such an experiment would be: if an adult experimenter directs a request (or command) towards, say, another experimenter, and this request is satisfied only fortuitously, does the child/ape show any sign of understanding that the adult's informative intention has in fact not been satisfied (even though their material goal has been satisfied)? For example, if the requester had not noticed that the request had been satisfied only fortuitously, perhaps the child would point this fact out to them, or show surprise, or show less trust in the addressee in a subsequent interaction. If they did so, that would be good evidence that they recognize that the requester had an informative intention (and that the audience did not recognize this). As I say, such an experiment has not, to the best of my knowledge, been conducted, with either children or apes. I would predict that children but not apes would succeed in a task of this sort.

The third of the four behaviours to consider is the recognition of communicative intentions i.e. of the fact that a signaller has an informative intention; or, more informally, of the fact that a signaller wishes to communicate in the first place. When asked of children, this question has been approached in a number of different ways, and these studies consistently show that children are indeed able to do this (e.g. Tomasello et al., 1997a; Behne et al., 2005; Gräfenhain et al., 2009; Moore et al., 2013). In one experiment, the child must look for a missing object, which is in a box. In the experimental condition an adult indicates this location ostensively: with a directed point to the box, accompanied by alternating gaze between the child and the box. In the control condition, the adult's behaviour is superficially similar, but is not in fact ostensive: the adult still points, but only as an incidental consequence of looking at her watch. Only in the ostensive condition do the children follow the point and hence fetch the object (Behne et al., 2005). This suggests that children can recognize and act upon others' communicative intentions. Another experiment used the same contrast, between ostensive and non-ostensive points, but used by one adult for another, as the child observes. Again, the children's subsequent behaviour shows that they understand which points express communicative intentions, and which do not (Gräfenhain et al., 2009). Even stronger evidence would be to observe the same pattern of results with a novel behaviour with which, unlike pointing, children are wholly unfamiliar. To my knowledge, the corresponding experiment with chimpanzees or any other non-human primate has not been conducted. One reason for this is that chimpanzees in general struggle to follow the points of others, even when motivated to do so (see below). Any task that involves the differentiation of different types of points is thus redundant.

The final behaviour to consider is the expression of communicative intentions. One behaviour that could be used as evidence for this is *hidden authorship* (Tomasello et al., 2007; Csibra, 2010). Suppose that I am a guest at a dinner party, and I finish my glass of wine, and would like more. However, suppose also that it would be impolite of me to directly ask my host for this. Instead, I move my empty glass surreptitiously (perhaps, say, when my host is out of the room), so that my host will, soon after, see the wine glass and hence notice that I have finished my wine. Here, I intend that my host understands that I have finished my wine, but I also intend that she does not believe that I intend that she understands that I have finished my wine. In other words, I have an informative intention (hence *authorship*), but also a separate intention that this informative intention is *not* recognized by my intended audience (hence *hidden*). (This analysis of hidden authorship is a slight departure from my previously stated view, that what is hidden in such cases is a communicative intention (see Grosse et al., 2013). I now think that what is hidden is an informative intention.)

Hidden authorship is not, incidentally, the same thing as other non-standard varieties of ostensive communication (see Table 4.1). It is in particular different from lying. There, an informative intention is manifest, but false. In hidden authorship, the informative intention is not manifest, but hidden. Hidden authorship is also different from indirect communication, where we only imply some aspects of the intended speaker meaning, and also absent authorship, in which although the signaller does not make her communicative intention manifest, neither does she try to hide it. For instance, when I place my credit card on the counter as the cashier

Table 4.1 *Non-standard varieties of ostensive communication.*

Type of communication	Communicative intention	Informative intention
Hidden authorship	n/a	Hidden
Absent authorship	Implied	Manifest
Indirect communication	Manifest	Implied
Lying	Manifest	Manifest, but false

processes my purchase, because I intend that the cashier sees it and infers that this is how I intend to pay, I may not draw the cashier's attention to my card, but equally I do not attempt to hide the fact that it was me who placed the credit card on the counter.

Even though hidden authorship does not itself directly involve communicative intentions, it is good evidence that an individual understands what a communicative intention is, and the role it plays in communication. Standard ostensive communication has the following recursive structure (see §3.4): I intend$_1$ that you understand$_2$ that I intend$_3$ that you understand$_4$ X, where X is the content of the stimulus (e.g. that the berries are edible). *Intend*$_1$ is the communicative intention; *intend*$_3$ the informative intention. Hidden authorship differs from this only in that it adds a single negative component: I intend$_1$ that you *don't* understand$_2$ that I intend$_3$ that you understand$_4$ X. As such, although *intend*$_1$ is in hidden authorship not strictly a communicative intention *per se* (because it is not an intention to make manifest an informative intention), it is an intention that has essentially the same relationship to an informative intention that a communicative intention normally has. In this way, it comprises good evidence of an understanding of what a communicative intention consists of, and its relationship with informative intentions.

Children are able to hide authorship, and understand when it is appropriate to do so. In an experiment I conducted with Michael Tomasello and the developmental psychologist Gerlind Grosse, children were placed in a situation in which they have information that would help an adult, but where that help was unwanted by the adult. Children found ways to inform the adult anyway, while simultaneously hiding the fact that this was what they were doing. They did this more often under these circumstances than in a control condition in which their help was not unwanted (Grosse et al., 2013). It should come as no surprise that nobody has conducted a similar experiment with any other species. Indeed, it is actually quite difficult to imagine what a suitable experimental design might look like – but if this methodological issue could be resolved, a direct comparison between great apes and human children could be very informative.

In sum, there are several open empirical questions about whether great ape communication is ostensive. For all four aspects of ostensive communication (the expression of informative intent; the recognition of informative intent; the expression of communicative intent; and the recognition of communicative intent) there are experimental studies that might prove conclusive, but for which we do not yet have data.

It is instructive to consider why these key experiments have not been conducted in great apes. One reason is methodological: there are significant practical issues associated with all of these experiments. Some of these may even be insurmountable. But there is also, I suspect, a more fundamental reason, namely a general skepticism among experts in the area that great apes will actually succeed at these tasks. Such skepticism is justified, because great apes perform poorly in various tasks that seem less cognitively demanding than those discussed above. For instance, in a task generally known as the object-choice task, an experimenter hides a prize (food for chimpanzees; a toy for children) in one of several opaque buckets. In a control condition, the experimenter knocks over the bucket with the prize in it, so the prize is visible. The buckets are then presented to the participant who, predictably, chooses the one with the prize. In the experimental condition the experimenter does not knock the bucket over, but instead simply points to it. Here, children choose the correct bucket, but, even after extensive training, captive chimpanzees choose at random (e.g. Tomasello et al., 1997a; Herrmann & Tomasello, 2006; but see Lyn et al., 2010, in which chimpanzees raised in rich socio-cultural environments performed more strongly). The persistent failure of captive chimpanzees in this task, and the almost complete absence of points among wild chimpanzees, must place serious doubt on whether or not they could succeed in the sorts of tasks, discussed above, which would most clearly illustrate command of the various different aspects of ostensive communication. This may explain, especially when combined with the various methodological challenges, why the key experiments have not been conducted: negative results are difficult to interpret and difficult to publish, and if this is what researchers most likely expect, they are left with little incentive to pursue such research.

I thus read the absence of the relevant studies as an implicit, collective acknowledgement on the part of researchers in the area that great apes would fail such tasks. Given the lively nature of this literature, and the resources currently and recently dedicated to the experimental study of ape cognition, it is reasonable to assume that such studies would have been conducted, if not for a collective skepticism about likely success (or perhaps these studies have been conducted but not reported, as is often the case with negative results). I will therefore assume, for the remainder of this book, that great ape communication is not ostensive. This assumption could be overturned, if great apes could be shown to succeed at the sorts of tasks described in this section. However, for the various reasons given above, I think this outcome unlikely.

There is, however, one non-primate species that does appear to use at least some of the components of ostensive communication: domestic dogs. Dogs have a suite of social cognitive skills that have apparently evolved as a result of their long history of domestication with humans (Hare et al., 2002; Miklósi et al., 2004; Kaminski, 2009). This includes the ability to differentiate between superficially similar behaviours that are expressed with and without communicative intent i.e. ostensively, or not, just as human children do (Kaminski et al., 2012).

One key difference between humans and dogs is that, whereas humans make use of communicated information even if they are not the intended audience of a signal e.g. when we eavesdrop on others, dogs make use of communicated information only if the communicative behaviour is directed specifically to them (Kaminski et al., 2012). This suggests that dogs interpret communicative behaviours as directive, rather than informative. In other words, they interpret such signals as commands, rather than as informative intentions. They show the same pattern with signal production: they signal in order to request but not simply to inform (Kaminski et al., 2011). Importantly, both these behaviours are explicable in associative terms. This fact suggests an important difference between dogs and humans: whereas humans use and interpret ostensive behaviour as evidence of the signaller's actual intentions, dogs seem to have instead evolved to communicate with humans in an associative way: certain types of human ostensive communication (e.g. points) are simply associated with certain responses, and certain states of the world (e.g. hunger) are associated with their production of certain signals. Consequently, there is no reason to conclude that mental states are necessarily involved, as there is with the child data. As such, human–dog communication seems to be an interesting case, where one species produces and interprets signals ostensively, while the other interprets and produces those same signals as part of a natural code. The overall situation comparing human children, dogs and chimpanzees is summarized in Table 4.2.

4.4 Do great apes communicate with natural codes?

If great ape communication is not ostensive, then does that imply that great ape communication must, therefore, be an instance of coded communication? There is, after all, no other account of the very possibility of communication (see Chapter 1). In this section I will present arguments that the code model is a good description of great ape communication. I should immediately reiterate that a communication system built upon codes need not be simple or unsophisticated. On the contrary, a system of coded communication could, in principle, be rather sophisticated indeed. In fact, we shall see in this section that this is likely the case with great ape communication.

To flesh this idea out, let me begin with the currently live debate about the origins of great ape gestural communication (see Liebal & Call, 2012 for a review). For some time now, the main explanation of this has been the process of *ontogenetic ritualization* (see §2.3). Several researchers have

Table 4.2 *A comparison of children's, dogs', and chimpanzees' abilities with respect to the different components of ostensive communication.* There are significant methodological challenges associated with many (perhaps all) of the entries that have not yet been directly studied. For some entries there is more than one relevant study; additional references are given in the main text.

	Type of intention	
	Communicative *(Can they differentiate between ostensive and non-ostensive behaviour?)*	**Informative** *(Do they understand that communication is about informing others i.e. about changing mental states?)*
Production	*Children:* Yes (Grosse et al., 2013) *Dogs:* Not (yet) directly studied *Chimpanzees:* Not (yet) directly studied	*Children:* Yes (Grosse et al., 2010) *Dogs:* No (Kaminski et al., 2011) *Chimpanzees:* Not (yet) directly studied
Reception	*Children:* Yes (Behne et al., 2005) *Dogs:* Yes (Kaminski et al., 2012) *Chimpanzees:* Not (yet) directly studied	*Children:* Not (yet) directly studied *Dogs:* No (Kaminski et al., 2012) *Chimpanzees:* Not (yet) directly studied

argued that great ape gestures originated exclusively or at least predominantly in this way (e.g. Call & Tomasello, 2007). The main objection to this claim has been that if the gestures were ontogenetically ritualized, then the actions involved should closely match those of the presumed original actions – but some detailed analyses suggest that this is not the case (Genty et al., 2009; Hobaiter & Byrne, 2011). The authors of these analyses thus argue that most gestures are part of a species-typical repertoire (*ibid.*). Debate continues: those that advocate the ontogenetic ritualization hypothesis have responded with new analyses in which they track instances of ontogenetic ritualization over time, and hence show that it is responsible for the creation of at least some great ape gestures (Halina et al., 2013). By the time you read this, the literature will likely have advanced further still.

Whether gestures are part of a species-wide repertoire, or whether they originate through ontogenetic ritualization, the key point for my purposes here is this: that either way, the end result is, according to both lines of argument, pairs of associations (one between states of the world and signals;

another between signals and responses) that together make a form of communication possible. In other words: a natural code. We do not (yet) have a complete list or understanding of the extent of these codes, mainly for methodological reasons. The relevant issues encompass questions such as: what counts as a gesture?; how should we determine whether two gestures are the same or different?; and how can we determine the intended meaning of any gesture? Some standard practices have been developed in response to these challenges, and the most recent data suggest that the repertoires may be significantly bigger than previously thought (e.g. Genty et al., 2009; Cartmill & Byrne, 2010; Hobaiter & Byrne, 2011; see Call & Tomasello, 2007 for a summary of earlier research). Significant work remains to be done here, but whatever this line of research reports in the future, the key point for the present issues is that the central debate in this area is about how these natural codes originate. That they exist is not in dispute, and there is no suggestion that these are mere conventional codes.

What is particularly interesting about these codes is that they seem to be used, in both production and reception, in a particularly flexible way. Indeed, flexibility is one of the criteria used to identify whether or not a signal is intentional (§4.3), and it is now widely accepted that the production of gestural signals in great ape communication is intentional (Call & Tomasello, 2007; Liebal et al., 2014). It is also possible that flexibility exists on the receiver's side. In fact, if there is signaller flexibility there surely must also be receiver flexibility, because otherwise how would receivers be able to interpret signals successfully? For example, detailed analysis of wild East African chimpanzee communication shows that their responses to gestural communication take into account the signaller's general behavioural intentions (Roberts et al., 2012a). There is also clear empirical evidence of flexibility in non-human primates' responses to vocal calls (including, it should be mentioned, the famous vervet alarm calls (Seyfarth & Cheney, 2010).

What makes this flexibility possible? The most likely answer is metapsychology. There is now good evidence that great apes are aware of what others know and intend (Call & Tomasello, 2008; but see Penn & Povinelli, 2007 for a skeptical view). Do apes make use of these abilities in signal comprehension? Conclusive demonstration of this, in the form of a playback experiment, would be difficult to achieve in the gestural modality, because of the methodological difficulties involved, but could perhaps be achieved in the vocal domain. Some present playback studies can be interpreted in these terms, but further experiments are necessary (see e.g. Engh et al., 2006; Arnold & Zuberbühler, 2013).

What we appear to have, then, is a system made possible by mechanisms of association, and made expressively more powerful by the existence of metapsychological abilities, which allow a natural code to be used in a flexible way. This is, interestingly, the very opposite of human language which, recall, is made possible by mechanisms of metapsychology, and made powerful by mechanisms of association (§1.5); see Table 4.3.

Table 4.3 *The difference between human ostensive communication and great ape gestural communication.* See main text for further discussion.

	What type of mechanism makes it *possible*?	**What type of mechanism makes it expressively *powerful*?**
Human ostensive communication	Metapsychological	Associative
Great ape gestural communication	Associative	Metapsychological

How could we tell the difference between these two different types of communication system? In a system made possible by metapsychology, its users should be able to use any behaviour at all for communicative ends, because they can perform it in a way that makes it apparent that this is what they are doing. Associations would then make it possible to expand the expressive scope of the system. If this set of associations is large enough and stable enough, this will mean that the users of this system will be able to express almost any proposition they wish to. Linguistic communication is certainly of this type.

In contrast, in a system made possible by association and enhanced by metapsychology we should expect to see a finite set of more-or-less loosely-defined prototypes (this is the coded foundation) which can be used in flexible ways (this is the effect of metapsychology). The most recent and detailed studies of chimpanzee gestural communication suggest that it is of this type: "adult chimpanzees have a multifaceted and complex repertoire of manual gestures, organised around prototypes, within which there is considerable variation" (Roberts et al., 2012b, pp. 586–587; see also Cartmill & Byrne, 2010 on orangutan gestures). This suggests that great ape gestural communication is very likely to consist of a natural code, although it is a particularly sophisticated instance of that genre, because the code is used in an intentional way. It is possible that the same is true of great ape vocal communication.

In Chapter 1 I discussed how it is a common intuition that language is made possible by the existence of associations, and made powerful by metapsychology. This intuition could be entrenched by the findings outlined above, that at least some forms of non-human primate communication involve codes enhanced by an awareness of others' minds. The difference with language would then become one of degree, and we would have a straightforward Darwinian picture: a small, simple code that is enhanced by limited metapsychological abilities evolved into a much larger, more complex code that is enhanced by rich metapsychological abilities. On this view, non-human primate communication would in an important sense be simply language-lite. But things are not this simple: as I have reiterated a number of times, the founding assumptions of this picture are simply wrong. Linguistic communication is not made possible by associations and made powerful by metapsychology; it is precisely the other way around (§1.5). As such, great ape gestural communication may in this sense be the very opposite of linguistic communication: made possible by associations, and expressively powerful by metapsychology (see Table 4.3).

One type of behaviour that great apes engage in which seems superficially akin to ostensive communication is attention-getting: behaviour that seems to serve no other function than to direct the attention of an intended audience to some subsequent behaviour (see Tomasello, 2008; Liebal et al., 2014 for reviews). Examples include slapping the ground, thumping the chest, or simply throwing things at the intended audience. The appropriate use of attention-getters is, recall, one of the criteria that is often used to identify whether or not a signal is used intentionally (see above). However, this is not ostensive communication. Even if they are used intentionally, attention-getters are only attempts to direct the attention of another individual. This does not amount, at least not necessarily so, to the same thing as an intention to make it apparent to the audience that you have an informative intention (to change the audience's beliefs, or other mental representations). One finding that demonstrates that attention-getters can be used through association (rather than metapsychology) is that operant conditioning, a process the very point of which is to create associations, can be used to teach chimpanzees how to use attention-getters (Russell et al., 2013). As such, although it is possible that attention-getters could be used in conjunction with metapsychology, and in that respect are relevant to our concerns here, they are not in and of themselves evidence of ostensive communication.

If non-human primate communication is not ostensive, as I have argued, then the prediction that follows is this: that they should also not possess the cognitive mechanisms, identified in the previous chapter, as those responsible for making ostensive communication possible in the first place. To have one and not the other would be a surprise, and difficult to explain. The next section investigates this prediction.

4.5 Mindreading in non-human primates

In the last 20 or so years, a great many controlled laboratory experiments have been conducted on the cognitive and communicative skills of great apes. Among them are numerous studies of their mindreading skills that we identified in the previous chapter as critical to the emergence of ostensive communication (see §3.4 and §3.5). Are the results of these studies consistent with the conclusion that great ape communication is not ostensive? One important point to make immediately is that in many tasks enculturated apes (i.e. those raised in rich socio-cultural environments in which human caregivers interact with them directly and from birth) outperform both wild apes and those raised in environments in which human interaction is limited to basic husbandry (e.g. Russell et al., 2011; see Call, 2011 for a review). Since most studies use unenculturated apes, it is possible that current research underestimates what chimpanzees are capable of, under the right circumstances. Whether this is actually the case is a question for future research.

So: are non-human primates able to entertain and manipulate mental metarepresentations i.e. to engage in recursive mindreading? The study of mental metarepresentation was spawned by a paper whose title asked just this question: "Does the chimpanzee have a theory of mind?" (Premack & Woodruff, 1978). Given the obvious importance of mindreading to human social life, the question of whether any other species, and in particular non-human primates, can represent others' mental states has been a lively topic of research and dispute ever since. Based on the classic criteria used in the infant studies, the answer to this question appears to be no: despite several attempts, there has been no convincing experimental demonstration that non-human primates can pass a false-belief task (Penn & Povinelli, 2007; Call & Tomasello, 2008).

Having said that, several species do behave in ways that are hard to explain if we assume that they are unable to mentally represent the minds of others. For example, several species of non-human primates, and some bird species, are able to distinguish between what others do and do not know, at least in some contexts (Hare et al., 2000; Flombaum & Santos, 2005; Clayton et al., 2007; but see Heyes, 1998; Povinelli & Vonk, 2003 for more skeptical views). Furthermore, there are now a significant number of experiments in which chimpanzees appear to demonstrate an understanding of others' intentions (Call & Tomasello, 2008).

Here is an example. The experimenter demonstrates to the chimpanzee, in one of two different ways, that pressing a button releases a reward. He then allows the chimpanzee to do the same. In one set of demonstrations, the experimenter is carrying a heavy load, and so can only press the button with his feet. In the other, the experimenter behaves in exactly the same way, but without the heavy load (i.e. he is bent over as if carrying the load, and he still presses the button with his feet). Now, if chimpanzees do not understand intentions, and can only comprehend the situation at the level of behaviour, there should be no difference between the conditions in how they press the button: they will use their hands in both conditions (like humans, this is the most convenient way for them). However, if chimpanzees understand the experimenter's intentions, then in the heavy load condition they will ascribe the use of feet to the fact that the hands were unavailable, and will hence use their own hands to press the button – but in the non-heavy load condition they will assume that the use of feet has something to do with why the experimenter gets a reward, and so they will copy this – and this is indeed what happens (Buttelmann et al., 2007). Fourteen-month-old human infants do the same (Gergely et al., 2002).

Here is a second example. The experimenter gives moves to give food to the chimpanzee, but fails for one of two reasons: either unable (because they are clumsy, and cannot fit it through the hole), or unwilling (they offer it, and then pull it away or drop it at the last moment). These are superficially similar behaviours, but they produce different responses in the chimpanzee: patience with the unable experimenter; frustration and anger with the unwilling one (Call et al., 2004). As before, this suggests that they understand the different intentions that lie underneath each behaviour. Also as before, human infants behave in the same way (Behne et al., 2005). So do capuchin monkeys (Phillips et al., 2009).

There are many more cases like this, where a change in the experimental condition produces a change in chimpanzee behaviour for which the most intuitive interpretation is that the chimpanzees understand that others act with intentions (see Call & Tomasello, 2008; Fitch et al., 2010 for reviews). It is always possible to construct killjoy explanations of such results (i.e. those expressed in terms of simpler cognitive mechanisms), but as the weight of evidence grows, it becomes increasingly parsimonious to conclude that chimpanzees do indeed understand others' behaviour in intentional terms. At the same time, however, this ability does not seem to have developed to the same extent as it has in humans – otherwise the multiple attempts to demonstrate false-belief understanding in chimpanzees would not have failed. Based on the present data, I concur with the conclusion that "chimpanzees, like humans, understand that others see, hear and know things ... [but they] probably do not understand others in terms of a fully human-like belief–desire psychology" (Call & Tomasello, 2008, pp. 190–191). The same may be true of some monkey species as well, although that literature has not yet developed the same weight of evidence as the ape literature has (see e.g. Marticorena et al., 2011).

Does this mean that chimpanzees have command of the mental metarepresentations required for ostensive communication? The first thing to say is that we simply do not know if the abilities that chimpanzees do have at this first level of mental metarepresentation translate up to the higher levels required. They may know$_1$ what others know$_2$, but do they know$_1$ what others know$_2$ about what others know$_3$? And what about even higher levels than that? The studies required to answer such questions simply have not been conducted. However, even if chimpanzees were shown to have such abilities, this would still not be sufficient to demonstrate the required levels of mental metarepresentation. This is because the sorts of mental metarepresentations involved in ostensive communication seem to be precisely those that involve intentions and beliefs (a "belief–desire psychology"), and not simply knowledge states. If great apes really do not have this, as the above conclusion indicates, then that would place ostensive communication out of reach. Of course, it remains possible that great apes will pass an appropriately-designed false-belief task at some point in the future, and if so these conclusions will have to be revised, but the present data suggest otherwise.

What about eye contact? In the previous chapter I highlighted how the use of eye contact is one possible way in which the metarepresentations required for ostensive communication can be made manifest. Do other species do this? Many species are able to detect gaze, and some are able to follow the direction of gaze (see Fitch et al., 2010 for a review). However, this is not yet evidence for mindreading, since we do not know if gaze direction is used to infer mental states (§3.5). Arguably the simplest mental state that could be inferred from gaze direction is attention – and the present data suggest that only humans and dogs are able to detect what others are looking at (Fitch et al., 2010). In fact, chimpanzees show a surprising inability to use gaze direction to infer attention (Call et al., 2000).

In sum, there is little evidence that chimpanzees have command of the type and extent of mental metarepresentation that have been identified as cognitive pre-requisites for ostensive communication. This conclusion is precisely in line with the conclusion that they do not communicate ostensively (§4.3). It seems, then, that ostensive communication is uniquely human. Certainly, I know of no other species for which there is any serious suggestion of ostensive communication.

Before we move on, let me make one final, general point about the theoretical choices available here. I have argued that great ape communication is likely not ostensive. The theorist who wants to argue otherwise, namely that great ape communication is not only intentional, but also ostensive, is faced with a couple of difficult questions. First: how could they do this, given the lack of evidence of the sort of recursive mindreading that is required? There are two possible responses here: either argue that ostensive communication does not require recursive mindreading, or argue that great apes can and do engage in recursive mindreading. Neither response looks tenable: §3.5 argued against the first; and this section has presented empirical data against the second. The second question for the apes-communicate-ostensively position is: if that is the case, then why don't apes also communicate linguistically, in even a basic way? After all, the potential of ostensive communication is massively enhanced by the development of conventional codes, and cultural norms do readily develop in great ape communities (Whiten, 2005). As such, if they do communicate ostensively, everything seems to be in place for them to communicate linguistically as well. But they do not. In contrast, if we accept that great apes do not communicate ostensively, then we have a ready-made explanation for why they don't have languages.

In sum, it seems likely that no other species communicates ostensively. If so, then the next question we should ask is: what caused humans, and only humans, to evolve the social cognitive capacities that made ostensive communication possible?

4.6 The social brain

Lists of collective nouns for animals make for curious reading. Some make intuitive sense, as good descriptions of what those groups are like: a *float* of crocodiles; a *stand* of flamingoes; an *ostentation* of peacocks; a *crash* of rhinoceroses; a *scurry* of squirrels. Others are more curious: a *school* of fish; a *murder* of magpies; a *parliament* of owls; a *zeal* of zebras. Wonderfully, the collective noun for a group of apes is this: a *shrewdness*. Now, here is the question: which type of collective noun is this? Is it the sort that describes some distinctive characteristic of the species, or the sort that requires a little more imagination to see the link, if there is one at all?

The *social brain hypothesis* says that it is the former. The basic idea is that what makes apes, and other primates, especially smart is not a general intelligence, equally adept in all domains, but rather a specifically social intelligence, which evolved to handle the increasingly complex social world of primate group living (Dunbar, 1998; 2003). In comparison to other vertebrates, primates have unusually large brains relative to body size and, according to the social brain hypothesis, this is the evolutionary consequence of living in large groups of interdependent individuals, in which it is critically important to be able to reason about the motives and intentions of others, keep track of the nature of others' relationships, manage one's own relationships, and decide who to deceive and who to trust. In other words: to be shrewd.

The basic insight of the social brain hypothesis, that the primate social world poses significant cognitive challenges that require a particular and sophisticated intelligence, is commonly said to originate in the work and observations of some mid 20th-century primatologists (Chance & Mead, 1953; Jolly, 1966). However, it can be traced back further: one survey finds roots in the writings of an early 20th-century writer named Eugene Marais: "Marais was a scientific pioneer because [unlike his contemporaries] he realized that the essence of baboon life was their society" (Cheney & Seyfarth, 2008, p. 29). Nevertheless, the idea that social factors can explain a great deal about primate intelligence and behaviour lay largely dormant through most of the 20th century. One reason for this may be sociological: "the history of...'comparative' psychology in the first half of the twentieth century is the history of the takeover of that science by quantitative, laboratory studies of learning in solitary animals" (Radick, 2007, p. 8). Methodological paradigms often have unintended consequences, and that may have been the case here: (comparative) psychology's quest for scientific control meant that animals, including our primate cousins, were habitually studied in isolation, an environment that meant that their capacity for social intelligence, and their similarities to humans in that respect, went largely unrecognized for many years (*ibid.*).

However, in more recent decades the social brain hypothesis has gained increasing acceptance, to the extent that it is now the dominant explanation of primate intelligence (Humphrey, 1976; Byrne & Whiten, 1989; Brothers, 1990; Dunbar, 2003). (In one of its earlier guises it was also called the Machiavellian Intelligence hypothesis, but that label is less used these days, presumably because of a recognition that social intelligence can be used not only subversively, but for pro-social reasons too.) It has a great deal of comparative evidence in its favour, not least the fact that relative brain size correlates with many indices of social complexity, such as group size, grooming clique size, the frequency of coalitions, male mating strategies, the prevalence of social play, the frequency of tactical deception, and the frequency of social learning, among others (see Dunbar & Shultz, 2007; Dunbar, 2012 for reviews). At the same time, it does not explain all the variation in brain size, intelligence, and cognitive ability between species, and so numerous modifications, refinements, qualifications, and partial alternatives have been put forward (e.g. Reader & Laland, 2002; Dunbar & Shultz, 2007; Holekamp, 2007; van Schaik et al., 2012). These details remain a matter of active research, but the basic idea that a great deal of primate social intelligence is explained by the complexity of their social lives is widely accepted.

What does the social brain hypothesis tell us about human social cognition? Humans live in particularly large and complex groups, even by primate standards. Correspondingly, we also have large brains relative to body size, and particularly advanced forms of social cognition (Dunbar, 2003; Frith & Frith, 2010; Whiten & Erdal, 2012). This advanced social cognition includes, among other things, recursive mindreading, which was identified in the previous chapter as critical to the very possibility of ostensive communication.

Numerous empirical findings are consistent with this picture. Here are three examples taken from the previous chapter. First, we track the beliefs of others automatically i.e. in a fast and efficient way, as part of our intuitive monitoring of the world around us (Cohen & German, 2009; Kovács et al., 2010; van der Wel et al., 2014). Monkeys, in contrast, do not (Martin & Santos, 2014). Second, we process false beliefs more quickly than we do equivalent public representations e.g. false maps and false photographs (Cohen & German, 2010). Third, we are highly motivated to engage with the social world, to the extent that when this motivation is absent we call it a disorder (Chevallier et al., 2012). And here are two further examples: we are extremely sensitive to cues that conspecifics may be observing us, whereas chimpanzees are not (Nettle et al., 2013); and while chimpanzees and human children have comparable skills of physical cognition (e.g. tool use, physical causality), human children vastly outperform chimpanzees and other great ape species in terms of social cognition (e.g. social learning, gaze following, reading intentions) (Herrmann et al., 2007). These facts, and many others like them, highlight the importance of sociality for understanding the human mind, and are consistent with the hypothesis that advanced social cognition evolved as a consequence of living in large and complex social groups: the socio-cognitive niche.

The evolution of advanced social cognition made it possible for our species to invent ostensive communication, and in doing so "to boldly go where no other species has been" (Frith & Frith, 2010, p. 165). Specifically, it allowed us to create a communication system with which we can directly express and recognize mental states. This is a revolution in a social species, and it was made even more so by the creation of shared communicative conventions, and hence languages. In short, the advent of ostensive communication made us 'language-ready'. In the next chapter we shall study the origins of these conventions in some detail. But before then, I want to flesh out exactly how ostensive communication might have emerged. Both Paul Grice, who did so much to bring attention to the importance of intentions in human communication, and Dan Sperber, who has written extensively on the cognitive basis of ostensive communication, have outlined how ostensive communication might have first emerged (Grice, 1982; Sperber, 2000). In this final section of the chapter, I will place their outlines into the bigger picture already developed.

4.7 The advent of ostensive communication

In §3.4 I described a series of scenarios – different ways in which Mary might eat berries, and how Peter might watch her do so – and I used them to explain why recursive mindreading abilities are required for ostensive communication to operate. Allow me to briefly recap. In scenario one, Mary is picking and eating berries, simply because the berries are edible. In scenario two, Peter watches her do this, and so forms a belief that the berries are edible. In scenario three, Mary wants Peter to believe that the berries are edible, and so she picks them precisely *because* this will cause Peter to believe that the berries are edible. In scenario four, Peter is aware that this is what Mary is doing. In all the scenarios up to here, Mary is picking berries in the same, standard way – she has no reason not to – but in scenarios five and six an important change occurs. In five, Mary wants Peter to believe that she wants him to believe that the berries are edible. In order to satisfy this intention, she picks the berries not as normal, but in a somewhat stylized or exaggerated way. This provides the evidence required to satisfy her (communicative) intention. In six, Peter correctly interprets this evidence, and consequently recognizes Mary's intention. This (and only this) is ostensive communication.

Dan Sperber has pointed out that the progressive development of these scenarios is suggestive of how ostensive communication could have emerged in the first place, as an offshoot of the evolution of sophisticated social intelligence (2000). As humans evolved greater social intelligence, and in particular as they became increasingly able to reason about the intentions and beliefs of others, they developed greater and better mindreading abilities, and in doing so they passed through stages in which each of the scenarios recalled above would have been possible. In most of these stages, the interactions are not communicative (by the terms of the definitions given in Chapter 1); instead, they are only attempts to manipulate attention, and to infer mental states. However, once the sixth scenario is reached, in which Mary expresses and Peter recognizes a communicative intention, we have ostensive communication proper. In our species' past, these first cases of ostensive communication would almost certainly have been very painstaking and haphazard, especially since at this point there would have been no cognitive adaptations to make ostensive communication operate smoothly and efficiently. The Communicative Principle of Relevance would probably not yet apply, and pragmatic competence would likely not yet exist (see §3.3). However over time, and especially as our ancestors started to develop shared communicative conventions, fluent ostensive communication would have become increasingly more straightforward.

Paul Grice sketched a very similar account of how a species might come to develop ostensive communication (1982; see also Wharton, 2006). Grice's story, which he proposed only as a speculative "myth" (p. 296), begins when organism *X* emits an involuntary yelp of pain. At the second stage, organism *X* gains voluntary control over the yelp, and organism *Y* is able to recognize this; that is, *Y* is able to differentiate between voluntary and involuntary yelps (i.e. they become intentional, in at least one sense; see §4.3). At the third stage, *X* yelps *in order that Y* infers that he is doing so voluntarily. In the fourth stage, *Y* recognizes that this is *X*'s intention but, unfamiliar with such behaviour, can only guess at why *X* might do this. At stage five, *Y* makes the inference that the reason *X* has this intention (that *Y* recognizes that he, *X*, is producing the yelp voluntarily) is that *X* is indeed in pain. We engage in such behaviour all the time: imagine a voluntarily produced yawn, used to communicate that I am tired. Although Grice does not label them extra stages, he goes on to discuss two further additions to this scenario: that *X* no longer produces the yelp itself, but in fact something "more loosely connected" (p. 295) to the pain; and that, because of this, *Y* is subsequently able to more easily infer that *X* is in pain. This is akin to yawning in an exaggerated and obvious voluntary fashion, and having the audience recognize as much. As I say, this story is in the essential details the same as the one we have already seen above: *X* is Mary, *Y* is Peter, pain is the edibility of the berries, and yelps are the eating of the berries.

The Gricean myth and the Sperberian scenarios are effectively accounts about how meaning$_N$ can transition into meaning$_{NN}$; or, if you prefer the terminology of animal communication theory, how cues can become ostensive signals. (I introduced the terms *meaning*$_{NN}$ and *meaning*$_N$ in §1.5, and *cue* and *signal* in §2.2.) Both accounts start with the exploitation by one individual (Peter/*Y*) of a correlation between some aspect of the behaviour of another individual (Mary eating berries/*X* yelping), and some fact about the world (that the berries are edible/that *X* is in pain). These correlations have meaning$_N$. To these beginnings are then added successive layers of mental metarepresentation, and these take us, eventually and quite plausibly via the stages described above, to ostensive signals that have meaning$_{NN}$.

These accounts thus expand on the bigger picture already developed in this chapter, and indeed throughout this book, which should by now be in focus. Changes in human group size led to the evolution of increased social intelligence, to the extent that it became possible to communicate in a hitherto unknown way: with ostension and inference, rather than with natural codes. The impact of this development, even before the advent of language, is hard to overstate. Without it, signals are used either inflexibly or, in some cases, flexibly but within limits (see §4.5), and new signals arise only through the cumbersome processes of ontogenetic ritualization, phylogenetic ritualization, and sensory manipulation (§2.3 and §4.5). With it, signals can be used to mean literally anything at all (§1.4), and they can be created far more easily, essentially out-of-the-blue (§2.5). Particularly productive yet still not linguistic examples of ostensive communication are pointing, nodding, screaming, some forms of eye contact, and many others. It was in this way that ostensive communication could have emerged without the prior existence of language.

The opposite – an account of how language might have emerged without the prior existence of ostensive communication – we do not have. On the contrary, in fact, a point long recognized by those who take the pragmatic basis of human communication seriously. For example, "an account of the genesis of language that supposed that first came literal meaning and then, as a derivative of that, utterer's meaning [speaker meaning], seems hard to conceptualize even in the barest and thinnest sort of outline" (Suppes, 1986, p. 113). In fact, the situation is worse than this: a code-first, pragmatics-later account is not just hard to conceptualize; it is, as I explained in some detail in Chapter 2, wholly implausible (see also Sperber & Origgi, 2010).

However, this conclusion has not yet been embraced. Most discussion of the origins of language acknowledges the importance of pragmatic competence in modern communication, but does not fully recognize its implications. I gave some examples of this in §2.7. Here is another, taken from a commentary on an article about the social cognition of children and nonhuman primates: "Very little understanding or sharing of intentions – perhaps little if any beyond what contemporary apes possess – would have been required to comprehend and act on the kind of single-unit utterances with which language must have begun" (Bickerton, 2005, p. 692). No substantive argument or evidence is offered for this claim, nor any references to where we might find such arguments developed. Exactly what these imagined forms of non-ostensive linguistic communication look like, and how we might get from there to here, is entirely unclear. The claim receives a blunt response: "If this is true, then why don't apes use symbolic utterances with one another today? Not only do they not use symbolic utterances with one another, they do not even point for one another or show things to one another" (Tomasello et al., 2005, p. 722). The importance of social cognition and pragmatics for language is often acknowledged, but too often only as lip service. Certainly, the evolutionary implications are too rarely embraced. Correspondingly, very few accounts of the origins of language provide any details of how pragmatic competence might have evolved. In this chapter we have identified a plausible account of this. In contrast, Chapter 2 showed how the alternative story, that language itself could have led to the development of ostensive communication, crumbles under scrutiny.

At this point the word *coevolution* may come to mind: perhaps language and ostensive communication 'co-evolved' with one another in some way or another (see e.g. Bickerton, 2005, p. 692; Hurford, 2011, pp. 571–572 for versions of this proposal). This is not a solution to the problem at hand. Coevolution is a process in which changes in one cause changes in the other, which in turn cause changes in the first trait, and so on and so on (Janzen, 1980; Thompson, 1994). As such, if this is the alternative story, then we need to know *what* changes in language caused *what* changes in ostensive communication, and vice versa. Without these details, which have been nowhere proposed, coevolution is just a black box – and as such, it is another question, not a solution.

In sum, there is only one account of the evolution of ostensive communication and hence language that is properly developed, coherent, and plausible: that ostensive communication emerged as a secondary adaptation of social intelligence, and this then, in turn, led to the creation of the first languages. I do not rule out the possibility that an alternative account will be developed in the future, but on our present knowledge, the former account seems inescapable.

The emergence of this new, especially expressive form of communication would have had a number of consequences, two of which are particularly relevant for our concerns here. The first is the natural selection of mechanisms designed to make ostensive communication run more smoothly and effectively than it otherwise would. Three likely examples of this are: white sclera (the opaque, protective outer layer of the eye), which make it far easier for others to identify gaze direction (Kobayashi & Kohshima, 2001); mental modules specifically dedicated to ostensive communication (Sperber & Wilson, 2002); and cognitive mechanisms that allow infants to detect when others are communicating with them (Csibra & Gergely, 2011). All of these would have been absent for the first users of ostensive communication, but each clearly enhances its effectiveness. The other consequence of the emergence of ostensive communication was the creation of communicative conventions that allow ostensive communication to be used more precisely and more easily than otherwise. These conventions would in time, through repeated use and cultural propagation, become languages. How that process occurs is the subject of the next chapter.

* * *

Chapter 4. *Non-human primates possess few of the crucial social cognitive mechanisms necessary for ostensive communication. Much non-human primate communication is intentional, but it is not ostensive. It is best characterized as a system of associations that is made expressively powerful by metapsychological abilities. Ostensive communication likely emerged among humans as a consequence of the increasing size and complexity of human groups, which led to the selection of sophisticated social cognition, including the recursive mindreading necessary to create ostensive communication in the first place.*

Chapter 5. *What were the first 'words', and how did they become culturally shared conventions? In what modality did language originate? How did structure in language evolve? What role does communication play in these processes? What can an evolutionary perspective tell us about the nature of languages?*

Chapter 5

Building a Language

5.1 Evolutionary linguistics

The comedian Chris Addison, in his spoof lecture series *The Ape That Got Lucky*, speculated that language developed spontaneously and in anger, when the rage felt by one half of a couple towards the other finally exploded, and they said the world's first ever proper words: "Arrrgggg, you tit!!!". "Oh, it's all coming out now, innit?", comes the reply. Comedy aside, there is a serious problem here. How *do* you get a language started? And where do complex grammatical constructions like "it's all coming out now" come from? These are among the defining questions of evolutionary linguistics (Scott-Phillips & Kirby, 2010; McMahon & McMahon, 2013). While the traditional task of linguistics is to document and explain the linguistic codes that exist and have previously existed, evolutionary linguistics studies, among other things, how these linguistic codes might have arisen in the first place, and what explains their continued stability within a population.

It is at this point useful and indeed necessary to distinguish between the words *language* and *languages*. *Languages* are the conventional codes used by a particular community (e.g. English, German, etc.; see §1.5). The word *language*, on the other hand, is often used specifically to refer to the suite of cognitive traits that allows us to acquire and use these languages. This chapter is concerned with the evolution of languages. We shall investigate how languages, as they are used and passed down from generation to generation, acquire the sort of characteristics that we associate with them. The evolution involved here is cultural: the languages change as they are used and acquired through various forms of social learning, rather than by the biological processes of genetic mutation and natural selection. In the next chapter, I will discuss whether there has also been any biological evolution of language i.e. of the cognitive capacity to acquire and use languages. (It is, note, hard to maintain a strict distinction in use between the terms *language* and *languages*. In particular, it is often natural to use simply 'language' for both intended meanings; indeed, I have already done so several times in this book. I do not think this is especially problematic, so long as the intended meaning is clear, and the correct term is used whenever there is the potential for misunderstanding.)

I will address these evolutionary questions about language and languages in the light of what we have already learnt about the ostensive character of linguistic communication. The vast majority of current research and discussion in this area does not do this (exceptions are Origgi & Sperber, 2000; Smith, 2008; Sperber & Origgi, 2010). Yet ostension and inference are, as I will show, critical to understanding both why and how languages evolve. We shall see that once we take ostension and inference into account, many of the most pertinent questions about the origins of language and languages come into sharper focus than they otherwise would.

In fact, there is an important point about ostension, inference, and language change that should be made here, at the outset. It is this: that the very phenomenon of language evolution is a consequence of the ostensive character of linguistic communication (Hoefler & Smith, 2009). The next four paragraphs explain why this is so.

There are two ways in which linguistic conventions can change (Hopper & Traugott, 2003; Heine & Kuteva, 2007). On the one hand, the speaker might use an existing form in a novel way; this is typically called *metaphor* (even though not all instances of this are actually metaphors e.g. metonymies). On the other, the listener might interpret an expressed form in a novel way; this is typically called *reanalysis*. Logically, there are no other possibilities. In both cases, if the new usages/interpretations are adopted by other users, in sufficient numbers, then the language will have changed.

How might such changes occur? In linguistic communication, like all ostensive communication, speakers must provide appropriate evidence for their intended meaning, and listeners must take the evidence provided to them and form the best inference they can about the speaker's intended meaning (§1.4). As such, a speaker who wishes to express a meaning but who is in a community in which no such convention exists would instead have to find some other way to do so. The best way to do this might well be to use an existing convention metaphorically. If this new metaphorical usage is successful, and if it recurs sufficiently often, then it may either supplant or sit alongside the existing conventions for the same or similar meanings; and if this occurs in a sufficient number of speakers within the community, then we can say that a new convention has developed, and that the language has changed (see Hoefler & Smith, 2009 for further discussion). Reanalysis can be dissected in a similar way (*ibid.*).

Let's work through an example (from Hoefler & Smith, 2009). The expression "going to" was once used exclusively as a verb to express spatial motion, but it now has an additional role, to mark future tense. Why might this have happened? Spatial motion is often associated with intention: when people intend to go somewhere, spatial motion usually follows. As such, a speaker who wishes to express intention, but whose language has no existing convention for this, might use spatial motion instead, and this would be an instance of metaphorical usage. This could work because the listener knows both that (i) spatial motion is often associated with intention; and

(ii) there is no existing convention in the language for intention. It would be especially effective if the context was such that spatial motion was unlikely to have any other possible meaning. In such circumstances, it would be entirely reasonable for the listener to infer that the use of the convention for spatial motion is intended to express intention, and indeed the speaker can reasonably assume that the listener will make such an inference. It is not hard to see how the process could then be repeated, with intention being used to express future tense.

This is all made possible only by the ostensive and inferential character of linguistic communication, since it depends upon the use of existing conventions as evidence for meanings that they are currently not associated with. In other words, the cognitive mechanisms that make human communication possible in the first place are also responsible for the subsequent cultural evolution of languages (Burling, 2005; Hoefler & Smith, 2009).

This fact has two important implications. The first is that once ostensive communication exists, no additional or special cognitive mechanisms are logically necessary to explain how languages come into existence. The second implication is that once humans had evolved the cognitive mechanisms that enabled ostensive communication in the first place, the processes by which those early, non-linguistic forms of ostensive communication would have developed into something like language would have begun more-or-less immediately. In other words, once we have ostensive communication, we also have the mechanisms required to create and modify the conventional codes that make ostensive communication expressively powerful. This chapter is about how that process actually occurs.

5.2 Early ostensive communication

During my teenage years our family went on a number of summer holidays to rural France. My uncle Frank was usually the first to rise each morning, and so took it upon himself to visit the local bakery and delicatessen to buy the bread and other provisions needed for breakfast. Having never been taught a foreign language, and with no particular desire to learn one, my uncle decided early on in these holidays that the best way to successfully communicate with the shop assistants was to simply give up on French, and to use other means instead. I joined him on a couple of these trips, and saw this strategy in action. To order bread, he would simply point to the pile of baguettes behind the counter, and then hold up the number of fingers required to indicate how many he wanted. More outlandishly, he would make noises and otherwise impersonate the animal whose meat he wished to buy. Frank never returned from any of these trips with anything less than what he planned to. This success illustrates just how much can be communicated with ostension and inference, even in the absence of language. Pointing in particular is an especially powerful form of ostensive communication.

One possible reaction to this anecdote is to point out that my uncle and the shop assistant are both already fluent users of language. Based on this observation, it might be possible to develop an argument that without this background and experience with linguistic communication, then the non-linguistic communication that they did engage in could not have been so successful. On this view, the use of ostensive communication in a wide range of non-linguistic settings depends and builds upon the prior experience of using ostensive communication in the more specific domain of linguistic interaction. However, empirical data show that this cannot be right. Specifically, there is at least one human group who, contrary to this view, are able to successfully use ostensive communication but who have had no direct experience of linguistic communication at all: infants. Ostensive communication precedes language in child development, and as such, the former cannot be dependent upon the latter (Tomasello, 2008).

I see no reason not to think that, once our ancestors had evolved the social cognitive abilities required for ostensive communication (see Chapter 4), then they would have used whatever means at their disposal to express their intended meanings, just as my uncle did. In fact, we know that when individuals with no shared language interact with one another repeatedly, they will create languages anew. The best examples of this are languages created by deaf children born to hearing parents (called homesign, previously mentioned in §2.6), and new sign languages, in particular Nicaraguan Sign Language (NSL) and Al-Sayyid Bedouin Sign Language (ABSL) (Senghas et al., 2004; Goldin-Meadow, 2005; Sandler et al., 2005; Aronoff et al., 2008).

Icons and indices are clearly important here. Icons are signs whose form has a physical resemblance (in whatever modality) to the thing it represents (and hence its meaning). ✂ looks like a pair of scissors, ✈ looks like a plane, and ☂ looks like an umbrella. Similarly, "moooo" sounds like a cow, and "cluck-cluck" sounds like a chicken. These physical similarities mean that all these examples, be they visual or auditory, are iconic. Icons can be contrasted with indices and symbols. Indices are signs whose form has a causal but not physical relationship to the thing it represents: dark clouds do not physically look like rain, but they do cause it. Symbols, however, have no relationship, either physical or causal, with the thing they represent. They are arbitrary. The classic example is (most) words, as Shakespeare's Juliet observed: "What's in a name? That which we call a rose / By any other name would smell as sweet".

The distinction between icons, indices and symbols are often blurred: there are many intermediate cases. For one thing, some signs have only a partial physical (or causal) link to the referent: does ⚡ *actually* look like lightning?; does "woof" *actually* sound like a dog? Second, some sounds seem to have a more natural association with some meaning than others. For instance, the overwhelming majority of people will judge *mal* as a 'larger' word than *mil*. People also agree on which words are which half of an antonym pair in foreign languages, and they are correct at above chance levels (e.g. when presented with, say, the Hindi words for 'big' and 'small', English speakers with no experience of Hindi are able to judge which is which at better than chance levels). This is *sound-symbolism*, and it illustrates how the traditional distinction between icons, indices and symbols is not as clean or as exhaustive as it first appears: words do not typically appear to be either iconic or indexical, but if they were truly symbolic, then the above results should not hold. Yet they do, which suggests that iconicity is more common than is generally recognized, both within mainstream linguistics, and by language users themselves (see Perniss et al., 2010 for a review of sound-symbolism).

Icons and indices are all ways in which signallers can produce new signals that have at least some evidence for the meaning they wish to express. This is, for instance, what we do when we play charades, what my uncle did in the French delicatessen, and what homesigners do when they create new languages. Early ostensive communication would have relied heavily on such signals. In other words, once humans had evolved the social intelligence that allowed them to start to communicate ostensively, they would have used whatever behaviours they had available – grunts, mimes, whatever – to make that communication work as best they could: "a free-for-all, catch-as-catch-can mode that utilised sounds, signs, pantomime and any other available mechanism that would carry intention and meaning" (Bickerton, 2007, p. 512).

This scenario of what early ostensive communication might have looked like is a rejection of a common dichotomy, namely whether language originated in the vocal or the gestural modality. When both modalities are available the vocal one plainly dominates (although gestures do play a significant role even here (McNeill, 2000)). As such, for some researchers the default assumption is that language originated in the vocal modality (e.g. Cheney & Seyfarth, 2005; Zuberbühler, 2005). However, the existence and study of sign languages shows that the full fruits of language can be enjoyed in either modality, and so the idea that language could have originated there is not at all an unreasonable one. In fact, gestural origins theories have a long history, and remain popular today (e.g. Hewes, 1973; Corballis, 2002; Armstrong & Wilcox, 2007; Arbib et al., 2008; Tomasello, 2008).

I do not see why we need to make any choice between vocal and gestural origins. There are some concepts for which one or the other modality would have been more effective: for some concepts vocalizations would be more useful (animals, perhaps?); for others, gestures would be (actions, say). The range of concepts that gestures are able to represent effectively is probably larger than the range of concepts that vocalizations are able to represent effectively. We know this because it has been tested experimentally: participants asked to communicate using only novel gestures are more successful than those asked to communicate using only novel vocalizations (i.e. without language and other existing conventions) (Fay et al., 2013). This is presumably because of gesture's capacity to better represent, through icons and indices, the speaker's intended meaning (Cartmill et al., 2012). This suggests that early ostensive communication probably involved a great deal of gesture and pantomime, but only for purely practical reasons. At other times it would have been vocal, and much of the time it would have been both. It is, after all, often fruitful to use both modalities: signals produced in two media are in general more effective than those produced in just one (Rowe, 1999). The default assumption must, therefore, be that early ostensive communication was neither exclusively vocal nor exclusively gestural, but multi-modal. Indeed, why *wouldn't* it be?

The only answer I know to this "why wouldn't it be?" question is the possibility that the users of this early ostensive communication did not have voluntary control over their vocalizations, and hence could only exercise the behavioural flexibility required for ostensive communication in the gestural modality. After all, we do not have voluntary control over all our behaviour (sneezing, for example). Proponents of a gestural origin of language sometimes argue that early humans probably did not have control of their vocal apparatus either. A significant part of the argument for this conclusion is that great ape vocal communication is involuntary. It is possible that this is true, although the matter is not as settled as some researchers believe (Slocombe et al., 2011). However even if it is true, the key question is: was it still involuntary after humans had evolved the social intelligence necessary for ostensive communication? It is not clear to me what sort of data would be able to answer this question in any definitive way, and so this detail may have to lie unresolved.

One pertinent question for this multi-modal approach to language origins is why, when both modalities are available, as they are for most modern language users, linguistic communication is predominantly vocal. The answer lies in the different strengths and weaknesses of vocalizations and gestures. Since gestures more easily facilitate iconicity, they may have dominated in early ostensive communication, when conventional codes were still only emerging. But vocalizations are quicker, and can be used without any line of sight, and so once a rich and precise set of vocal conventional codes exists, they have the advantage. The transition from one dominant modality to another is not hard to explain: sounds could have been used in conjunction with the more iconic gestures, but once that association is established, then the sounds alone would suffice. More of a challenge is to explain how conventions, in any modality, actually emerge in the first place.

5.3 The first symbols

While non-linguistic ostensive communication is a potent tool, there are some meanings that will have been very difficult, if not impossible, to communicate without language. There are some meanings, such as complex propositions and many abstract nouns, for which natural icons and indices do not exist. To get beyond icons and indices, the first properly conventional codes would have had to develop. This is, in effect, a change in the division of labour, from a scenario in which pragmatic factors are doing all of the work, to one in which communicative conventions and hence literal meaning take on some or even most of that load (but never all of it: see Chapter 1).

Evolutionary linguistics has in recent years embraced the use of experiments with human participants, in which the evolution of communication systems can be observed in real-time (see Scott-Phillips & Kirby, 2010; Galantucci & Garrod, 2011 for reviews). These studies are not attempts to recreate the origins of language in the laboratory. Instead, they are designed to investigate how the various different processes involved in language evolution actually work (Scott-Phillips & Kirby, 2010). In this section we are concerned with one such process in particular: how does a pair or group of interacting individuals converge upon a shared symbolic convention in the first place?

The pioneering study that kick-started this experimental turn in language evolution research was focused on precisely this question (Galantucci, 2005). Pairs of participants controlled different characters within a small maze, and had to coordinate their behaviour with the other player. This required them to communicate with one another. A communication channel was provided for this purpose, but the channel was designed such that the signals were distorted in a way that prevented the use of existing, conventional words or symbols. Instead, the participants had to invent novel symbols. In at least some cases they were able to do this, but it often proved difficult, and some pairs failed altogether (Galantucci, 2005). This first study did not include any experimental manipulations. That is, it did not conduct any controlled comparisons to establish, say, the different conditions under which participants failed or succeeded. Rather, its main contribution was, to my mind, exploratory; a proof-of-concept, if you will. It showed that it was possible to investigate the emergence of symbolic communication systems in real-time, in the laboratory. It also, in passing, nicely illustrates a point I touched upon above: that even putting aside the problems of signalling signalhood (discussed in previous chapters), early ostensive communication was likely to be very painstaking and haphazard, with no guarantee of success, even in relatively simple scenarios. If already fluent language users in the closed environment of a simple psychology experiment sometimes struggle with this activity, then non-language users in an open-ended environment are almost certain to.

Not long after this, a series of experiments were conducted based upon the party game Pictionary, in which players must draw words, but without using any letters or other conventional symbols. The general structure of the Pictionary experiments is that one player has to draw and the other guess one of a pre-defined set of concepts, such as 'cartoon', 'art gallery', and 'homesick'. These concepts are drawn and guessed again and again, so that it is possible to observe how the drawings for each of the concepts change over time. The most salient change is a change from iconic to symbolic: at first the drawings are (necessarily) iconic or, occasionally, indexical, just as early ostensive communication must have been; but over time, they lose this form–meaning relationship, and become symbolic (Garrod et al., 2007; Healey et al., 2007; see Figure 5.1). This process has been dubbed the "drift to the arbitrary" (Tomasello, 2008, p. 220). It has also been observed outside of the laboratory, for instance in the natural evolution of writing systems (Garrod et al., 2007; Figure 5.1). Various experimental manipulations demonstrate the importance of interaction in this process, as well as in the initial emergence of the conventions. The conventions are not simply created by one individual and then adopted (or not) by another. Rather, their form is arrived at through an interactive process of use and feedback. When this is absent, conventions do not emerge (Garrod et al., 2007; Healey et al., 2007; Tan & Fay, 2011).

It is then not difficult for these conventions to spread through a population. For example, one experiment showed that observers of such systems,

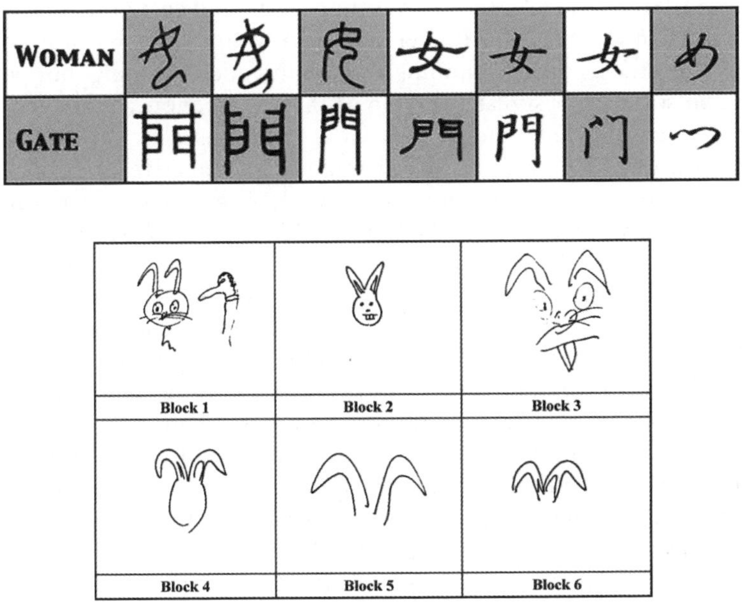

Figure 5.1 *The drift to the arbitrary (figures from Garrod et al., 2007).* The top figure shows the evolution of two Chinese writing symbols, the bottom figure the evolution of a drawing for 'cartoon' in one of the Pictionary-style experiments (Garrod et al., 2007). In all cases, the signs started off with some degree of iconicity, but became increasingly symbolic over time.

who were not privy to the original creation of the conventions and hence do not perceive them to have any iconic or indexical features, simply learn them as arbitrary signs (i.e. as symbols), and use them accordingly (Caldwell & Smith, 2012). Another showed that if participants are paired with different people for each interaction, continually swapping communicative partners, then the conventions emerged at this group level (Fay et al., 2008). That is to say: conventions do not have to be negotiated upon by a pair or small group first, and then subsequently rolled out to the larger community. Instead, this negotiation and propagation can occur simultaneously.

In many respects, the results of these experiments, and the broader picture that I am developing here, should not be too surprising. The emergence of new forms of symbolic communication proceeds in a more-or-less predictable way, given its ostensive character. Indeed, on the few occasions when specialists in linguistic pragmatics have speculated on the origins of language, what they have outlined is remarkably close to what the above experiments have demonstrated in the laboratory. Here is one example: "Surely, language must have begun from attempts at [ostensive] communication between a few individuals. At first these efforts at communication did not have very much stability of literal meaning. Only [later]...did a stable community of users lead to the abstract concept of literal meaning" (Suppes, 1986, p. 113). Here is another: "At a given point, the success of communication need no longer depend on any prior natural connection between the ostensive stimulus and the intended meaning, but perhaps instead on some prior stylised version of that connection... more generally, it doesn't matter what kind of behaviours were used in early inferential communication – existing coded warning calls, instinctive emotional calls, mimes, gestures, facial expressions; what we have is a plausible, naturalistic framework on which to build" (Wharton, 2009, pp. 189–190).

The emergence of these first communicative conventions would have been a boon to the effectiveness of ostensive communication. Consider a world in which, post the advent of ostensive communication, a more-or-less stable communicative convention has developed around the notion of, say, 'animal'. This convention could, very plausibly, have been used to indicate any of the following intended speaker meanings: "Dinner", "Please bring some meat back from the hunt", "There's an animal behind that bush!", "I'm hungry" and, indeed, a great many others too – the vast majority of which would have been very difficult to express without that convention. Note also that even just this simple example illustrates how the underdeterminacy of ostensive communication – which, because it can lead to ambiguity, is often thought of as a defective quality – is in fact often an asset, since it allows us to express a large range of propositions in an efficient way.

Despite the boost in expressivity that these early conventions would have given ostensive communication, they would still not be as expressively powerful as fully-developed languages are. This additional level of expressiveness relies upon several other factors, most pertinently *grammar*:

the organization of these conventions within a language. Where does grammar come from? To begin to answer this question, we must first look at what a language without grammar might look like: a 'proto-language', if you like.

5.4 A pragmatic perspective on protolanguage

He was not the first to use the term, but the widespread adoption of the term *protolanguage* owes a great deal to the work of the linguist Derek Bickerton (1990). It has since entered the jargon of evolutionary linguistics, as a useful way to refer to the earliest languages, those that have not yet developed the sort of properties we associate with more developed languages. Exactly what form protolanguages took, and how they subsequently developed into languages proper, are both disputed topics. However, like too much research on the origins of language, the importance of pragmatics, and in particular of ostension and inference, is sorely neglected in these discussions (an exception is Smith, 2008). In this section I will describe what a pragmatic perspective tells us about the nature of protolanguage.

There are two established schools of thought with regards the evolution of protolanguage. The first is the *synthetic* approach, so called because it emphasizes how different elements are synthesized together. It is also sometimes called the *compositional* approach, because it emphasizes how larger units are created by the composition of smaller units. The basic idea is that languages develop as linguistic elements that are then combined together in increasingly complex ways. The first conventions are, in effect, the building blocks with which more complex constructions are created. Newcomers to the topic typically assume, quite reasonably, that this is how early languages must have developed, for it is initially hard to imagine any alternative.

An alternative does exist, however, and it has a surprisingly long history, dating back at least as far as the 18th-century philosopher and political radical Jeremy Bentham (better known as one of the founders, alongside John Mill, of utilitarianism). He advocated an account of the origin of language in which "single primitive utterances were equivalent to whole sentences" and where "linguistic progress…came with analysis…the breaking down of primitive one-word sentences into their component parts" (Stam, 1976, p. 42). Much the same idea has been independently developed by several modern-day scholars (e.g. Wray, 2000).

The idea, then, is that early linguistic utterances were equivalent to whole phrases, and that the component parts of languages emerged when two such phrases had both a sound and a part of meaning in common, so these two parts might be analysed as being related to one another. For example, suppose that 'tebima' means 'give that to her', and that 'kumapi' means 'share this with her'. Then the syllable 'ma' might be analysed as meaning 'female' (or maybe 'female beneficiary'), since both the sound and that aspect of meaning are common to both words (example from Wray, 2000). This is the *analytic* approach to protolanguage, so called because it emphasizes how existing linguistic objects are analysed into their component parts. It is also sometimes called the *holophrastic* approach, because it similarly emphasizes how the earliest utterances would have been equivalent to whole phrases, or sentences. The sorts of phrases proposed as examples are sometimes very and unnecessarily elaborate: "go and hunt the hare I saw five minutes ago behind the stone at the top of the hill" (Mithen, 2005, p. 172); "Take your spear and go around the other side of that animal and we will have a better chance together of being able to kill it" (Arbib, 2005, p. 118).

The difference between the analytic and the synthetic approaches is ultimately the difference between putting things together (synthesis), or taking them apart (analysis), and the often vexed debate between these two views is typically presented as an either/or matter (see Hurford, 2011 for a recent overview). To this end, several theoretical arguments and computational simulations have been developed that speak in favour of one side or the other, and the debate was in 2008 the focal topic of a special issue of the journal *Interaction Studies* (see e.g. Bickerton, 1990; Wray, 1998; Tallerman, 2007; Arbib & Bickerton, 2008).

I will not review the details of this debate here, because to do so would be to implicitly grant that the dichotomy between the two views is a coherent one – and I do not think this is the case. When we examine protolanguage through a pragmatic lens, the distinction between analytic and synthetic approaches becomes far more fuzzy than most discussions recognize (Smith, 2008). There is in fact no forced choice to make. The rest of this section develops this point, and in doing so outlines what protolinguistic communication must have looked like. We shall see that both the synthetic and analytic views contain important insights, but also that they both overstate other aspects of the situation, in order to make them consistent with the insights that they rightly argue must be correct.

To begin, I must reiterate the points made in §5.2 and §5.3, above: that because they were being used as part of ostensive-inferential communication, early linguistic conventions were able to express a diverse range of meanings. In this sense, early protolanguage *must* have been holophrastic: single, isolated units used to express whole propositions. For example, 'animal' can, *even now*, be used to express any and all of "Dinner", "Please bring some meat back from the hunt", "There's an animal behind that bush!", and so on – and if established languages with many semantic conventions and a grammar to organize them still use single expressions to express whole propositions, then it is entirely plausible that protolanguage must have done. In fact, given the inherently flexible nature of ostensive communication, it seems inevitable.

However, there is no reason to think that any particular convention was *consistently* used to express any particular, specific phrase. On the contrary, given that protolanguage must have had a far smaller vocabulary than modern languages (this is true almost by definition), then protolanguage would likely have been *more* semantically promiscuous than modern languages are. The relationships between specific words/phrases and specific propositions in protolanguage would have been no more rigid than they are in modern languages, and probably far less so.

This semantic promiscuity implies something very problematic for the analytic account of protolanguage. The analytic account depends upon the existence of signals that are used *repeatedly* and more-or-less *exclusively* to express particular complex meanings. If the signals were not used repeatedly, there would be nothing to analyse: you cannot generalize from a single usage. Similarly, if the signals were not used to express more-or-less the same meanings on each occasion, then there would be no reliable consistency between form and meaning, and again we would be left with nothing to analyse. By way of illustration, suppose that the same phrase was used to express each of the meanings mentioned above: "Dinner", "Please bring some meat back from the hunt", and "There's an animal behind that bush!" The only thing these meanings have in common is the base concept 'animal', not some more complex concept that can be analysed into its component parts. It is a necessary condition for the analytic account that there should be some "phonetic similarity in two utterances that also had some aspect of meaning in common" (Wray, 1998, p. 55), yet the fact of semantic promiscuity means that this condition is unlikely to be satisfied: "complex meaning[s]...would have almost no chance of being *repeatedly replicated* across communicative episodes and by different individuals" (Smith, 2008, p. 106, italics in original). In sum, the realities of ostension and inference imply an underdeterminacy and semantic promiscuity that makes any exclusively analytic approach to protolanguage implausible.

What we have instead is ostensive communication augmented by a limited number of more-or-less stable communicative conventions, which speakers will use as best they can. Their task is to provide the best evidence they can for their intended meaning, and conventional codes are one tool they can use to achieve that. Modern humans are able to and in general do provide the right amount of evidence for their intended meaning, and this efficacy owes a lot to both the quantity and diversity of the conventional codes we have available to us (and also to the existence of cognitive mechanisms dedicated to the task; see Sperber & Wilson, 2002). With fewer conventions, some speaker meanings will be difficult and perhaps impossible to express.

This problem can be overcome with a diversification of both the quantity and type of available conventions. This could and indeed must have included the combination of existing conventions in new ways. In fact, not only is this possible, but in the right contexts it causes no problems of comprehension. Pidgin languages are new languages developed by human adults who need to communicate with one another but who speak unrelated and mutually incomprehensible languages. Here, translated into English, is a pidgin dialogue between two sea captains, a Norwegian and a Russian, bartering over an exchange of fish for flour (from Bickerton, 1990, p. 121):

> R: What say? Me no understand.
> N: Expensive, Russian – goodbye.
> R: Nothing. Four half.
> N: Give four, nothing good.
> R: No brother. How me sell cheap? Big expensive flour on Russia this year.
> N: You no true say.
> R: Yes. Big true, me no lie, expensive flour.

Here, various conventions (the individual words) have been combined to express a wider range of speaker meanings (the intended meaning of each of the utterances). It is not as easy to infer the intended speaker meanings as it is with more developed languages, but neither is it impossible. Far from it, in fact: it is possible for the reader to follow at least the gist of the conversation, even without further details of the context.

In short, ostension and inference makes it possible to create and then combine conventions together, to express a growing range of different speaker meanings, even in the absence of grammar. There is, for instance, very little grammar in the example above: there are very few grammatical items (most of the words are content words: nouns, adjectives, a few verbs, and so on), and word order is not especially fixed. There are a number of other 'languages' that make similarly little use of grammar, and some have no grammar at all (Bickerton, 1990; Heine & Kuteva, 2007): the language of human toddlers, under two years of age (e.g. 'I no can see you'); the communication of some language-trained chimpanzees (e.g. 'Toothbrush there, me toothbrush'); the language of isolated children, such as Genie, who was deprived of any exposure to language until she was 13 (e.g. 'Applesauce buy store'); and the language of homesigners (e.g. 'Move palm eat'). These 'languages' thus give us a window on what protolanguages might have looked like: numerous content words, each with a more-or-less stable literal meaning, but no grammatical words, and few if any norms about how words are or should be combined (*ibid.*). In the jargon of linguistics, they have a lexicon, but little or no syntax (see Heine & Kuteva, 2007, p. 206 for a more detailed list of the typical qualities that these languages possess).

In sum, the emergence of protolanguage involved aspects of both analysis and synthesis. Early conventions would indeed have been holophrastic, as the analytic account argues, but rather than being dissected, they would have been combined together in production, as the synthetic account argues. In short, once we recognize the ostensive and inferential character of linguistic communication, then it becomes clear what protolanguage must have been like (heavily semantically promiscuous), and the differences between the two supposedly opposing accounts of protolanguage are "no longer so fundamental" (Smith, 2008, p. 108).

Of course, the addition of grammar would further enhance the expressive power of protolanguage. Compare, say, "man bites dog" with "dog bites man": these expressions are indistinguishable in protolanguage, but they become quite different once grammar is added to the mix. Both the synthetic and analytic approaches attempt to explain the origins of grammar, but by dissolving the difference between them, we have also dissolved the explanations of the origins of grammar these two accounts offer. Where, then, does grammar come from?

5.5 A short note on grammaticalization

One phenomenon commonly mentioned at this point is a process called *grammaticalization* (e.g. Heine & Kuteva, 2007; Tallerman, 2007; Hurford, 2011). As languages change, the grammatical role played by a particular linguistic item can change. A classic example is the English word 'back'. Originally it was only used as a noun, to refer to a body part. Over time, it began to be used as an adverb, to describe travel or movement in a particular direction (e.g. "He moved back a step"). More recently, in US English it has taken on a role as a preposition, as part of the construction 'in back of', to mean 'behind' (e.g. "She's in back of the shop"). We saw another example earlier in the chapter, namely 'going to', which was originally used only as a verb, to express motion (e.g. "We are going to Windsor to see the King"), but has since taken on an additional role as a future tense marker, even when there is no motion involved (e.g. "We are going to get married in June") (examples from Bybee, 2003).

If you take an overview of all the different ways in which linguistic elements change their role, what you find is that these changes are overwhelmingly unidirectional (Heine & Kuteva, 2002b; Hopper & Traugott, 2003). Specifically, they move away from the expression of content, and towards grammatical functionality. Although languages do sometimes change in the other direction, this is the exception. That is, it is quite common for, say, nouns to become adverbs, for adverbs to become tense markers, for verbs to become negators, and so on and so on, but the opposite is far less common (Heine & Kuteva, 2007). The process, the ongoing adoption of an increased grammatical role, is called *grammaticalization*, and it is very well-attested and well-documented across many different languages (Heine & Kuteva, 2002b; Hopper & Traugott, 2003).

Grammaticalization seems, then, to offer us an answer to the question of where grammar comes from. The early conventions must have been content words, in particular nouns and verbs: there would be no point having grammatical words if there are no content words to be grammatical about. These conventions then became grammatical, over the course of time, by the inexorable process of grammaticalization: "Once actual nouns and verbs have evolved, then words of other classes can be taken to be derived from them, just as they are in full language, by well-understood processes of grammaticalization" (Tallerman, 2007, p. 602); "Grammaticalization is the only theory in town purporting to explain how languages, in their syntax and morphology, get to be the way they are" (Hurford, 2011, p. 673). I agree with the general sentiment here, that the process of grammaticalization could have led to the emergence of grammar, and that there is no need to invoke any other process. However, I do not think this point *explains* why grammar emerges. Rather, it is a description of *how* grammar emerges. In this respect, it is not an answer to our present questions, but rather a description of the problem. We must go beyond the observation that grammaticalization can give us grammar, and ask *why* it does.

I suggest that the answer to this question lies in pragmatics. Ostensive communication is about the provision and interpretation of evidence for an intended speaker meaning (§1.4), and, put simply, it is far more likely that a content word can be used as good evidence for a grammatical function than it is that a grammatical word can be used as good evidence for content. We have already seen an example of a content word being used for a grammatical function, in §5.1: the expression 'going to' took on a role as a future tense marker precisely because it could be used as good evidence for intention and hence for future behaviour. Same for 'back', mentioned above, and it is not difficult to imagine further examples (I could, for instance, use 'sky' to refer to things above me, and if that usage caught on, it would be a case of grammaticalization). However, it is harder, I think, to imagine how grammatical words could be used as content: how could 'of' be used as a verb, or noun, for example? I'm sure there are contexts in which this could occur; my suggestion is simply that they are fewer and less likely than contexts in which content words could be used for grammatical functions. As an idea for future research, it would be interesting and worthwhile to develop some objective way to evaluate this suggestion, since if correct, it can help to explain why grammaticalization is unidirectional, and hence how a protolanguage can develop grammar.

5.6 Cultural attraction, and the naturalness of languages

For a great many years the study of languages was essentially a historical exercise, with the goal being to adduce the form of earlier languages, and in particular of languages such as (what we now call) proto-Indo-European, the common ancestor of several distinct Eurasian language families. The study of historical languages continues today, but now as just one part of the modern-day discipline, which has a far broader remit. This change in the discipline's domain of enquiry is often traced back to the work of Ferdinand de Saussure in the early part of the 20th century, and in particular to the publication of his *Cours de Linguistique Générale* (*Course in General Linguistics*) (1916). In the *Cours*, Saussure brought attention to the way in which languages are organized and structured. This organization subsequently became the central object of study for the discipline, and remains the focus of mainstream linguistics to this day. The question 'Why are languages the way they are?' is central for modern-day linguistics, just as the question 'Why are organisms the way they are?' is central for modern-day biology. Darwin's theory of natural selection answers this latter question. In this section we shall develop the outlines of an evolutionary answer to the former question.

Let's start with a simple, specific example. The region of the colour spectrum referred to by a given colour term, say 'red', does not have clear boundaries, but it does have a focal point which is seen as prototypical red. Why? When a child learns the meaning of 'red', she does not take the first instance of 'red' as prototypical, nor does she average over all instances of 'red'. Instead, her colour-perception system, and specifically the red cone cells in her eye, influences how she interprets the word. Because these dispositions are more-or-less the same across all individuals, then common meanings for basic colour terms can become stable, both within and between languages (Berlin & Kay, 1969; Kay & Regier, 2006; Regier et al., 2007). In contrast, the meanings of non-basic colour terms, for instance 'crimson' or 'indigo', are not stabilized in this way, and are hence more likely to vary between individuals, and between languages.

This process has been investigated experimentally. The colour spectrum was depicted on 330 different-coloured chips, which differed from one another in terms of both hue and lightness. Participants were first asked to learn how an invented language labelled a subset of these 330 different colours. The number of colour words in the invented language varied between two and six words, depending on condition. The participants were then asked to label all 330 colours. Next comes the crucial step: the labels they produced in this second stage were used as the labels that the next participant had to learn. In this way, the artificial language is passed from participant to participant, similar to how it is passed between individuals in the children's game Chinese Whispers (called 'Broken Telephone' in the US), in which one person whispers something to another, who then whispers it to a third person, and so on. What happens is that, like the whispers in Chinese Whispers, in each 'generation' the language is liable to be changed slightly. However, these changes are not random. On the contrary, they operate in a particular direction: the language comes to label the different areas of the colour space in a way that closely matches not the native language of the experimental participants (English), but instead our basic, shared perceptual categories (Xu et al., 2013). (Like all languages, English has idiosyncrasies that make it slightly different to these basic categories.) In sum, each individual reinterprets the language they learn, and this reinterpretation often acts not randomly, but systematically in a particular direction, determined by the material facts about how human colour perception works. The result is that over time the language gravitates towards particular forms.

This process is called *cultural attraction*, and it applies to all cultural traits, not just languages (Sperber, 1996; Claidière et al., 2014). The main idea is that the mechanisms of imitation and ostensive communication, and the other cognitive mechanisms involved in the acquisition of cultural traits, themselves change those cultural traits in non-random ways. (These changes need not and indeed typically are not deliberate or even conscious.) The result is that the traits tend to be drawn towards particular forms, and away from others. In the example above, the language is drawn towards forms that match the perceptual categories of the human visual system. These forms to which cultural traits are drawn are called *attractors*, and attractors themselves arise due to *factors of attraction*. Cultural attraction has the potential to explain a great deal about why languages are the way they are (Evans & Levinson, 2009). We have already seen one example of this, namely the evolution of primary colour terms. Here is another.

Some languages are *tonal*. This means that pitch conveys an aspect of meaning. English, like most European languages, is not tonal: whether I say "cat" with high or low pitch makes no difference to meaning. However, tonal languages are common in several other regions of the world, especially Asia. Indeed, the language with most native speakers in the world, Mandarin Chinese, is tonal: words said with different pitches often have different meanings. A few years ago, a remarkable discovery was made: the distribution of tonal languages in the world is closely correlated with the distribution of two genes associated with brain growth and development, named *ASPM* and *Microcephalin* (Dediu & Ladd, 2007). Crucially, this correlation is not spurious. Detailed, in-depth statistical analysis of a large dataset showed this relationship between genes and languages cannot be explained by a common history or geography, or any other non-causal factors (*ibid.*). Instead, the data suggest that the relationship is causal. Variations in the methods and datasets used do not change this result (Dediu, 2011).

Why? One explanation might be that tonal languages can only be acquired if you have these genes. But this cannot be correct, since there are many individuals who do not have these genes but who still acquire the languages without any problems. All infants born into societies with tonal languages acquire those languages, whether or not they have these genes. Instead, the likely explanation is in terms of cultural attraction: through their effect on brain development, the genes create particular cognitive biases in a significant proportion of the population, which in turn influence the direction of change as the language propagates through a community and between generations. Specifically, the genes lead to a small preference in individuals for tonal rather than non-tonal languages – and even if this preference is tiny, it can cause the language to become tonal, if a sufficient number of the speakers share the preference (Dediu, 2008). This is the same process of cultural attraction that we saw with primary colour terms: as the language is passed from individual to individual, it is reinterpreted at each stage. The collective effect of these reinterpretations will be to draw the language in the direction of the cognitive bias for tonal languages.

Cultural attraction has obvious analogies with the process of natural selection that shapes the biological evolution of organisms, but there are some deep and important disanalogies too (Claidière & André, 2012; Claidière et al., 2014). The most fundamental of these is that whereas biological evolution is replicative, cultural evolution is re-productive. What this means is that cultural items are not simply copied, or replicated, as biological DNA is; instead, they are re-produced, or re-constructed, anew in each case. For instance, a student taking notes in a lecture does not simply copy any spelling from a lecturer's presentation (i.e. she does not simply *reproduce* the spelling), but will in fact correct the error, and in doing so *re-produce* the correct spelling. Put another way, the function of the mechanisms of cultural transmission is not simply to replicate, as in the biological case, but rather to re-produce inputs and if necessary adjust them so that they best serve the individual's needs (Claidière et al., 2014). This aspect of how cultural traits spread between individuals has profound implications for understanding how cultural evolution works, and hence why cultures and cultural traits, of which languages are an example *par excellence*, take the form that they do (Sperber, 1996; Claidière et al., 2014).

Nevertheless, at one level factors of attraction do for culture what environments do for biology: given enough time, they modify cultural/biological traits into those forms that best fit those factors of attraction/biological environments. If the factors were different, the languages would be different. If, for example, *ASPM* and *Microcephalin* had a different effect on the human brain, then languages would be different. Most obviously, there might not be tonal languages. In this way, factors of attraction can explain why languages and other cultural traits take the form that they do (*ibid.*). In this sense, there is a naturalness to languages that we also see in other social institutions, for instance marriage systems, legal norms, and kinship systems, among others: in each case, cultural attraction has modified them and hence caused them to take forms that fit the natural intuitions and dispositions of the human mind, and the goals of human behaviour (Boyer, 1998; Boyer & Petersen, 2012).

Note also that cultural attraction is not unique to humans. Just as humans acquire their languages from previous generations, young songbirds acquire their songs from adults. If, for instance, a juvenile zebra finch is unexposed to singing males during its development, it will not develop the prototypical zebra finch song. However, if this isolated individual's non-standard song is then used as the first generation in a series of songs, where each new generation only hears the song of the birds in the previous generation, then eventually the song will converge back to the prototypical version (Fehér et al., 2009). This too is cultural attraction.

Clearly, numerous attractors are important for the cultural evolution of languages. I identified two above, for the purposes of exposition (colour terms and tonal languages), but there will be many more. Here is another example. Young children have a tendency to segment and linearize information. This is shown clearly in an experiment in which participants watched a video in which a shape moved across a screen, and were then asked to indicate with their hands what had happened. Young children indicated the manner (e.g. bouncing, sliding, rotating) and path (e.g. up, down) of the movement separately (i.e. with two distinct gestures), whereas older children and adults tended to indicate both aspects of the movement in one gesture (Clay et al., in press). Since languages are passed on through young children, then this tendency causes languages to gravitate towards segmentation (Senghas et al., 2004). This tendency is, then, another factor of attraction that affects the evolution of languages, and it makes segmented languages (i.e. languages with distinct words for, say, manner and path) attractors.

More generally, most of the traits that numerous authors have identified as pre-adaptations for language are likely to have affected language in this way, as factors of attraction that will influence the cultural evolution of linguistic form (see e.g. Hauser et al., 2002; Christiansen & Kirby, 2003; Hurford, 2003 for lists of such pre-adaptations). For instance, the fact that humans are able to learn hierarchical structures from serially presented information is an important factor of attraction in explaining why languages tend be organized the way they are. Identification of the various factors of attraction that affect the cultural evolution of languages should be the central question for language evolution in the coming years.

I have so far only discussed factors of attraction that are aspects of human biology (including cognition). However, there is also another sort of attractor altogether, namely those associated with the observable *use* of cultural traits (Claidière et al., 2014). In the case of language, that means communication. The next section discusses how the use of languages in ostensive communication influences how those same languages evolve.

5.7 The role of communication in language evolution

In the examples of cultural attraction given in the previous section (primary colour terms; tone; functional segmentation), the source of the attractor is a feature of human biology: the physiology of the eye in one case; genes in another; infant cognition in the third. Attractors can, however, arise from other sources too. One particularly important source is a functional one: *usage*. Languages are attracted to forms where they actually serve a useful function for language users; in other words, to forms where they can usefully enhance ostensive communication. This is true in both a trivial way, and in a more insightful way. The trivial point is simply that if the languages were not useful, they would not be used, and hence there would be nothing to pass on to the next generation. The more insightful point, which I shall develop in this section, is that the need to be useful is itself a factor of attraction that, in conjunction with other factors of attraction, can and does influence the direction of the cultural evolution of languages and other communicative conventions.

Let me begin with another Chinese Whispers style experiment, this time concerned with the emergence of linguistic structure (Kirby et al., 2008). Participants were asked to learn an 'alien' language, which consisted of a set of 27 different meaning–word mappings. Each 'meaning' comprised one of three different shapes (square, triangle, circle), which could each be in one of three different colours (red, blue, black), and which were associated with one of three different types of movement (straight, rotation, bounce). The words associated with these meanings were randomly created, and without meaning in English (e.g. 'pukema', 'topi', 'kegemaku', etc.). So for the first participant, the language was essentially a set of 27 distinct associations, between meanings and previously unknown words, that had to be learnt (e.g. a red bouncing square labelled 'topi'). Having been shown this language, the participant was then tested on it: shown all the shapes again, and asked to type in the corresponding word. Next comes the Chinese Whispers step: the language the participant produced in this second stage was used as the training data that the next participant had to learn, and this process was repeated for 10 generations. When the experiment proceeded in this way, the languages degenerated: within a few generations, many meanings had the same word associated with them (for example, all the squares might be called, say, 'bukame', regardless of their colour or type of movement). Sometimes participants in the later generations of these experiments even sought to rationalize this feature of the language, for instance saying in debrief interviews after the experiment that they assumed that the aliens were colour-blind.

What does this result tell us? We have already seen from previous examples that languages will, as they pass from individual to individual, gravitate towards cultural attractors, just as other cultural traits do. In this case, important factors of attraction are the limits of human learning and memory: languages that pose challenges for learning and memory are likely to be adjusted in the direction of increasing simplicity. As such, we should expect the language to gravitate towards forms that are easier and easier to learn and recall – and this is precisely what it does.

In another condition, the language was filtered after each generation: all cases of homonymy were removed from the training data. (Homonymy is where two or more different meanings have the same word associated with them, such as 'bank', which refers to both the side of a river, and to financial institutions.) So, if a participant in the test phase entered the same word for both, say, {red-square-rotation} and {blue-square-rotation}, then one of these, chosen at random, was simply removed from the training data for the next generation. What happened in this case is that, as the generations passed, the language became increasingly structured: the language began to develop distinct syllables for each shape, colour, and movement. For instance, there was a distinct morpheme for all black shapes ('ne'), another for blue shapes ('la'), and a third for red shapes ('re'); similarly, there were morphemes for each shape (e.g. squares were 'ho') and for each movement (e.g. 'pilu' for bounce). (A morpheme is a meaning carrying unit that cannot be subdivided into smaller meaning carrying units e.g. in this language 'pilu' is a morpheme, meaning 'bounce', but 'pi' and 'lu' are not morphemes, because they do not mean anything independently of one another.) These morphemes then combine in different ways, to refer to the various different meanings (e.g. 'lahopilu' was {blue-square-bounce}). In other words: linguistic organization began to emerge (Kirby et al., 2008).

What role is this homonymy filter playing? Its immediate effect is to ensure that there are unique words for each individual meaning. This fact adds a second attractor to the mix: the first attractor, to do with ease of learning, is now supplemented by a second one, to do with homonymy. These two attractors both exert an influence on the language. The result is then as we might expect: the language gravitates towards the form that is easiest to remember, given this additional demand of unique words for each meaning. Specifically, the languages gravitate towards forms that minimize the number of distinct elements that must be remembered: just 9, if the language is fully structured (one for each shape, colour, and type of movement), as opposed to 27 if there is no structure (one for each distinct object). In sum, just as colour terms are attracted to forms that fit the basic perceptual categories of the human visual system, and just as some languages are attracted to tonality because it fits the cognitive biases of (most of) the relevant population, word structure is attracted to a form that keeps the demands on learning to a minimum, while at the same time ensuring that there is a unique word for each meaning.

What does this result tell us about real-world languages? After all, there is no homonymy filter in the real world. This is where (ostensive) communication becomes important. The real world does not have a homonymy filter, but it does involve the use of languages for communication – and languages with lots of homonymy are no good for this. To take the extreme case, a language that has the same word for multiple different meanings is no good for communication at all. It must be possible for the language to express the meanings that its users want it to. Experimental studies show that in the process of learning a new language, learners will often change the language in order to make it more communicatively efficient (Fedzechkina et al., 2012). The homonymy filter is, then, a proxy for this: a functional factor of attraction that pulls languages in the direction of expressive utility.

The language is thus manipulated by two different factors of attraction, learnability and expressive utility, with the end result that a type of linguistic structure emerges (Smith et al., 2013). If only one or the other of these attractors is absent, the system converges to other, predictable forms: if there is no need for the language to be expressive, it degenerates (see above); and if there is no need for it to be learnt by each new generation, it becomes less learnable (Fay & Ellison, 2013). Experiments that directly test this analysis, in which the homonymy filter is replaced by an actual communication task, so that both attractors are present, are ongoing. Early results are consistent with the above conclusion: when languages must be both used for communication and learnt anew by each generation, they are attracted towards forms that are both learnable and expressive at the same time (Tamariz et al., 2012).

How far does the influence of the expressivity attractor extend? One possible answer to this question is that the influence of communicative expressivity cannot be too great, since languages contain some properties, most obviously ambiguity, that make them ill-suited for communication: "The natural approach has always been: Is [language] well designed for use, understood typically as use for communication? ... If you want to make sure that we never misunderstand one another, for that purpose language is not well designed, because you have such properties as ambiguity" (Chomsky, 2002, p. 107). In the remainder of this section, I shall explain why this intuitive thought is incorrect (Piantadosi et al., 2012).

The context in which an utterance is produced tells us something about its likely meaning. I began Chapter 1 with the example of "Wait until these people have all gone and I'll dig her out and have a good old fiddle". This could mean one thing when uttered by a keen but shy violinist at a party, but quite another when uttered by a guest at a funeral. The fact that context is informative about the likely speaker meaning means that although there is ambiguity in this and indeed all utterances (see §1.6), this poses no substantive or general problems for communication, if the context is informative about the speaker's likely intended meaning.

The fact has two important consequences for linguistic communication. The first is that speakers who wish to be efficient in what they do *should* be ambiguous, to the extent that this ambiguity can be resolved by the context. Why say something that is already apparent from the context? We have in fact already met a version of this prediction previously. It follows directly from the Communicative Principle of Relevance, which says that ostensive signals should tend to be maximally relevant for their intended audience (see §3.3). To do this, the signal should keep the processing effort required of the listener to a minimum (recall that relevance is the trade-off between processing effort, and worthwhile cognitive effects). This means that when given the choice between two utterances, one of which would, if not for context, have the greater ambiguity but require less processing effort, and the other of which would have less ambiguity but require more processing effort, it is the former that will be produced. I discussed some experimental tests of this prediction in §3.3, the results of which support this analysis.

The second important consequence of ambiguity is directly relevant to our concerns in this section, about the role that communication plays in the cultural evolution of languages. The insight is this: that languages will be attracted to forms that are easiest to use, *even if those forms are ambiguous*, because context can resolve those ambiguities at no cost to ease-of-use. One obvious example is pronouns (e.g. I, we, you, it, they, etc.), which are necessarily indeterminate (who is 'he'?), but also short and concise, and hence easy to use. Other examples are word length (speech is slow and cumbersome in comparison to inference, and so shorter words are easier to use) and word frequency (more common words are easier to use, because they place fewer demands on memory retrieval). The specific prediction that follows from these insights is that those words and other linguistic units that are easiest to use should be re-used wherever possible, and should hence be *more* ambiguous (i.e. have more possible literal meanings) than those that are harder to use. This prediction has been tested in English, German, and French, and in all three cases those words that are most easy to use are also those that have the highest number of different possible meanings (Piantadosi et al., 2012).

This result is good evidence for the following conclusion: that Chomsky's intuitive analysis is exactly backwards. Ambiguity is precisely what we *should* expect to see in an efficient system of ostensive communication (*ibid.*). This is because languages are attracted to those forms that are most easy to use in ostensive communication, even at the cost of ambiguity, so long as that ambiguity can be resolved by context. Viewed this way, ambiguity is arguably the wrong term to begin with, because when used in context, utterances are generally *not* ambiguous. This is in essence the key point here: "Why do people tolerate... ambiguity? The answer is that they do not. There is nothing ambiguous about 'take' as it is used in everyday speech. The ambiguity appears only when we, quite arbitrarily, call isolated words the unit of meaning" (Miller, 1951, pp. 111–112). As I have emphasized, meaning in ostensive communication comes not from a literal interpretation of the conventional code, but instead from speakers' use of that code in ostensive-inferential communication. When we bear this in mind, the supposed problem of ambiguity does not even arise.

The suggestion that emerges from this and the preceding section is that all linguistic form may be the consequence of cultural attraction of one sort or another (Kirby et al., 2007; Evans & Levinson, 2009). It is not hard to develop hypotheses about aspects of human biology, cognition or behaviour that may be factors of attraction that cause languages to evolve in ways they do. We have seen numerous examples of this already in this chapter (the colour-perception system; the genes *ASPM* and *Microcephalin*; children's tendency to segment information; the ability to infer hierarchical structure from serial information; the need for languages to be useful in communication). There will be many more. Individual hypotheses should then be tested, and the claims refined, if necessary. The end goal should be to understand the full gamut of factors of attraction that influence the evolution of languages. This project has the potential to answer the question I raised at the beginning of this section – why are languages the way they are? – and I am sure that it will be the subject of a great deal of attention in the coming years. Indeed, a wide and diverse set of existing results and analyses can be interpreted as contributions to it, even if they are not presented in such terms (e.g. Jackendoff, 2002; Fitch & Hauser, 2004; Seyfarth et al., 2005; Wray & Grace, 2007; Lupyan & Dale, 2010; Smith & Wonnacott, 2010; Piantadosi et al., 2011; Culbertson, 2012; Nettle, 2012; Verhoef et al., 2014; and many others).

However, further development of this project is not my objective here. Indeed, it is a research agenda worthy of a book-length treatment of its own. Rather, I have articulated it to make two more modest points. The first is to sketch how the account of the origins of language that I have developed in this book could have subsequently led to the emergence of languages as we know them. Communicative conventions were first created in the service of making ostensive-inferential communication more expressively powerful than it otherwise would have been (§5.2–§5.5), and the process of cultural attraction would then have moulded them into forms that we now call languages. The second, related point is to highlight the importance of ostensive communication in this process, which both prevents the degeneration of languages into uselessness, and actually influences the forms that languages will be attracted towards. Just as with the creation of the first symbols (§5.3), and the emergence of protolanguage and grammar (§5.4 and §5.5), ostension and inference play a critical role in the origins of linguistic form.

The thesis that linguistic form is the result of a process of cultural attraction has been used to argue against other theories of why languages take the forms that they do (see e.g. Kirby et al., 2007; Christiansen & Chater, 2008; Evans & Levinson, 2009). The main target of these arguments is Noam Chomsky's thesis that languages take the form that they do because of a *Universal Grammar* – an innate cognitive mechanism that specifies the underlying grammatical structure of languages (Chomsky, 1988). The next chapter, in which I take an adaptationist perspective on communication and language, will begin with discussion of whether and how Universal Grammar fits into this book's larger thesis.

* * *

Chapter 5. *Language evolution is the process by which the conventions that make ostensive communication expressively powerful emerge. These early conventions were holophrastic, and they would have been expressed in whatever modality, vocal or gestural, was most appropriate for the* *intended speaker meaning. Protolanguage would have developed through the combination of these conventions, and over time some of them would have taken on a grammatical function. The subsequent development of languages was driven by a process of cultural attraction, in which languages were progressively modified to fit the human mind and human behaviour. Ostensive communication is a critical factor of attraction in this process.*

Chapter 6. *What can an adaptationist perspective tell us about language, and about human communication? What are the evolutionary functions of language and linguistic communication? What are the ultimate and proximate explanations of the evolutionary stability of human communication? Was the origin of language a major transition in the evolution of life?*

Chapter 6

Evolutionary Adaptation

6.1 Adaptationism

Charles Darwin's theory of natural selection is lauded as one of the landmark achievements in all of science. The reason for this high regard is that it gives us a naturalistic explanation of the most general and basic observation we can make about the natural world: that organisms appear to be well-adapted to the environments in which they live; and, furthermore, the different parts of organisms appear to work together, towards a common goal, as if they have been designed for a common purpose. For the biological sciences, this empirical pattern of adaptation is of "pervasive importance" (Williams, 1966, p. 5). Darwin's explanation was that heritable characteristics associated with greater reproductive success will tend to accumulate in a population, those associated with lesser reproductive success will not, and given sufficient time, these differences will lead to adaptation (1859). This does not mean that everything in nature is perfectly adapted. The form that organisms take is always subject to constraints of history, genetic architecture, trade-offs, and other contingencies. Nonetheless, the theory of natural selection answers the question of adaptation, and this answer is supported by an overwhelming amount of empirical evidence. There is no alternative naturalistic explanation of non-random design in nature. (Some language evolution researchers have argued otherwise. Specifically, they have argued that the processes of cultural attraction described in the previous section provide an alternative to natural selection as a source of design in nature. I will discuss and reject this argument at the end of the next section.)

An important set of conceptual and methodological tools follow Darwin's insight. They collectively go by the name *adaptationism*. *Evolutionary psychology* is adaptationism applied to the human mind (Pinker, 1997; Cosmides & Tooby, 2013). Both these terms, 'adaptationism' and 'evolutionary psychology', are much abused and misunderstood. This chapter is about using adaptationism to study human language and communication, and so given the confusion around the term, I want to begin by clarifying, as concisely as possible, exactly what adaptationism is, and why it is essential for evolutionary study.

I'd like to start with a quotation from a professor of the psychology of perception: "all vision scientists are basically evolutionary psychologists both in theory and practice" (Scholl, 2010). This is because vision scientists all, as a matter of routine, make an assumption about the adaptive function of visual perception, and use it to derive their hypotheses about how perception actually works. Specifically, they all assume that the function of visual perception is, of course, to see; or, more precisely, to "recover the structure of the local environment (so as to better interact with it)" (*ibid.*). This assumption guides their subsequent research, both theoretical and empirical. This is ordinary adaptationism: hypothesize or assume an adaptive function, and then use that to derive testable hypotheses about how a trait actually works. If vision scientists are not thought of as adaptationists, that is only because the adaptive function of visual perception is so obvious that it does not normally need stating. But it is adaptationism all the same.

Of course, while the adaptive function of visual perception is clear, the same is not true of many other traits, where the function is often opaque. In some cases, there is no dedicated function at all. This is where adaptationism can be a very powerful theoretical tool. Once we entertain a particular hypothesis about function, then the question becomes: *if* you were going to design a trait with that function, how would you do it, and how would it differ from a trait designed to perform other candidate functions, or no function at all? Answers to these questions can give you testable predictions about how the proximate mechanisms involved actually work (I introduced the distinction between proximate mechanisms and ultimate functions in §1.5; see Scott-Phillips et al., 2011). The data can then be used to choose between different hypotheses about function (including the hypothesis that there is no function). In this way, adaptationism is reverse-engineering (Dennett, 1995).

Again, we can use vision as an example. In motion-induced blindness (MIB), fully visible objects that are superimposed over background movement patterns become 'unseen' to the conscious mind: we do not 'see' them, even though they are there (see http://www.yale.edu/perception/MIB/ for examples). Above I endorsed the statement that the function of visual perception is to recover the structure of the local environment. What wasn't stated was which aspects of the local environment this is true of. One hypothesis would be that the function is to recover *all* aspects of the local environment, since that gives the brain all the possible information it might need. This hypothesis cannot explain MIB, except as a flaw: MIB describes a context in which the visual system simply fails to perform its purported function. Perhaps, however, this is not a flaw. There is a plausible alternative hypothesis, on which MIB is actually an adaptation (New & Scholl, 2008). Sometimes the eye is damaged, leading to a permanent, blank spot in the visual field, called a scotoma. The best that the visual system of an individual with scotomas can do is to fill the gaps in as best it can, given what is known about surrounding objects. This would result in MIB. This is a testable hypothesis: if it is correct, then MIB should occur under certain specific circumstances, and not others. The vision scientist I quote above,

Brian Scholl, and a then postdoctoral fellow in his lab, Joshua New, tested these predictions, and their results are consistent with their adaptationist hypothesis, and inconsistent with the MIB-as-flaw hypothesis (*ibid.*). As such, their data suggest that the human visual system appears to be *designed* to ignore small objects that are invariant against changes in the visual field, since doing so actually enhances the visual system. This is a clear example of adaptationism: a hypothesis about the function of a particular trait was used to generate testable predictions about mechanisms, and the results of the subsequent experiments were used to assess the claim about function.

Not all cases are as clean as this, not by a long shot. It is easy for the owner of the adaptationist hammer to see nails everywhere, including where there are none. We should of course be alert to this possibility. Nevertheless, adaptationism is "about as basic to biology as the atomic theory is to chemistry. And about as controversial" (Daly, 1991, p. 219). For the evolutionist, it is "not optional" (Dennett, 1995, p. 238). It has provided the foundation for countless major breakthroughs in all branches of the natural sciences. It is particularly central to disciplines such as social evolution and, especially, behavioural ecology (Davies et al., 2012). The central tenet of evolutionary psychology is that we should also use adaptationism to study the human mind (Tooby & Cosmides, 1992).

A naïve observer would be forgiven for assuming that the field of language evolution would, in terms of its scope and methodologies, look much like the field of evolutionary psychology, but with a particular emphasis on language. However, this hypothetical naïve observer would be wrong. In its short history, language evolution has, as a discipline, shown a great deal more interest in diachronic questions of evolutionary history than it has in synchronic analyses of what an adaptationist perspective can tell us about the cognitive mechanisms involved in language and communication (Scott-Phillips, 2010c). While I certainly do not wish to discourage research on evolutionary history, I do think this imbalance of attention is regrettable. This chapter surveys the adaptationist terrain.

6.2 Language and adaptation

I begin with the capacity for language itself. In Chapter 1 I briefly mentioned one of the classic papers in the study of language evolution, Steven Pinker and Paul Bloom's 'Natural language and natural selection' (1990). A great deal of ink has been spilt discussing this paper and its arguments: it is a common topic for student essays, and it has been the topic of much subsequent analysis (e.g. Botha, 2003). It is also frequently cited as one of the major triggers for the current enthusiasm for research into language origins and evolution.

Pinker and Bloom were rightly exercised by the fact that much of mainstream linguistics had at the time an antipathy towards evolutionary thinking of any sort. The most well-known and influential illustration of this is Noam Chomsky's many assertions that natural selection has nothing to say about language and linguistics, or indeed about the human mind in general. Here are two examples: "The processes by which the human mind achieved its present stage of complexity and its particular form of innate organization are a total mystery... it is perfectly safe to attribute this development to 'natural selection', so long as we realize that there is no substance to this assertion, that it amounts to nothing more than a belief that there is some naturalistic explanation for these phenomena" (1972, p. 97); "What kind of biological evolution [is language the result of]?... We can make up lots of stories. It is quite easy: for example, take language as it is, break it up into fifty different things (syllable, word, putting things together, phrases and so on) and say: 'OK, I have the story: there was a mutation that gave syllables, there was another mutation that gave words, another one that gave phrases... another that (miraculously) yields the recursive property (actually, all the mutations are left as miracles).' OK, maybe, or maybe something totally different... the story you choose is independent of the facts, pretty much" (2002, p. 146). There are many more statements in a similar vein (Pinker and Bloom's paper contains several examples).

It was in response to such views that Pinker and Bloom were motivated to apply adaptationism to language. They argued that language shows evidence of design for communication ("grammar is a complex mechanism tailored to the transmission of propositional structures through a serial interface" (1990, p. 707)) and hence, following the logic of adaptationism, that language is a biological adaptation. Their logic is undeniable. The question is whether one accepts the premises of their argument, which are two.

Their first premise is the adaptationist point that if we find evidence of design in nature, the only naturalistic explanation we have of that design is natural selection (see §6.1). The second premise is the assumption that humans actually have 'language', in the way that Pinker and Bloom are using the term. This is important. Pinker and Bloom adopt an explicitly Chomskyan perspective on language and linguistics, in which language is *defined* as an innate cognitive mechanism that allows for the acquisition and processing of languages, and which explains why, underneath their many differences, there are also many similarities in the way that languages are organized. (Here 'innate' means that it develops gradually and inexorably in the early years of life, much like, say, wings do in chickens.) This mechanism is sometimes called a Universal Grammar (UG). The substance of Pinker and Bloom's article was the combination of these two premises: an attempt to conjoin Darwinian biology and Chomskyan linguistics ("Since we are impressed both by the synthetic theory of evolution and by the theory of generative grammar, we hope that we will not have to choose between the two" (1990, p. 708)).

However, the existence of UG is disputed. Chomsky's central argument is that children are able to acquire languages only because they are innately primed to do so. If they were not primed in this way, they would not be able to acquire their native language, because the natural language they are exposed to does not contain sufficient data for them to actually acquire them completely (Chomsky, 1980; Laurence & Margolis, 2001; Berwick et al., 2011b). Others have argued, against this view, that language acquisition is possible in a purely data-driven way i.e. that in order to learn their native tongues, children need no more linguistic input than that which they naturally encounter (e.g. Tomasello, 2003; Goldberg, 2006).

These debates are not about whether humans are, in some way or another, biologically pre-disposed to acquire languages; they clearly are. The issue is rather what that pre-disposition consists of, and in particular whether it includes anything that is specific to grammar and syntax: "Our biological endowment is what separates us from the Amazon horned frog and is what ultimately ensures that humans have language while frogs do not. This is not the issue; the question is whether what separates us includes unlearned linguistic ... representations concerning syntax" (Goldberg, 2008, p. 523); "Certainly, humans are endowed with some sort of predisposition toward language learning. The substantive issue is whether a full description of that predisposition incorporates anything that entails specific contingent facts about natural languages" (Pullum & Scholz, 2002, p. 10). I will not here enter into the details of these debates. The proposed UG may exist, or it may not, and if it does, it may take one of several different possible forms.

The point I do want to make is that Pinker and Bloom's claim, that a Chomskyan UG is an adaptation, makes sense *only if you accept their premise that such a UG exists in the first place*. As such, the position one takes in the above summarized debates, about whether UG is necessary to explain language acquisition, should determine whether one thinks it is coherent to talk about a Chomskyan language faculty as an evolutionary adaptation: if you accept Pinker and Bloom's premise that there is a UG, which appears to be designed to aid language acquisition and processing, then their logic that it is an adaptation is unarguable – since the only naturalistic explanation of apparent design is natural selection. If, on the other hand, you disagree with them about UG, then their claim should be nonsensical to you.

For those that do argue for the existence of a UG of some sort, other important questions are what form it takes, and when and why it would have evolved. I made an important point about this in passing in §2.7, and repeat it here: if there are mechanisms specifically designed to aid in the acquisition and use of languages, then the natural selection of those mechanisms must have occurred *after* the emergence of the first (proto-)languages i.e. after the processes described in the previous chapters had occurred. The right selective environment for the natural selection of any UG is a world in which communicative conventions have already made ostensive communication more precise and hence powerful than it otherwise would be, but where the acquisition of those conventions does not run as smoothly as it might do. If such an environment existed, then mechanisms to aid language acquisition may have evolved. If so, it is these mechanisms that, if anything, should be called 'UG': "The important questions ... are twofold: (1) Do mechanisms exist that evolved because of their beneficial fitness effects on language acquisition? and (2) what are the computational properties of these mechanisms?" (Barrett et al., 2008, p. 511). From an evolutionary perspective, this is the only notion of UG that makes any sense: numerous aspects of human psychology are involved in language acquisition but did not evolve for that purpose (memory, sound perception, inference, etc.), and we do not label these UG. Any other conception of UG is "an odd way to carve up evolved structures" (*ibid.*).

It is sometimes argued that the process of cultural attraction described in the previous chapter, or something much like it, challenges *both* premises of Pinker and Bloom's argument. For instance: "Cultural transmission ... provides an alternative to traditional nativist [UG] *and* adaptationist explanations for the properties of human languages" (Kirby et al., 2007, p. 5241, italics added; see also e.g. Kirby, 2000). The first part of this claim is true, but the second part is not, as I shall now explain.

Cultural attraction provides an alternative explanation to the nativist UG claim because it describes a way in which languages can be very similar to one another in the absence of a UG (Christiansen & Chater, 2008; Evans & Levinson, 2009). Specifically, if the attractors that act upon languages are similar in each case (and they are), then the process of cultural attraction will cause the different languages to become organized in similar ways. This can in turn lead to strong statistical tendencies ('universals') in the forms that different languages take, without a UG.

At the same time, cultural attraction does *not* provide an alternative to adaptationist explanations of design in nature, because this supposed contrast, between cultural evolution and natural selection, is in fact a false dichotomy. It conflates two separate levels of analysis. Specifically, it conflates ultimate and proximate explanations (Scott-Phillips et al., 2011). (I introduced the ultimate/proximate distinction in §1.5.) This difference between ultimate and proximate explanations can be seen even in the research of those who make the claim that cultural evolution provides an alternative to adaptationist approaches. In one computational simulation, languages evolve culturally within a population of two different types of simulated agents: those that have a (very) small bias to acquire structured languages, and those that do not. Furthermore, there is natural selection of agents that use structured languages (regardless of whether or not the agents have a bias for such languages). What happens is that the languages in the population become structured, and agents without any bias to prefer such languages become extinct (Smith & Kirby, 2008). What explains this result? In one sense, the answer is natural selection: those agents with the 'biology' that results in unstructured languages are selected against. In another sense, the answer is cultural evolution, for it is that process that transforms the agents' small bias for structure into a pervasive feature of the language. In fact, both these answers are correct, because these are two quite different levels of analysis: the first is an ultimate explanation, concerned with why a particular trait (the bias) exists in a population; the second is a proximate explanation, concerned with the workings of the trait in question, in other words, with the mechanics of how that bias contributes to the generation of structured languages.

We can tell that these are different levels of analysis because if the particulars of one of these two explanations change, that does not have any necessary consequences for the particulars of the other. If, on the one hand, we change which set of agents achieve the greater fitness, from those using structured languages to those using unstructured ones, that has no implications for the fact that it is cultural attraction that explains why some languages are structured and others are not. If, on the other hand, it is not cultural attraction but, say, UG that explains how languages become structured, that would have no implications for the fact that natural selection explains why some types of agent become common in the population, while others are selected against. These facts show that questions about the role of natural selection and the role of cultural attraction in language evolution are orthogonal to one another, and can vary independently.

When Gregor Mendel's work on heritability and genetics first became widely known, it was thought to challenge rather than complement Darwin's theory of evolution by natural selection. This was because, whereas Darwin's theory emphasized continuity, Mendelian genetics is discrete (Provine, 2001). This apparent tension was resolved once it was recognized that these two accounts of evolution describe two distinct levels of analysis: while Darwin's theory was about the logic of natural selection (the ultimate level), Mendel's work was about its mechanics (the proximate level). This insight, and the subsequent demonstration that discrete replicators can produce gradual natural selection, resolved the apparent tension between Darwinian natural selection and Mendelian genetics, and led directly to the development of what is now called the modern neo-Darwinian synthesis (Fisher, 1930; Wright, 1931; Haldane, 1932). Indeed, this theory is called a synthesis precisely because it synthesized these two different levels of analysis. We should not repeat this mistake with cultural evolution.

I have digressed, but with good reason. In this section, I have argued that, if there is a UG worthy of the name, then Pinker and Bloom were right to follow adaptationist logic and conclude that it is a biological adaptation. They felt the need to make this argument because several linguists and cognitive scientists of that time, most prominently Noam Chomsky, argued otherwise, and suggested that some factor other than natural selection could explain the appearance of design in nature. Pinker and Bloom addressed those supposed alternatives in their article. However, dissent from adaptationist orthodoxy has not passed: some linguists and cognitive scientists of the present era also reject it, and suggest that the process of cultural attraction provides an alternative to natural selection. My digression was necessary to address those arguments.

6.3 Linguistic communication as social navigation

As a highly interdisciplinary topic, language evolution attracts researchers from a diverse set of backgrounds, and these backgrounds frame not only the sort of tools that different researchers use, and the conclusions they draw, but also the very questions they ask in the first place. What is important or interesting to the evolutionary biologist is not always so to the linguist, and vice versa. Questions about evolutionary function and possible adaptation are a good illustration of this. Those linguists and cognitive scientists that have considered such questions have tended to ask them about the internal, cognitive mechanisms discussed in the previous section. In contrast, those evolutionary biologists and evolutionary psychologists that have considered the same questions have tended to ask them about the more public face of language, namely its use in communication. This section is concerned with this latter set of questions. Is linguistic communication an adaptation, and if so, what is its evolutionary function?

These are not (yet) well-formed questions. In Chapter 2 I emphasized how communication is not a single behaviour or trait, but rather the product of two distinct behaviours. As such, it makes little sense to ask whether ostensive communication (linguistic or otherwise) is an adaptation. We must instead ask this question once about signal production, and once again about signal comprehension. In other words, about ostension, and about inference.

The difficulty is that, because these two distinct behaviours are interdependent, it is not immediately clear what adaptive behaviour should even look like, for either signallers or receivers. For many biological traits, such as vision, what is good design is often more-or-less clear. But that is not the case here, where the interactivity of communication complicates matters. The listener's goal is to come to believe or know or understand something worthwhile that they did not believe or know or understand beforehand (in the jargon of Relevance Theory, their goal is to achieve positive cognitive effects (see §3.3)). The speaker also wants the listener to come to believe or know or understand something that they previously did not. The rub is that these may not be the same things that the listener cares about. We must therefore do some preliminary work to understand how these different interests of speaker and listener interact with one another, in order to establish what would constitute good design in the first place.

For listeners, the matter is straightforward: they must avoid attending to irrelevant stimuli. If they do not, they would expend a great deal of cognitive effort on processing stimuli of no use to themselves. They must find some way to filter for relevance the stimuli they are exposed to. If I say to you "this is a spoon", one thing that follows is that the object I am holding is conventionally referred to as a spoon. But other things logically follow too, for example that it is not a knife. Or a fork. Or a house, a potato, a field, an idea, a computer, a lobster ... and so on. What I am trying to illustrate with this random list is that the potential new beliefs and knowledge that follow from even this most simple of stimuli are literally infinite (in artificial intelligence this is called the *frame problem*). Even for such superficially simple utterances as this, listeners must have some way to limit exactly what conclusions they do draw to only those that are actually worthwhile deriving.

Speakers too must limit their efforts. There is no point telling your audience everything you have ever known or thought. If listeners filter for relevance, as they should (see above), then telling them everything regardless of relevance is a waste, since it will not have any effect. Better to save your energy. And this is not to mention the fact that persistent irrelevance is likely to lose you your friends (recall Satchel the dog, from the *Get Fuzzy* cartoon in Chapter 3; Figure 3.1).

As such, the design features for competent ostensive communication are that (i) listeners' cognitive systems should be built to maximize the relevance of the inputs they receive (i.e. they must filter out irrelevant information); and (ii) speakers should produce ostensive stimuli only if they are actually relevant for the intended audience (Scott-Phillips, 2010d). These are, you may well have noticed, the Cognitive and Communicative Principles of Relevance (see §3.3). In other words, these two principles are computational descriptions of how the mechanisms involved in ostensive communication should work, if they are well-designed for that purpose (*ibid.*).

The question now is: does ostensive communication actually work this way? And the answer is yes. We have already reviewed the relevant data: in §3.3 I discussed how many empirical studies have shown that the mechanisms involved in ostensive communication do indeed work in the way predicted by Relevance Theory. Following the adaptationist logic I described in §6.1, these data are excellent evidence that humans are indeed adapted for ostensive communication, that is, to express and recognize communicative and informative intentions, and in doing so better navigate their social environment.

This conclusion has some important implications. The first regards continuity and discontinuity in the origins of linguistic communication. In §2.7 I critiqued a common assumption that linguistic communication is evolutionarily related to non-human primate communication. The account I have developed since then, especially in Chapter 4 where I argued that great ape communication is likely not ostensive, reinforces this point. However, although there is not continuity between humans and great apes in terms of communication, there is continuity in a different domain: social navigation. Primate social intelligence evolved because, in a social species like humans, large group sizes make for a very politicized existence. In this world, the ability to read others' minds, and to manipulate them wherever possible, are key adaptations (Humphrey, 1976; Byrne & Whiten, 1989; see also §4.6). Note that although the everyday meanings of 'mindreading' and 'manipulation' have overtones of a conflict of interest, I am using them here, and in what follows, more neutrally than that. In particular, the everyday meaning of 'manipulation' is typically associated with nefarious motives, but here it is being used to describe any attempt to influence the audience's behaviour, for good or ill.

Humans and other primates do both these tasks, mindreading and manipulation, even without communication – but if we have the other party's acquiescence and assistance in the matter, then we can use ostensive communication to do them far more directly. (This is one reason why many researchers view ostensive communication as a *joint* activity; see §3.6.) As such, although ostensive communication is not evolutionarily continuous with non-human primate communication (Chapter 4), it is continuous with non-human primate social cognition. Great apes in particular are adept social navigators. What humans have evolved is an additional form of social navigation, called ostensive communication, with which we literally speak our minds. The development of languages, which allows us to use ostensive communication in particularly precise and powerful ways, builds the cake even higher (§1.5).

What about evolutionary function? There has been much speculation regarding possible selective scenarios that might have triggered the emergence of language, too much of it simply unconstrained. Example scenarios include gossip, mate attraction, sexual competition, planning for hunting, the advent of throwing, the emergence of politics, changes in human life history, and many others (see Számadó & Szathmáry, 2006 for a review). What these suggestions have in common is that they each point to different tasks for which linguistic communication would be functionally useful, and then propose that language evolved to fill that void.

There are at least two problems with this approach. The first problem is that all sorts of species have all sorts of goals for which something like language would be of great assistance, but language did not evolve in any of those cases – so the observation that it would be useful in some context or another that humans find it useful in is really no argument at all.

The second, deeper problem is a failure to distinguish between *direct* and *derived* functions (see Millikan, 1984; Origgi & Sperber, 2000). A trait's *direct function* is the function that is historically responsible for the reproduction of the item in question. In §2.2 I illustrated this idea with the example of hearts, which make noise, contribute to body weight, and pump blood – but it is only the last of these that, because it explains why hearts are reproduced from one generation to the next, is a heart's direct function. In contrast, an item's *derived functions* are those sub-functions that the item performs in order to satisfy its direct function. For example, while the direct function of, say, a chameleon's ability to change the pigmentation of its skin is to allow it to disguise itself in a variety of different environments, the derived function of *this* chameleon changing its skin to *this* colour is that it allows the chameleon to camouflage itself in *this* particular environment.

This distinction brings the evolutionary function of linguistic communication into clear light (Scott-Phillips, 2010c). Ostensive communication evolved as an adaptation for social navigation (see above), and as such, the direct function of ostension – the function that is historically responsible for its reproduction in the next generation – is the manipulation of others' mental states (Origgi & Sperber, 2000). Similarly, the direct function of inference is the mindreading of others' mental states (*ibid.*). One classic paper in the history of animal communication theory used the idea of mindreading and manipulation as a metaphor to describe the payoffs available to each side in animal communication (Krebs & Dawkins, 1984). It turns out that in the case of human ostensive communication, that insight is not metaphorical, but literal: ostensive communication is a form of extended social navigation, in which signallers try to mentally manipulate their audience, and audiences try to mindread their signallers. In contrast, all of the functions invoked by the various speculations summarized above (sex, politics, planning, etc.) are *derived* functions of linguistic communication: they are tasks to which linguistic communication is applied, as instances of the more general direct function. Once this point is understood, it follows that there is no need to identify any particular evolutionary function for early linguistic communication, over and above the mindreading and manipulation of others' mental states.

6.4 Vigilance and argumentation

Throughout this book, and again in the section above, I have emphasized how communication is not a single trait, but rather the product of two other traits, namely mechanisms for signal production, and mechanisms for signal reception. Interactive, social behaviours of this sort present the adaptationist with a raft of interesting questions, to do with how the interests of the different parties play off against one another in evolution (Davies et al., 2012). In the case of communication, the headline questions of this sort are questions about the possibility of deception and dishonesty (Maynard Smith & Harper, 2003). Other people's minds are a powerful and important source of information about the world, but what if that information is false? Similarly, mental manipulation is a powerful and important way to influence others, but what if they don't believe you? These are the ecological problems faced by the users of ostensive-inferential communication. In this section I shall discuss whether we are well-adapted to handle these problems, as both speakers and listeners.

Let's look first at the listener. Ostensive communication is a potentially rich source of useful information. However, it does not come without the above-mentioned risks: listeners can be misinformed. This means that listeners need to filter the information they receive, such that useless or false information is rejected. Speakers who are either malevolent (those liable to deceive) or incompetent (those who do not know what they are talking about) should be ignored, to the extent that it is possible to detect malevolence and incompetence in advance. If listeners are able to do this effectively, they will maximize the utility of ostensive communication as a source of information about the world.

Clearly, listeners do this: they filter incoming information. That is to say, there is a difference between comprehension and acceptance. We can understand what changes to our mental representations a speaker wants to achieve, without having to actually change them. If you tell me that there is cake for dessert, what I understand is that you intend that I believe that there is cake for dessert. Whether I actually *do* subsequently believe there is cake for dessert is a different matter. I can choose not to believe it, and there are two types of reason why I might do this: I might think you untrustworthy; or I might think you mistaken. In other words, suspicions about a speaker's benevolence or her competence are both possible reasons why a listener might comprehend but not accept the meaning of an ostensive stimulus.

This filtering of incoming information is called *epistemic vigilance*, and it is specific to ostensive communication (Sperber et al., 2010). It involves satisfying a speaker's communicative intention, while holding open the possibility of not satisfying the corresponding informative intention. That is to say, the listener can accept that the speaker intends that the listener understands that the speaker has an informative intention, while at the same time the listener can choose not to accept the content of that informative intention. There are by definition no such similar intentions in code model communication, and so no such epistemic vigilance is possible there.

Is our epistemic vigilance effective? There has been a great deal of psychological research on whether and how both adults and children detect malevolence, and some on the detection of incompetence, but there has, perhaps surprisingly, been almost none on whether we filter information acquired via ostensive communication as usefully as possible, given the inherent uncertainties involved (Sperber et al., 2010). Given the central role that ostensive communication plays in human life, it is quite plausible that the mechanisms involved in ostensive communication are adapted for this purpose. There are sizeable literatures on the dissemination and persistence of misinformation, and on how accent and other para-linguistic features of dialects are sometimes used as heuristic markers of group identity, and hence of whom one should or should not trust and cooperate with (Cohen, 2012; Lewandowsky et al., 2012; Roberts, 2013). However, to the best of my knowledge nobody has yet done quantitative empirical work on the effectiveness of epistemic vigilance. This is an important topic for future research.

I turn now to speakers, whose goals are to change the listener's mental representations in some way. The existence of epistemic vigilance, however basic, is a barrier to the speaker's goals. The speaker aims to manipulate the receiver's mental states, but the receiver's epistemic vigilance prevents this from happening willy-nilly. There are of course occasions when listeners do not exercise epistemic vigilance, specifically when there are good reasons to assume that the speaker is both benevolent and competent (e.g. when I ask my friend, who is wearing a watch, for the time). Equally, however, such speakers are not so common that the default setting should be to exercise no epistemic vigilance at all. I have no reason to assume that my parents, for instance, would be malevolent in their communication with me, but they, like everybody else, may not always be competent. As such, I must still be vigilant, and not simply accept as true whatever they might say. Put concisely: the opposite of vigilance is not trust, it is blind trust; and in general, listeners are not blindly trusting (Sperber et al., 2010).

How can speakers overcome this? That is, how can speakers encourage listeners to accept what is being said? This literally cannot be done through physical force: despots throughout history have tried, and have always failed. Instead, speakers must give good reasons why listeners really should adopt their point of view. They must convince. If they cannot, listeners are liable and indeed likely to reject the proffered information, since listeners do not in general trust speakers blindly. As such, adaptive behaviour for the speaker includes the ability to generate good reasons why what you say should be accepted. The best way to do this may be to be good at generating good reasons in the first place. In other words, to be good at reasoning.

This is the *argumentative theory of reasoning*: that the proper function of human reasoning skills is to devise and evaluate arguments intended to persuade (Mercier & Sperber, 2011). This is a counter-intuitive claim, since it goes against a common assumption that the function of reasoning is to improve knowledge and in doing so make better decisions. The argumentative theory does not, of course, suggest that reasoning is not used to improve one's own knowledge and make better decisions, or that it is not good for this. The claim is simply that using reasoning in this way is like using a chair to hold open a door: it works, most of the time, and often very well, but not always, and that is not what it is designed for. The function of reasoning is instead to persuade others in ostensive communication.

This claim makes a number of specific, otherwise counter-intuitive predictions that are supported by the empirical data, and which are hard to account for under the more traditional view. The clearest (but not the only) example of this is confirmation bias: the well-attested phenomenon that people tend not to systematically evaluate both the arguments in favour of and those against existing beliefs or new ideas, but instead interpret new data in a highly partial way, and consider only or predominantly those that support already existing beliefs (see Nickerson, 1998 for a review). This tendency has been noticed by scholars throughout history, and has been demonstrated in a great many psychology experiments, to the extent that "confirmation bias is perhaps the best known and most widely accepted notion of inferential error to come out of the literature on human reasoning" (Evans, 1989, p. 41).

Here is one classic example (Wason, 1960). Participants are shown a sequence of three numbers that satisfy a secret, unstated rule, and their challenge is to work out what that rule is. To do this, they must suggest further sequences of three numbers. The experimenter then tells them whether those sequences comply with the rule, or not. When the participants believe they have identified the rule, they are asked to write it down. What happens? If, for instance, the original sequence is {2, 4, 6}, participants typically suggest sequences like {8, 10, 12} or {20, 22, 24}. The experimenter confirms that these sequences are correct, and the participants then write down that the rule is sequences of successive even numbers. However, the evidence they have amassed does not warrant that conclusion. The rule may, for instance, simply be 'any sequence of successive numbers' i.e. they do not have to be even, or have equal differences between them. If so, then, say, {1, 8, 125} would also be correct. What this possibility highlights is that the most effective strategy to determine the actual rule is not to generate an initial hypothesis based on the original sequences, and then seek data that are consistent with it. This is confirmation bias. A more effective strategy would be to test sequences that falsify it, for instance {2, 2, 2}, or {28, 51, 9}. Yet very few people actually do this.

Now, from the perspective of the traditional and intuitive view – that human reasoning is about improving one's own knowledge and making better decisions – confirmation bias is simply a flaw: it hinders rather than aids the purported goal. However, from the perspective of the argumentative theory, it is precisely what should be expected. The goal of reasoning is to provide listeners with reasons to accept your claims, and as such, our reasoning skills are designed to seek arguments (further sequences of numbers) in favour of our existing view (that the rule is successive even numbers) because it is these arguments that are most useful for the generation of arguments intended to persuade others (Mercier & Sperber, 2011).

This argument is analogous to the example of visual perception, which I discussed in §6.1. There, we considered motion-induced blindness, which, according to traditional assumptions of what the visual system is for, is simply a flaw. However, an alternative hypothesis was proposed, in which motion-induced blindness is in fact adaptive. Empirical data were then sought to distinguish between the competing hypotheses. Much the same is true here: the traditional assumption is that confirmation bias is simply a flaw, but an adaptationist analysis suggests a different view, which turns out to be strongly supported by the existing empirical data. That different view is, in short, that reasoning allows speakers to persuade others as best they can, which is necessary because listeners exercise epistemic vigilance, in order to protect themselves against misinformation. In this way, argumentation and vigilance are two sides of the same communicative coin.

6.5 The boy who cried 'Wolf!', and how he might be stopped

In an episode of *The Simpsons* called 'Marge gets a job', Bart is told by his teacher, Ms. Krabappel, that he has to take a test. To avoid this, he fakes an illness, and Grampa is called to take him home. The next day, his teacher again asks him to do the test, and again he pretends to be ill and is taken home. This same thing happens the following day too, but this time, while Bart is waiting to be collected from school, an Alaskan timber wolf escapes from the set of a show being made at KrustyLu Studios. In its wandering through Springfield, the animal finds its way to Bart who, panicking, calls "Wolf!" – but, because he has lied so often lately, his cry for help is ignored, leaving him to be attacked by the beast. This is, of course, a reference to Aesop's fable *The Boy Who Cried Wolf*, in which a shepherd boy is asked to watch over a flock of sheep, but who raises the alarm in jest once too often, so that when a wolf does eventually come, nobody responds, and the sheep are eaten. (In some versions of the story the boy is eaten too.)

Honesty among non-kin poses a real theoretical problem for the evolution of communication, just as it does for the child who cannot resist the temptation to lie. If dishonesty pays, at least on average, then we should expect dishonest signals to evolve. If so, the receiver's best reaction is simply to ignore them, and so we should expect this indifference to evolve too. If that occurs then the end result is that the system has collapsed: an evolutionary re-telling of Aesop's fable (and Bart's fate). Communication systems in which this outcome is avoided are *evolutionarily stable*, and explaining evolutionary stability is the defining problem of animal signalling theory (Maynard Smith & Harper, 2003; Searcy & Nowicki, 2005). Several researchers have emphasized the importance of this problem for a complete understanding of the evolution of human communication and language (e.g. Számadó & Szathmáry, 2006; Bickerton, 2009; Fitch, 2010). In this section I shall discuss the various solutions to the general problem, and in the next section I shall explain how they apply to human ostensive communication in particular.

Before I begin, I would like to clarify what the question here is *not*. Several authors have characterized the social evolutionary problem as one of information transmission (e.g. Dessalles, 2007; Hurford, 2007): why do we give so much information away to others? But this is no problem to explain at all: we talk so much because there is so much we want to do to others' minds. There is no paradox here, as there is with deception (why is any system stable, given that signallers always have some incentives to deceive?). There would be a paradox if it were the case that we talk *even when doing so is clearly against our own interests*. But there is no good evidence that this is the case.

What, then, maintains the evolutionary stability of human ostensive communication? Shortly after the 2008 credit crunch I read a newspaper article about the culture of drinking and drug taking during work hours that existed in some parts of the City of London prior to the crisis. Apparently some clients *expected* such behaviour from their brokers, because it proved how good they must be at their job: if they could trade successfully even under influence, they must be extremely good traders indeed! This is an example of what is by far the most discussed explanation of the evolutionary stability of communication: the *handicap principle*. The central idea is that excess works as a guarantee: I could only afford to be this wasteful, such signals say, if I really do have lots to spare. Less able traders could not do the same.

The thought that such handicaps can stabilize communication was independently proposed by the biologist Amotz Zahavi and the economist Michael Spence (Spence, 1973; Zahavi, 1975). The classic example used to illustrate the idea in biology is the peacock tail. Large tails make peacocks less dexterous and slower than they would otherwise be, a handicap that only the highest quality peacocks can afford. As such, peahens should be most attracted to these peacocks, and hence the handicap of a cumbersome tail is selected for. The thought that natural selection could lead to the existence of such wasteful traits was initially rejected as implausible: natural selection just doesn't trade in such excess! However, subsequent mathematical models demonstrated otherwise, and described the necessary conditions for it to do so (Grafen, 1990; Maynard Smith, 1991; Lachmann et al., 2001; see Grose, 2011 for a review).

The criteria necessary for handicaps to work are more restrictive than is generally understood (see Számadó, 2011 for an overview). There has in particular been a failure to appreciate that the costs necessary to make the handicap principle work are *differential* costs (Grose, 2011; Számadó, 2011). What this means is that the costs of signal production must correlate with signal meaning, and be greater for dishonest rather than honest signallers. As the eponymous lead character in the film *Withnail and I* puts it, these things are "Free to those that can afford it, very expensive to those that can't". Peacock tails are a plausible example of a handicap because the size of the tail correlates with quality, and the costs that a given tail incurs are greater for lower rather than higher quality individuals. Mathematical models show that the handicap principle *requires* that the costs of signal production are differential in this way: without this, the handicap principle simply does not work (Grose, 2011; Számadó, 2011).

A second common point of misunderstanding is whether handicaps are *necessary* to stabilize communication. The findings of the mathematical models have sometimes been interpreted to mean that signals *must* involve excess. Zahavi himself has certainly made this claim: "in order to be reliable, signals *have to be* costly" (Zahavi & Zahavi, 1997, p. xiv, italics added; see Számadó, 2012 for further quotes). Many other researchers, especially those that study human communication, have followed Zahavi's interpretation. For example: "resistance to deception has *always* selected against conventional [cost free] signals" (Knight, 1998, p. 72, italics added). Yet these claims are, as numerous reviews have made clear, "simply wrong" (Grose, 2011, p. 686; see also Maynard Smith & Harper, 2003; Számadó, 2011, 2012). Handicaps *can* stabilize communication, but that does not mean that they are the only way to do so. For one thing, there is not always any incentive to be dishonest anyway. In those situations the problem of stability does not even arise, which makes handicaps entirely unnecessary. Think of a train timetable: the train company has no incentive to deceive you. They might be incompetent, but they are not malevolent! But even when the interests of signaller and receiver are not aligned, handicaps are still not always necessary, because handicaps are not the only way in which communication can be kept stable. There are several other ways in which stability can be ensured (Lachmann et al., 2001; Maynard Smith & Harper, 2003; Számadó, 2011). In fact, clear, unambiguous examples of handicaps in nature are in fact harder to find than is widely recognized: "All in all, there is not a single biological example that could be claimed as handicap beyond doubt" (Számadó, 2012, p. 281).

Indices are one alternative to handicaps. Red deer roar to one another before fights. The formant dispersal of these roars is negatively correlated with the size of the deer, and hence with fighting ability: larger deer have smaller formant dispersal (Clutton-Brock & Albon, 1979; Reby & McComb, 2003). (Formant dispersal is a measure of the distribution of the characteristic pitch constituents of vocalizations.) Dishonesty would in this case involve a smaller formant dispersal than predicted by the deer's size. However, it turns out that physical constraints make this impossible. A smaller formant dispersal requires a lower larynx. Deer already lower their larynx when they roar, but that process seems to have gone as far as it can: natural selection cannot lower a deer's larynx any further, at least not without fatally compromising other aspects of the deer's anatomy (Fitch & Reby, 2001). Consequently, it is not even possible for red deer to be dishonest. This is an example of an *index*: a signal that cannot be faked, because of some causal relationship between the signal and the thing being signalled. Other examples of indexical signals include male jumping spiders, who expose the ventral surface of their abdomen as an indicator of their current condition, and snapping shrimps, who advertise their claws to each other as a way to avoid physical conflict (Maynard Smith & Harper, 2003).

It is easy to confuse handicaps and indices. Indeed, handicaps are a type of index. Because of differential costs, there is a causal relationship between the signal (the handicap) and its meaning (wealth, quality, etc.). Heavy drinking at work is an index of the fact that you can drink heavily and still function (or not!). Note that this does not imply that handicaps and indices are the same as one another. Handicaps are a type of index, but the converse is not true: not all indices are handicaps. In fact, the vast majority are not.

As an example, consider conspicuous consumption. The term was coined by Thorstein Veblen, an early 20th-century sociologist, in his book *The Theory of the Leisure Class* (1899), as a way to describe how the affluent classes advertise their wealth. After all, if you can afford to spend money on objects like diamond rings and designer clothes, whose non-signalling functions could be equally well fulfilled by far less expensive purchases, you must be wealthy indeed. For this reason, conspicuous consumption is frequently used in textbooks and other pedagogical contexts as an illustration of the idea of the handicap principle, and indeed is sometimes studied as such (e.g. Sundie et al., 2011). However, it is not a great example, because it is not, in fact, a handicap at all. This is because there are no differential costs involved. Put simply, jewellers do not have different prices for different customers (and if they did, it would probably be in the opposite way to that required for the handicap principle: discounts would be available to the poor customers, not the affluent ones). Conspicuous consumption is an *index* of wealth, but it is not a handicap.

Here is another way in which stability can be ensured without handicaps. Many bird species have throat bibs or forehead patches, and the size and coloration of this plumage often varies between individuals. What is most interesting is that many of these variations correlate with what animal behaviour researchers call 'resource-holding potential' (RHP), a composite measure of all factors that influence fighting ability. These variations in plumage are signals. However, they are neither handicaps (there are no excess costs) nor indices (there are no physical facts that prevent dishonesty). Nevertheless, honesty is still the norm. This is because birds with similar sized bibs tend to have agonistic interactions with one another, and so those whose bibs indicate a higher RHP than they actually have tend to get into fights they are unlikely to win. This *deters* dishonesty, without the need for handicaps (Lachmann et al., 2001). This deterrent arises from the fact that conflict among closely ranked birds is common. Another possible source of deterrents is repeated interaction: if individuals are likely to interact with the same individuals again in the future, so long as previous interactions have been honest, then the immediate benefit of deception may be outweighed by the benefits of future interactions (Silk et al., 2000). In such cases, dishonesty should not evolve.

There is a critical difference between deterrents like these, and handicaps (Lachmann et al., 2001; Scott-Phillips, 2008b). Handicaps are costs paid by *honest* signallers, as a guarantee of honesty; in other words, as part of the very act of being honest. Deterrents, on the other hand, are paid by *dishonest* signallers when they *deviate* from honesty. Put another way, the costs in handicaps *have* to be paid for the handicap to work, but the costs associated with deterrents do not have to be paid, if you are honest. This distinction is very clear in the formal mathematical models of honest communication, but it is, as I shall shortly document, not properly applied in much of the literature on human communication.

In sum, the evolutionary stability of communication can be ensured in a number of different ways. I have here outlined one general, high-level taxonomy, which makes a three-way distinction between common interest, deterrents, and indices, of which handicaps are a special case. The reason why this is a high-level taxonomy is that each of these is distinct from the others, and collectively they exhaust all the known possibilities. Which of these applies in any given case is an empirical question. So, what about humans? We are prepared to lie, at least some of the time, if it best serves our interests. What keeps us honest?

6.6 The evolutionary stability of human communication

In general, students of human behaviour have been far too keen to argue that human communication involves handicaps. That is to say, in many cases the handicap principle has been invoked as an explanation when the criteria for a signal to be a handicap simply do not apply. In particular, the requirement that signals are *differentially* costly (see above) is often ignored (Grose, 2011). That is, the costs incurred must correlate with the signal's meaning, and be greater for dishonest rather than honest signallers.

Here are some examples. The first is blood donation (Lyle et al., 2009). To show that this is a handicap, one would have to show that *the act of donation itself* is somehow less costly to donors (in general) than to non-donors. Even if there are evolutionarily relevant costs associated with blood donation, I would be surprised if these are greater for non-donors than for donors. Certainly, no evidence of this sort has been provided. Another example is costly apologies (e.g. gifts), which have been proposed as handicaps on the grounds that they signal a sincere desire to repair a relationship (the idea being that insincere individuals would only produce non-costly apologies) (Ohtsubo & Watanabe, 2009). This suggestion also ignores the requirement that signal costs be different for honest and dishonest signallers. A third example is Duchenne (i.e. not faked) smiles, which some researchers have suggested are handicaps, because they are difficult to fake (Schmidt & Cohn, 2001; Centorrino et al., 2011). But again: no differential costs. A fourth example is self-harm among prisoners, which may signal volatility: if I am crazy enough to do this to myself, these signals say, just think what I might do to you (Gambetta, 2009). Such signals are certainly costly to produce, but, yet again, it is not at all clear that they are *differentially* costly: there are no data to suggest that self-harm is more costly to dishonest rather than honest signallers. Both self-harm and Duchenne smiles are indices rather than handicaps. It is a regrettable fact that for the most part, "human scientists do not take into account the fact that handicaps are defined by virtue of their strategic cost" (Számadó, 2012, p. 284).

This misapplication of the handicap principle has also seeped into the study of linguistic communication. One example is the suggestion that linguistic self-expression is a handicap because of the potential loss of credibility that can result if that self-expression is found to be insincere (Green, 2009). Another example is the suggestion that politeness is a handicap, because it places the speaker in the listener's debt (for example, the utterance "I don't suppose there'd be any possibility of you…" can be read as an announcement that the speaker is prepared to incur some social cost in order to ensure that their wish is satisfied) (van Rooij, 2003). A third example is the suggestion that the very act of speech production is a handicap, because it involves physical and developmental costs (Locke, 2008). All these cases fail the first criterion for a signal to be a handicap, namely that the signal itself, and not its consequences, must be costly. They probably also fail the equally important criterion that the costs be differential.

Linguistic and indeed ostensive communication is not a handicap. Whatever costs are involved in signal production (e.g. energy costs), there is no reason to think they are differential. On the contrary, in fact: the costs involved in the production of linguistic utterances clearly do not vary according to whether the content of the signal is honest or not. Put bluntly, the criteria that must be satisfied for the handicap principle to work are far more stringent than many researchers in the human sciences recognize, and they are simply not satisfied in the case of linguistic communication.

Linguistic communication is kept stable by other means. Specifically, it is kept stable by deterrents, and in particular by reputation (Scott-Phillips, 2008b). Individuals that lie are likely to be ignored or ostracized in the future, and this possibility stops people from lying. The loss of reputation that can result from dishonesty is a major cost in a highly social species like humans, who continually monitor and gossip about each other's behaviour, and form judgements accordingly (Tennie et al., 2010; Sperber & Baumard, 2012). Adam Smith, the father of economics, argued that humans value reputation above even profit. When he is stripped of his rank in Shakespeare's *Othello*, Cassio laments: "Reputation, reputation, reputation! Oh, I have lost my reputation! I have lost the immortal part of myself, and what remains is bestial. My reputation, Iago, my reputation!" And of course, it is the importance of reputation that Aesop's fable is designed to illustrate. Research on the stability of human cooperation recognizes the critical importance of reputation (e.g. Milinski et al., 2002; Lyle & Smith, 2014). Research on the stability of human communication should do the same.

Of course, I do not mean to suggest that ostensive communication is never used deceptively. Clearly it is. But if it were regularly or systematically used deceptively, then communication would break down, just as it did in Aesop's fable – but this has not and does not happen, and the reason why is reputation. If this is correct, then people should be more willing to lie when they believe they can do so without damage to their reputation i.e. when they think that they won't be caught (or that nobody will care). In collaboration with the evolutionary biologists Max Burton-Chellew and Stu West, I have recently tested this prediction in a controlled experimental setting, and our results show that human communication can indeed be kept stable in this way (unpublished data).

I would like here to make a brief aside on the infrequency of handicaps. As I mentioned in §6.5, the literature on handicaps has largely been driven by theoretical models rather than any well-attested empirical examples (Grose, 2011). Over the course of the last three sections, we have identified a number of conditions that must be satisfied for handicaps to work as a viable means by which to ensure honesty. They are: (i) signal honesty should be hard to verify by other means (why bother paying the costs if they are unnecessary?); (ii) the potential benefits are significant enough to warrant the costs involved; (iii) the costs associated with the signal must be differential costs; and (iv) that there must be a possible costly signal for the given meaning (there is, for instance, no possible costly signal that could convince you that my great grandfather won his school chess championship in 1894; handicaps are a type of index, and this fact limits the range of possible signals that can actually be employed as handicaps). None of these conditions is trivial, and so the chances that all four conditions are satisfied in a given case is probably very small. (iii) and (iv) are particularly pertinent, since they render the very possibility of handicaps in linguistic communication impossible. This restrictive set of conditions may explain why, contrary to the level of attention the handicap principle has received in the theoretical literature, there are few if any clear cases of handicaps in the empirical literature (Cotton et al., 2004; Számadó, 2012).

Let me now summarize this and the previous section. Stability is a critical issue for an evolutionary analysis of any communication system. Its importance to accounts of the origins of language is widely recognized (e.g. Számadó & Szathmáry, 2006; Bickerton, 2009; Fitch, 2010). However, there is substantial confusion in the human sciences about what the theoretical literature says about the different ways in which this question can be answered. As a result, the obvious explanation has been ignored: ostensive communication does not collapse for the simple reason that the immediate benefits of dishonesty are outweighed by the loss to one's reputation and other social costs (Lachmann et al., 2001; Scott-Phillips, 2008a). In a few cases, this does not work, because the veracity of signals cannot be verified in any way, and in those cases handicaps might work as an alternative means by which to stabilize communication – but for the majority of the time, and in particular for all linguistic communication, stability is ensured by the threat of the potential loss of reputation.

6.7 A major transition in the evolution of life?

I would like to end this chapter, and the book, by zooming out to the broadest possible biological perspective. In 1995 the evolutionary biologists John Maynard Smith and Eörs Szathmáry published a seminal book, *The Major Transitions in Evolution* (1995). It presented a novel picture of the evolution of life on earth, one based upon information, and the different ways in which it is passed between organisms. In this light, they identified eight major transitions: the emergence of fundamentally new ways for information to be transmitted between individuals and across generations. For example, the third major transition is from a world in which both genes and enzymes are made of RNA, to a world in which genes are made from DNA, and enzymes from RNA. The important point about this change is that because of its unique double-helix structure, DNA provides a form of proof-reading for the replication process, so that the number of transcription errors is reduced, and a new process of information transmission is thus made possible (this description is of course an oversimplification, for the purposes of exposition). Other major transitions include the evolution of chromosomes, the evolution of sex, the evolution of multicellular organisms – and, lastly, the origins of language (Figure 6.1).

Why did Maynard Smith and Szathmáry choose to include the origins of language on this short list? They did not list firm criteria for the major transitions. Instead, they stated what they considered the major transitions to be, and described a number of features common to them. Those features are: (i) previously independently replicating units come together to form a higher-level unit; (ii) contingent irreversibility (i.e. once the change has occurred, it cannot be reversed); (iii) central control (the higher-level unit in some way polices the behaviour of its component units); (iv) division of labour (different units within the new unit perform different functions); and (v) the emergence of new ways of transmitting information. It was this last criterion that motivated Maynard Smith and Szathmáry to consider the origins of language one of the major transitions in evolution.

I am not so sure that the origins of language really belongs on this list. Evolutionary biologists have also been skeptical. The idea of the major transitions is nicely summarized by a metaphor used in one of the reviews of the original book: "If you imagine the history of life as a giant cosmic card game, previous thought on major evolutionary transitions has focused on particular high scores – how well this or that strategy (e.g., aerobic

Replicating molecules → Populations of molecules
Independent replicators → Chromosomes
RNA as gene and enzyme → DNA + protein as genetic code
Prokaryotes → Eukaryotes
Asexual clones → Sexual populations
Protists → Animals, plants, fungi
Solitary individuals → Colonies
Primate societies → Human societies with **language**

Figure 6.1 *The major transitions in evolution.*

metabolism, photosynthesis, invasion of land) performs. This work focuses instead on the rules of the game and how they come to be modified. How many cards are there and of what type? How are they shuffled and re-dealt between generations?" (Queller, 1997, p. 184). Whether particular rule changes qualify as major transitions depends on whether they "lead to such consistently high scores that they spread widely throughout the living domain" (*ibid.*). It is not clear to me how language fits this description. Indeed, the review goes on to say that while the major transitions are in general about the changes in the rules of the game, "the principal exception is human language". Another way to think about the major transitions is that they are about the origins of new forms of *individuality* (Bourke, 2011; see also Queller, 2000). Think of the origin of multicellular organisms: prior to this transition, cells were biological individuals in their own right, subject to biological evolution; post the transition, they were part of a new type of individual, subject to biological evolution only as part of this new conglomerate. Here too it is hard to see how the origins of language fit.

The origins of language may not, then, be a major transition in any sense that is especially useful. It does not change the rules of the biological game, or create new forms of biological individuality. Having said that, it may qualify on a looser reading of the idea of a major transition, one focused on novel ways to transfer information. Even here, however, there is room for argument. As I have argued at length in this book, the real novelty is not in the origins of language *per se*, but rather in the origins of ostensive-inferential communication. This is probably uniquely human, and it enables us to use any behaviour at all in a communicative way – a new form of information transfer indeed. What languages do is make that novelty extra special.

* * *

Chapter 6. *If there is a dedicated language faculty, its evolutionary function is to enhance linguistic communication. More generally, the evolutionary function of ostensive communication, of which linguistic communication is a special case, is mindreading (for the listener) and the manipulation of others' mental states (for the speaker). As such, ostensive communication is a tool for social navigation, and is evolutionarily continuous with the social intelligence of other primate species. Both speakers and listeners have evolved cognitive adaptations to make ostensive communication more effective and useful for them than it otherwise would be. Ostensive communication can be kept stable in a variety of ways, but the most important is social reputation, which acts as a deterrent to dishonesty. The origins of language is at best a major transition only in a broad, loose sense of the term.*

Epilogue. *What are the big questions that are asked about the origins of language? How does the account developed in this book answer them?*

Epilogue

The Big Questions Answered

What I hope to have shown in this book is that, once we take into account ostension and inference, to which insufficient attention has been paid in the past, the origins of language are far less mysterious than they otherwise would be. By way of demonstration, I know of five publications that provide lists of the central questions we might ask about language origins (Számadó & Szathmáry, 2006; Kirby, 2007; Bickerton, 2007; 2009; Odling-Smee & Laland, 2009). I have in this book addressed all these questions. Table 7.1 summarizes my answers.

Table 7.1 *Key questions for any theory of language origins.* Superscripts indicate which publications list each question: [1] Számadó & Szathmáry, 2006; [2] Kirby, 2007; [3] Bickerton, 2007; [4] Bickerton, 2009; [5] Odling-Smee & Laland, 2009.

Question	Answer
Uniqueness [1,2,3,4,5]: Why do only humans have language?	Because of all primate species, only we began to live in social groups so large and complex that there was natural selection for the sort of advanced social cognition (in particular recursive mindreading) that made ostensive-inferential communication, and hence language, possible (see Chapter 4).
Honesty [1,4,5]: What explains the evolutionary stability of human communication?	Social reputation: being known as dishonest is a major deterrent in a social species like humans (see §6.5 and §6.6).
Function and ecology [2,3,4]: What is the evolutionary function of language, and in what selective environment did it evolve?	The evolutionary function of linguistic communication is, like all ostensive communication, mindreading and mental manipulation (see §6.3). It evolved within a specifically social ecology, as a way to better navigate that environment (again, see §6.3). If there is a dedicated language faculty, its evolutionary function is to make the acquisition and processing of languages more straightforward than it would otherwise be (see §6.2).

Continued

Table 7.1 *Continued*

Question	Answer
Expressivity (1,5): What explains the expressive power of human language?	The capacity for ostensive-inferential communication, which is probably uniquely human, allows us to create new signals at will (see Chapter 2), and to use them in highly flexible, expressive ways (see Chapter 1).
Form (2,3): Why does language have the form and structure that it does (e.g. syntax, phonology, etc.)?	As languages propagate through a community, they are changed in non-random ways, such that they gravitate towards particular forms, which are more compatible with human goals and dispositions, and away from others. This process is called cultural attraction (see §5.6 and §5.7).
History (2,3): What is the evolutionary history of language?	Humans evolved advanced forms of social cognition which allowed us to create ostensive communication. This in turn allowed us to create shared conventional codes, which over time became ossified into what we now call languages (see Chapters 2, 4, and 5).
Groundedness (1): How were the first symbols grounded (i.e. how could speaker and listener agree on meaning)?	Early ostensive-inferential communication relied heavily on metapsychology. Any behaviour that could give some clue to meaning would have been used. Over time, these behaviours would have become culturally-shared norms i.e. the first words and other constituent parts of language (see Chapter 5).
Selfishness (4): Why are speakers so willing to talk and hence share information?	Speakers speak in order to affect the mental states of their listeners. We speak so much because, as a highly social species, there is so much we want to do to others' minds (see §6.3).
Coherence (5): Does the proposed account depend only on well-understood evolutionary mechanisms, or is it more speculative?	My proposals depend on well-understood evolutionary mechanisms alone.

The only question to appear in all five publications is 'Why do only humans have language?' Elsewhere, one of the authors of these lists highlights the dearth of good answers to the question: "the fact that humans alone, but no other species, not even those closest to us, have acquired language poses a serious problem for explanations of how language evolved... nobody has ever even suggested [a solution]" (Bickerton, 2008, p. 285). Well, they have now. Of all primate species, only we began to live in social groups so large and complex that there was natural selection for the sort of advanced social cognition that made ostensive-inferential communication possible. Then, once that had evolved, our ancestors began to enhance this novel form of communication with suites of shared communicative conventions – which in time became ossified into what we now call languages. That, in short, is how language emerged, and why we are the only species that has it.

Glossary

Parentheses denote the section in the main text where the concept/definition is first introduced. Italics denote terms that are defined elsewhere in the glossary.

attractor (§5.6)
The end point of the process of *cultural attraction*.

code model (§1.2)
A model of *communication* in which the message is encoded by the signaller, and then decoded by the receiver. To be contrasted with the *ostensive-inferential model*.

coercion (§2.2)
An interaction in which an action causes a reaction, where the action but not the reaction is designed to be part of the interaction. See also *cue* and *communication*.

Cognitive Principle of Relevance (§3.3)
That human cognition tends to be geared towards the maximization of *relevance*.

combinatorial communication (§2.1)
Communication using a system with at least one *composite signal*.

common ground (§3.4)
The information (the mental *representations*) that is known to two (or more) individuals, and which both of them know, or believe, that the other knows (see Clark, 1996).

communication (§2.2)
An interaction in which an action causes a reaction, where both the action and the reaction are designed to be part of the interaction.

communicative intention (§1.3)
An intention to make it manifest to the audience that one has an *informative intention*.

Communicative Principle of Relevance (§3.3)
That every ostensive stimulus carries a presumption of its own optimal *relevance*.

composite signal (§2.1)
A signal whose form is the combination of two (or more) other signals, but whose *meaning* is not simply the sum of the meanings of the component signals.

conventional code (§1.5)
A reliable association between *signal* and *meaning* that holds by virtue of the fact that every member of the community agrees that it holds. To be contrasted with *natural code*.

cue (§2.2)
An interaction in which an action causes a reaction, where the reaction but not the action is designed to be part of the interaction. Also called public information.

cultural attraction (§5.6)
The process by which cultural traits gravitate towards particular forms, and away from others.

direct route to communication (§2.5)
A third route, in addition to the two well-known routes of *ritualization* and *sensory manipulation*, by which a *communication* system might emerge. This route requires that signals *signal* not only their meaning, but also their own signalhood.

function, derived (§6.3)
Those sub-tasks that an item performs in order to satisfy its *direct function*.

function, direct (§6.3)
The task that an item performs that is historically responsible for its reproduction. When 'function' is used without a prefix (*direct* or *derived*) this is usually what is meant.

inference (§1.4)
The recognition of *communicative intentions* and *informative intentions*. Along with ostension, it is one half of *ostensive-inferential communication*.

informative intention (§1.3)
An intention to change the audience's *representation(s)* of the world; more colloquially, an intention to inform the audience. Informative intentions are embedded inside *communicative intentions*.

intentional communication (§4.3)
Communication that involves the purposive production of *signals*. Related to, but not the same as, *ostensive communication*.

language (§5.1)
The suite of cognitive traits that allows us to acquire and use *languages*.

languages (§1.5)
Rich, structured collections of *conventional codes* that exist within a community, and which collectively augment the expressive capacity of *ostensive communication*.

literal meaning (§1.1)
The literal, 'decoded' meaning of a linguistic utterance. To be contrasted with *speaker meaning*. Sometimes also called 'linguistic meaning' or 'utterance meaning'.

meaning (§1.6)
Used in two different ways. Within *pragmatics*, and when discussing *ostensive-inferential communication*, it is usually used to refer to *speaker meaning*. Within

evolutionary biology, and when discussing *communication* within the *code model*, it is usually used to refer to a *signal's (direct) function*. These two usages share in common the notion that *signals* do things to other organisms.

metarepresentation (§3.4)
A *representation* of a *representation*.

natural code (§1.5)
Codes that operate according to the *code model*.

ontogenetic ritualization (§4.5)
A process by which *signals* emerge. It proceeds through exactly the same stages as *ritualization*; the only difference is that ontogenetic ritualization happens within an individual's lifetime, rather than over evolutionary time.

ostension (§1.4)
The expression of *communicative intentions* and *informative intentions*. Along with inference, it is one half of *ostensive-inferential communication*.

ostensive communication
See *ostensive-inferential communication*.

ostensive-inferential communication (§1.4)
The expression and recognition of intentions; specifically, *communicative intentions* and *informative intentions*.

ostensive-inferential model (§1.4)
A model of *communication*, in which *communication* is *ostensive-inferential*. To be contrasted with the *code model*.

pragmatic competence (§3.1)
The ability to use *ostensive communication* in a competent way i.e. to provide the right sort of evidence for the intended *speaker meaning* (as signallers), and to make the right sort of *inferences* about the evidence we do receive (as listeners).

pragmatics (Preface)
The branch of linguistics that studies *meaning* and language use in context. Also, relatedly, the study of the communicative basis of language use.

protolanguage (§5.4)
The hypothesized early forms of *languages*' evolutionary history, before they developed the sort of properties we associate with the established *languages* with which we are familiar.

relevance (§3.3)
The trade-off between worthwhile changes to one's *representations* (e.g. new, useful, and true information), and the processing effort required to achieve these changes.

representation (§3.4)
Anything that is produced by an information processing device as a way to hold information about something, so that it may later be used by another (or the same) information processing device.

response (§2.2)
The reaction in *communication* i.e. the reaction that is caused by an action in another organism, where both action and reaction are designed to be part of the interaction.

ritualization (§2.3)
The process by which *cues* evolve into *signals*, with corresponding *responses*. One of two well-established ways by which *communication* can emerge (the other is *sensory manipulation*).

sensory manipulation (§2.3)
The process by which *coercion* evolves into a *response*, with corresponding *signals*. One of two well-established ways by which *communication* can emerge (the other is *ritualization*).

signal (§2.2)
The action in *communication* i.e. the action that causes a reaction in another organism, where both action and reaction are designed to be part of the interaction.

speaker meaning (§1.1)
The *meaning* that the speaker intends to communicate with a linguistic utterance. To be contrasted with *literal meaning*. Sometimes also called 'intended meaning' or 'utterer's meaning'.

underdeterminacy (§1.1)
The fact that the *literal meaning* of an utterance does not fully determine the *speaker meaning*.

References

Anderson, S. R. (2006). *Doctor Dolittle's Delusion: Animals and the Uniqueness of Human Language*. New Haven, CT: Yale University Press.

Apperly, I. A. (2011). *Mindreaders: The Cognitive Basis of 'Theory of Mind'*. New York, NY: Psychology Press.

Apperly, I. A., & Butterfill, S. A. (2009). Do humans have two systems to track beliefs and belief-like states? *Psychological Review*, *116*(4), 953–970.

Arbib, M. A. (2005). From monkey-like action recognition to human language: An evolutionary framework for neurolinguistics. *Behavioral and Brain Sciences*, *28*(2), 105–167.

Arbib, M. A., & Bickerton, D. (Eds.) (2008). *Interaction Studies*, *9*(1) (special issue on 'Holophrasis, Compositionality and Protolanguage').

Arbib, M. A., Liebal, K., & Pika, S. (2008). Primate vocalization, gesture, and the evolution of human language. *Current Anthropology*, *49*(6), 1053–1076.

Armstrong, D. F., & Wilcox, S. E. (2007). *The Gestural Origin of Language*. Oxford: Oxford University Press.

Arnold, K., & Zuberbühler, K. (2006). Semantic combinations in primate calls. *Nature*, *441*, 303.

Arnold, K., & Zuberbühler, K. (2008). Meaningful call combinations in a non-human primate. *Current Biology*, *18*(5), R202–R203.

Arnold, K., & Zuberbühler, K. (2012). Call combinations in monkeys: Compositional or idiomatic expressions? *Brain & Language*, *120*, 303–309.

Arnold, K., & Zuberbühler, K. (2013). Female putty-nosed monkeys use experimentally altered contextual information to disambiguate the cause of male alarm calls. *PLoS One*, *8*(6), e65660.

Aronoff, M., Meir, I., Padden, C., & Sandler, W. (2008). The emergence of linguistic organization in a new language. *Interaction Studies*, *9*(1), 131–150.

Atlas, J. D. (2005). *Logic, Meaning and Conversation: Semantic Underdeterminacy*. Oxford: Oxford University Press.

Austin, J. L. (1955). *How to Do Things with Words*. Oxford: Oxford University Press.

Baillargeon, R., Scott, R. M., & He, Z. (2010). False-belief understanding in infants. *Trends in Cognitive Sciences*, *14*(3), 110–118.

Bara, B. G. (2010). *Cognitive Pragmatics: The Mental Processes of Communication*. Cambridge, MA: MIT Press.

Bar-Hillel, Y. (1971). Out of the pragmatic wastebasket. *Linguistic Inquiry*, *2*(3), 401–407.

Bar-On, D. (2013). Origins of meaning: Must we 'go Gricean'? *Mind & Language, 28*(3), 342–375.

Baron-Cohen, S. (1995). *Mindblindness: An Essay on Autism and Theory of Mind.* Cambridge, MA: MIT Press.

Barrett, H. C., Frankenhuis, W. E., & Wilke, A. (2008). Adaptation to moving targets: Culture/gene coevolution, not either/or. *Behavioral and Brain Sciences, 31*(5), 511–512.

Barrett, H. C., Broesch, T., Scott, R. M., He, Z., Baillargeon, R., Wu, D., Bolz, M., Henrich, J., Setoh, P., Wang, J., & Laurence, S. (2013). Early false-belief understanding in traditional non-Western societies. *Proceedings of the Royal Society of London B*, *280*(1755), 20122654.

Behne, T., Carpenter, M., & Tomasello, M. (2005). One-year-olds comprehend the communicative intentions behind gestures in a hiding game. *Developmental Science*, *8*(6), 492–499.

Berlin, B., & Kay, P. (1969). *Basic Color Terms: Their Universality and Evolution.* Berkeley, CA: University of California Press.

Berwick, R. C., Okanoya, K., Beckers, G. J. L., & Bolhuis, J. J. (2011a). Songs to syntax: The linguistics of birdsong. *Trends in Cognitive Sciences*, *15*(3), 113–121.

Berwick, R. C., Pietroski, P., Yankama, B., & Chomsky, N. (2011b). Poverty of the stimulus revisited. *Cognitive Science*, *35*(7), 1207–1242.

Bickerton, D. (1990). *Language and Species.* Chicago, IL: University of Chicago Press.

Bickerton, D. (2005). Language first, then shared intentionality, then a beneficent spiral. *Behavioral and Brain Sciences*, *28*(5), 691–692.

Bickerton, D. (2007). Language evolution: A brief guide for linguists. *Lingua*, *117*(3), 510–526.

Bickerton, D. (2008). Ancestors of meaning. *Language & Communication*, *28*(3), 282–290.

Bickerton, D. (2009). *Adam's Tongue: How Humans Made Language, How Language Made Humans*. New York, NY: Hill and Wang.

Blackburn, P. (2007). *The Code Model of Language: A Powerful Metaphor in Linguistic Metatheory*. SIL International.

Botha, R. P. (2003). *Unravelling the Evolution of Language.* Oxford: Elsevier.

Bourke, A. F. (2011). *Principles of Social Evolution.* Oxford: Oxford University Press.

Boyer, P. (1998). Cognitive tracks of cultural inheritance: How evolved intuitive ontology governs cultural transmission. *American Anthropologist*, *100*(4), 876–889.

Boyer, P., & Petersen, M. B. (2012). The naturalness of (many) social institutions: Evolved cognition as their foundation. *Journal of Institutional Economics*, *8*(1), 1–25.

Bradbury, J. W., & Vehrencamp, S. L. (1998). *Principles of Animal Communication.* Sunderland, MA: Sinauer Associates, Inc.

Breheny, R. (2006). Communication and folk psychology. *Mind & Language*, *21*(1), 74–107.

Brothers, L. (1990). The social brain: A project for integrating primate behaviour and neurophysiology in a new domain. *Concepts in Neuroscience*, *1*, 27–51.

Bryant, G. A., & Aktipis, A. (2014). The animal nature of spontaneous human laughter. *Evolution and Human Behavior, 35*(4), 327–335.

Burling, R. (1993). Primate calls, human language, and nonverbal communication. *Current Anthropology*, *34*(1), 25–53.

Burling, R. (2005). *The Talking Ape: How Language Evolved*. Oxford: Oxford University Press.

Buttelmann, D., Carpenter, M., Call, J., & Tomasello, M. (2007). Enculturated chimpanzees imitate rationally. *Developmental Science*, *10*(4), F31–F38.

Buttelmann, D., Carpenter, M., & Tomasello, M. (2009). Eighteen-month-old infants show false belief understanding in an active helping paradigm. *Cognition*, *112*(2), 337–342.

Bybee, J. L. (2003). Cognitive processes in grammaticalization. In: M. Tomasello (Ed.), *The New Psychology of Language: Cognitive and Functional Approaches to Language Structure* (pp. 145–167). Mahwah, NJ: Lawrence Erlbaum.

Byrne, R. W., & Bates, L. A. (2006). Why are animals cognitive? *Current Biology*, *16*(12), R445–R448.

Byrne, R. W., & Whiten, A. (1989). *Machiavellian Intelligence: Social Expertise and the Evolution of Intellect in Monkeys, Apes, and Humans*. Oxford: Oxford University Press.

Caldwell, C. A., & Smith, K. (2012). Cultural evolution and perpetuation of arbitrary communicative conventions in experimental microsocieties. *PLoS One*, *7*(8), e43807.

Call, J. (2011). How artificial communication affects the communication and cognition of the great apes. *Mind & Language*, *26*(1), 1–20.

Call, J., & Tomasello, M. (Eds.) (2007). *The Gestural Communication of Apes and Monkeys*. Mahwah, NJ: Lawrence Erlbaum.

Call, J., & Tomasello, M. (2008). Does the chimpanzee have a theory of mind? 30 years later. *Trends in Cognitive Sciences*, *12*(5), 187–192.

Call, J., Agnetta, B., & Tomasello, M. (2000). Cues that chimpanzees do and do not use to find hidden objects. *Animal Cognition*, *3*(1), 23–34.

Call, J., Hare, B., Carpenter, M., & Tomasello, M. (2004). 'Unwilling' versus 'unable': Chimpanzees' understanding of human intentional action. *Developmental Science*, *7*(4), 488–498.

Caron, A. J. (2009). Comprehension of the representational mind in infancy. *Developmental Review*, *29*(2), 69–95.

Carruthers, P. (2013). Mindreading in infancy. *Mind & Language*, *28*(2), 141–172.

Carston, R. (2002a). *Thoughts and Utterances: The Pragmatics of Explicit Communication*. Oxford: Blackwell.

Carston, R. (2002b). Linguistic meaning, communicated meaning and pragmatics. *Mind & Language*, *17*(1–2) , 127–148.

Cartmill, E. A., & Byrne, R. W. (2010). Semantics of primate gestures: Intentional meanings of orangutan gestures. *Animal Cognition*, *13*(6), 793–804.

Cartmill, E. A., Beilock, S., & Goldin-Meadow, S. (2012). A word in the hand: Action, gesture and mental representation in humans and non-human primates.

Philosophical Transactions of the Royal Society of London, B, *367*(1585), 129–143.

Centorrino, S., Djemaï, E., Hopfensitz, A., Milinski, M., & Seabright, P. (2011). Smiling is a costly signal of cooperation opportunities: Experimental evidence from a trust game. *TSE Working Papers*, no. 11-231. Toulouse School of Economics (TSE), http://EconPapers.repec.org/RePEc:tse:wpaper:24351.

Chance, M. R. A., & Mead, A. P. (1953). Social behaviour and primate evolution. *Symposia of the Society for Experimental Biology*, *7*, 395–439.

Cheney, D. L., & Seyfarth, R. M. (2005). Constraints and preadaptations in the earliest stages of language evolution. *The Linguistic Review*, *22*(2–4), 135–159.

Cheney, D. L., & Seyfarth, R. M. (2008). *Baboon Metaphysics: The Evolution of a Social Mind*. Chicago, IL: University of Chicago Press.

Chevallier, C., Kohls, G., Troiani, V., Brodkin, E. S., & Schultz, R. T. (2012). The social motivation theory of autism. *Trends in Cognitive Sciences*, *16*(4), 231–239.

Chomsky, N. (1972). *Language and Mind*. New York, NY: Harcourt Brace Jovanovich.

Chomksy, N. (1980). *Rules and Representations*. Oxford: Blackwell.

Chomsky, N. (1988). *Language and Problems of Knowledge: The Managua Lectures*. Cambridge, MA: MIT Press.

Chomsky, N. (2002). *On Nature and Language*. Cambridge: Cambridge University Press.

Christiansen, M. H., & Chater, N. (2008). Language as shaped by the brain. *Behavioral and Brain Sciences*, *31*(5), 489–558.

Christiansen, M. H., & Kirby, S. (2003). Language evolution: Consensus and controversies. *Trends in Cognitive Sciences*, *7*(7), 300–307.

Claidière, N., & André, J.-B. (2012). The transmission of genes and culture: A questionable analogy. *Evolutionary Biology*, *39*(1), 12–24.

Claidière, N., Scott-Phillips, T. C., & Sperber, D. (2014). How Darwinian is cultural evolution? *Philosophical Transactions of the Royal Society of London*, *369*, 20130368.

Clark, H. H. (1996). *Using Language*. Cambridge: Cambridge University Press.

Clay, Z., Pople, S., Hood, B., & Kita, S. (in press). Young children make their gestural communication systems more language-like: Segmentation and linearisation of semantic elements in motion events. *Psychological Science*.

Clayton, N. S., Dally, J. M., & Emery, N. J. (2007). Social cognition by food-caching corvids: The western scrub-jay as a natural psychologist. *Philosophical Transactions of the Royal Society of London, B*, *362*(1480), 507–552.

Clutton-Brock, T. H., & Albon, S. D. (1979). The roaring red deer and the evolution of honest advertising. *Behaviour*, *69*, 145–170.

Cohen, A. S., & German, T. C. (2009). Encoding of others' beliefs without overt instruction. *Cognition*, *111*, 356–363.

Cohen, A. S., & German, T. C. (2010). A reaction time advantage for calculating beliefs over public representations signals domain specificity for 'theory of mind'. *Cognition*, *115*(3), 417–425.

Cohen, E. (2012). The evolution of tag-based cooperation in humans: The case for accent. *Current Anthropology*, *53*(5), 588–616.

Corballis, M. C. (2002). *From Hand to Mouth: The Origins of Language*. Princeton, NJ: Princeton University Press.

Cornforth, D. M., Popat, R., McNally, L., Gurney, J., Scott-Phillips, T. C., Ivens, A., Diggle, S. P., & Brown, S. P. (2014). Combinatorial quorum-sensing allows bacteria to resolve physical and social uncertainty. *Proceedings of the National Academy of Sciences, 111*(11), 4280–4284.

Cosmides, L., & Tooby, J. (2013). Evolutionary psychology: New perspectives on cognition and motivation. *Annual Review of Psychology, 64*, 201–229.

Cotton, S., Fowler, K., & Pomiankowski, A. (2004). Do sexual ornaments demonstrate heightened condition-dependent expression as predicted by the handicap hypothesis? *Proceedings of the Royal Society of London, B, 271*(1541), 771–783.

Csibra, G. (2010). Recognizing communicative intentions in infancy. *Mind & Language, 25*(2), 141–168.

Csibra, G., & Gergely, G. (2011). Natural pedagogy as evolutionary adaptation. *Philosophical Transactions of the Royal Society of London, B, 366*(1567), 1149–1157.

Culbertson, J. (2012). Typological universals as reflections of biased learning: Evidence from artificial language learning. *Language and Linguistics Compass, 6*(5), 310–329.

Cummings, L. (1998). The scientific reductionism of Relevance Theory: The lesson from logical positivism. *Journal of Pragmatics, 29*(1), 1–12.

Daly, M. (1991). Natural selection doesn't have goals, but it's the reason organisms do. *Behavioral and Brain Sciences, 14*, 219–220.

Danchin, É., Giraldeau, L. A., Valone, T. J., & Wagner, R. H. (2004). Public information: From nosy neighbors to cultural evolution. *Science, 305*(5683), 487–491.

Darwin, C. (1859). *On the Origin of Species*. London: John Murray.

Darwin, C. (1872). *The Expression of the Emotions in Man and Animals*. London: John Murray.

Davies, N. B., Krebs, J. R., & West, S. A. (2012). *An Introduction to Behavioural Ecology*. Oxford: Wiley-Blackwell.

Davila Ross, M., Owren, M. J., & Zimmermann, E. (2009). Reconstructing the evolution of laughter in great apes and humans. *Current Biology, 19*(13), 1106–1111.

Dawkins, R. (1986). *The Blind Watchmaker: Why the Evidence of Evolution Reveals a Universe Without Design*. New York, NY: WW Norton & Co.

Deacon, T. W. (1997). *The Symbolic Species: The Co-evolution of Language and the Brain*. New York, NY: WW Norton & Co.

Dediu, D. (2008). The role of genetic biases in shaping the correlations between languages and genes. *Journal of Theoretical Biology, 254*(2), 400–407.

Dediu, D. (2011). A Bayesian phylogenetic approach to estimating the stability of linguistic features and the genetic biasing of tone. *Proceedings of the Royal Society of London, B, 278*(1704), 474–479.

Dediu, D., & Ladd, D. R. (2007). Linguistic tone is related to the population frequency of the adaptive haplogroups of two brain size genes, *ASPM* and *Microcephalin*. *Proceedings of the National Academy of Sciences, 104*(26), 10944–10949.

Dennett, D. C. (1978). Beliefs about beliefs. *Behavioral and Brain Sciences*, *1*(4), 568–570.

Dennett, D. C. (1995). *Darwin's Dangerous Idea: Evolution and the Meanings of Life*. London: Penguin.

de Ruiter, J. P., Noordzij, M. L., Newman-Norland, S., Newman-Norland, R., Hagoort, P., Levinson, S. C., & Toni, I. (2010). Exploring the cognitive infrastructure of communication. *Interaction Studies*, *11*(1), 51–77.

de Saussure, F. (1916). *Cours de Linguistique Générale*.

Dessalles, J.-L. (2007). *Why We Talk: The Evolutionary Origins of Language*. Oxford: Oxford University Press.

di Paolo, E. A. (1997). An investigation into the evolution of communication. *Adaptive Behavior*, *6*(2), 285–324.

Doucet, S., Soussignan, R., Sagot, P., & Schaal, B. (2009). The secretion of areolar (Montgomery's) glands from lactating women elicits selective, unconditional responses in neonates. *PLoS One*, *4*(10), e7579.

Dunbar, R. I. M. (1998). The social brain hypothesis. *Evolutionary Anthropology*, *6*(5), 178–190.

Dunbar, R. I. M. (2003). The social brain: mind, language, and society in evolutionary perspective. *Annual Review of Anthropology*, 163–181.

Dunbar, R. I. M. (2012). Social cognition on the internet: Testing constraints on social network size. *Philosophical Transactions of the Royal Society of London, B*, *367*, 2192–2201.

Dunbar, R. I. M., & Shultz, S. (2007). Evolution in the social brain. *Science*, *317*(5843), 1344–1347.

Dyer, F. C. (2002). The biology of the dance language. *Annual Review of Entomology*, *47*(1), 917–949.

Engh, A. L., Hoffmeier, R. R., Cheney, D. L., & Seyfarth, R. M. (2006). Who, me? Can baboons infer the target of vocalizations? *Animal Behaviour*, *71*(2), 381–387.

Evans, J. St. B. T. (1989). *Bias in Human Reasoning: Causes and Consequences*. Hillsdale, NJ: Erlbaum.

Evans, N., & Levinson, S. C. (2009). The myth of language universals: Language diversity and its importance for cognitive science. *Behavioral and Brain Sciences*, *32*(5), 429–492.

Everett, D. L. (2005). Cultural constraints on grammar and cognition in Pirahã. *Current Anthropology*, *46*(4), 621–634.

Fay, N., & Ellison, T. M. (2013). The cultural evolution of human communication systems in different sized populations: Usability trumps learnability. *PLoS One*, *8*(8), e71781.

Fay, N., Garrod, S., & Roberts, L. (2008). The fitness and functionality of culturally evolved communication systems. *Philosophical Transactions of the Royal Society of London, B*, *363*(1509), 3553–3561.

Fay, N., Arbib, M., & Garrod, S. (2013). How to bootstrap a human communication system. *Cognitive Science*, *37*(7), 1356–1367.

Fedzechkina, M., Jaeger, T. F., & Newport, E. L. (2012). Language learners restructure their input to facilitate efficient communication. *Proceedings of the National Academy of Sciences*, *109*(44), 17897–17902.

Fehér, O., Wang, H., Saar, S., Mitra, P. P., & Tchernichovski, O. (2009). De novo establishment of wild-type song culture in the zebra finch. *Nature*, *459*(7246), 564–568.

Fisher, R. A. (1930). *The Genetical Theory of Natural Selection*. Oxford: Clarendon Press.

Fitch, W. T. (2000). The evolution of speech: A comparative review. *Trends in Cognitive Sciences*, *4*(7), 258–267.

Fitch, W. T. (2010). *The Evolution of Language*. Cambridge: Cambridge University Press.

Fitch, W. T., & Hauser, M. D. (2004). Computational constraints on syntactic processing in a nonhuman primate. *Science*, *303*(5656), 377–380.

Fitch, W. T., & Reby, D. (2001). The descended larynx is not uniquely human. *Proceedings of the Royal Society of London, B*, *268*(1477), 1669–1675.

Fitch, W. T., & Zuberbühler, K. (2013). Primate precursors to human language: Beyond discontinuity. In: E. Altenmüller, S. Schmidt, & E. Zimmermann (Eds.), *The Evolution of Emotional Communication: From Sounds in Nonhuman Mammals to Speech and Music in Man* (pp. 26–48). Oxford: Oxford University Press.

Fitch, W. T., Huber, L., & Bugnyar, T. (2010). Social cognition and the evolution of language: Constructing cognitive phylogenies. *Neuron*, *65*(6), 795–814.

Flombaum, J. I., & Santos, L. R. (2005). Rhesus monkeys attribute perceptions to others. *Current Biology*, *15*(5), 447–452.

Frith, U. (2003). *Autism: Explaining the Enigma*. Oxford: Blackwell.

Frith, U., & Frith, C. (2010). The social brain: Allowing humans to boldly go where no other species has been. *Philosophical Transactions of the Royal Society of London, B*, *365*(1537), 165–176.

Futuyma, D. J. (2005). *Evolution*. Sunderland, MA: Sinauer.

Galantucci, B. (2005). An experimental study of the emergence of human communication systems. *Cognitive Science*, *29*(5), 737–767.

Galantucci, B., & Garrod, S. (2011). Experimental semiotics: A review. *Frontiers in Human Neuroscience*, *5*.

Galantucci, B., & Sebanz, N. (Eds.) (2009). *Topics in Cognitive Science*, *1*(2) (special issue on 'Joint Action').

Gambetta, D. (2009). *Codes of the Underworld: How Criminals Communicate*. Princeton, NJ: Princeton University Press.

Gardner, A. (2009). Adaptation as organism design. *Biology Letters*, *5*(6), 861–864.

Garner, R. L. (1892). *The Speech of Monkeys*. London: William Heinemann.

Garrod, S., Fay, N., Lee, J., Oberlander, J., & MacLeod, T. (2007). Foundations of representation: Where might graphical symbol systems come from? *Cognitive Science*, *31*(6), 961–987.

Gelstein, S., Yeshurun, Y., Rozenkrantz, L., Shushan, S., Frumin, I., Roth, Y., & Sobel, N. (2011). Human tears contain a chemosignal. *Science*, *331*(6014), 226–230.

Genty, E., Breuer, T., Hobaiter, C., & Byrne, R. W. (2009). Gestural communication of the gorilla (*Gorilla gorilla*): Repertoire, intentionality and possible origins. *Animal Cognition*, *12*(3), 527–546.

Gergely, G., Bekkering, H., & Király, I. (2002). Rational imitation in preverbal infants. *Nature*, *415*(6873), 755.

Gervais, M., & Wilson, D. S. (2005). The evolution and functions of laughter and humor: A synthetic approach. *The Quarterly Review of Biology*, *80*(4), 395–430.

Gibbs, R. W. (1994). *The Poetics of Mind*. Cambridge: Cambridge University Press.

Gibbs, R. W., & Bryant, G. A. (2008). Striving for optimal relevance when answering questions. *Cognition*, *106(*1), 345–369.

Gibbs, R. W., & Tendahl, M. (2006). Cognitive effort and effects in metaphor comprehension: Relevance theory and psycholinguistics. *Mind & Language*, *21*(3), 379–403.

Girotto, V., Kemmelmeir, M., Sperber, D., & van der Henst, J.-B. (2001). Inept reasoners or pragmatic virtuosos? Relevance and the deontic selection task. *Cognition*, *81*, 69–76.

Glüer, K., & Pagin, P. (2003). Meaning theory and autistic speakers. *Mind & Language*, *18*(1), 23–51.

Goldberg, A. E. (2006). *Constructions at Work: The Nature of Generalization in Language*. Oxford: Oxford University Press.

Goldberg, A. E. (2008). Universal Grammar? Or prerequisites for natural language? *Behavioral and Brain Sciences*, *31*(5), 522–523.

Goldin-Meadow, S. (2005). *The Resilience of Language*. Abingdon: Psychology Press.

Gómez, J. C. (1994). Mutual awareness in primate communication: A Gricean approach. In: S. T. Parker, R. W. Mitchell, & M. L. Boccia (Eds.), *Self-Awareness in Animals and Humans* (pp. 61–80). Cambridge: Cambridge University Press.

Grafen, A. (1990). Biological signals as handicaps. *Journal of Theoretical Biology*, *144*(4), 517–546.

Gräfenhain, M., Behne, T., Carpenter, M., & Tomasello, M. (2009). One-year-olds' understanding of nonverbally expressed communicative intentions directed to a third person. *Cognitive Development*, *24*, 23–33.

Green, M. S. (2009). Speech acts, the Handicap Principle and the expression of psychological states. *Mind & Language*, *24*(2), 139–163.

Green, S., & Marler, P. (1979). The analysis of animal communication. In: P. Marler & G. Vandenbergh (Eds.), *Handbook of Behavioral Neurobiology, Vol. 3: Social Behavior and Communication* (pp. 73–158). New York: Plenum.

Grice, H. P. (1957). Meaning. *The Philosophical Review*, *66*(3), 377–388.

Grice, H. P. (1969). Utterer's meaning and intention. *The Philosophical Review*, *78*(2), 147–177.

Grice, H. P. (1975). Logic and conversation. In: P. Cole & J. Morgan (Eds.), *Syntax and Semantics III: Speech Acts* (pp. 41–58). New York, NY: Academic Press.

Grice, H. P. (1982). Meaning revisited. In: N. Smith (Ed.), *Mutual Knowledge*. London: Academic Press.

Grice, H. P. (1989). *Studies in the Way of Words*. Cambridge, MA: Harvard University Press.

Grose, J. (2011). Modelling and the fall and rise of the handicap principle. *Biology & Philosophy*, *26*(5), 677–696.

Grosse, G., Behne, T., Carpenter, M., & Tomasello, M. (2010). Infants communicate in order to be understood. *Developmental Psychology*, *46*(6), 1710–1722.

Grosse, G., Scott-Phillips, T. C., & Tomasello, M. (2013). Three-year-olds hide their communicative intentions in appropriate contexts. *Developmental Psychology*, *49*(11), 2095–2101.

Gyger, M., Karakashian, S. J., & Marler, P. (1986). Avian alarm-calling: Is there an audience effect? *Animal Behaviour*, *34*, 1570–1572.

Hailman, J. P. (1977). *Optical Signals: Animal Communication and Light*. Bloomington, IN: Indiana University Press.

Haldane, J. B. S. (1932). *The Causes of Evolution*. New York, NY: Harper's.

Halina, M., Rossano, F., & Tomasello, M. (2013). The ontogenetic ritualization of bonobo gestures. *Animal Cognition*, *16*, 155–163.

Hare, B., Call, J., Agnetta, B., & Tomasello, M. (2000). Chimpanzees know what conspecifics do and do not see. *Animal Behaviour*, *59*, 771–785.

Hare, B., Brown, M., Williamson, C., & Tomasello, M. (2002). The domestication of social cognition in dogs. *Science*, *298*(5598), 1634–1636.

Harvey, P. H., & Pagel, M. D. (1991). *The Comparative Method in Evolutionary Biology*. Oxford: Oxford University Press.

Hauser, M. D. (1996). *The Evolution of Communication*. Cambridge, MA: MIT Press.

Hauser, M. D., Chomsky, N., & Fitch, W. T. (2002). The faculty of language: What is it, who has it, and how did it evolve? *Science*, *298*(5598), 1569–1579.

He, Z., Bolz, M., & Baillargeon, R. (2012). 2.5-year-olds succeed at a verbal anticipatory-looking false-belief task. *British Journal of Developmental Psychology*, *30*(1), 14–29.

Healey, P. G., Swoboda, N., Umata, I., & King, J. (2007). Graphical language games: Interactional constraints on representational form. *Cognitive Science*, *31*(2), 285–309.

Heine, B., & Kuteva, T. (2002b). *World Lexicon of Grammaticalization*. Cambridge: Cambridge University Press.

Heine, B., & Kuteva, T. (2007). *The Genesis of Grammar: A Reconstruction*. Oxford: Oxford University Press.

Helming, K. A., Strickland, B., & Jacob, P. (2014). Making sense of early-false-belief understanding. *Trends in Cognitive Sciences, 18*(4), 167–170.

Henderson, A. M. E., Sabbagh, M. A., & Woodward, A. L. (2013). Preschoolers' selective learning is guided by the principle of relevance. *Cognition*, *126*(2), 246–257.

Henderson, J. M., Malcolm, G. L., & Schandl, C. (2009). Searching in the dark: Cognitive relevance drives attention in real-world scenes. *Psychonomic Bulletin & Review*, *16*, 850–856.

Herrmann, E., & Tomasello, M. (2006). Apes' and children's understanding of cooperative and competitive motives in a communicative situation. *Developmental Science*, *9*(5), 518–529.

Herrmann, E., Call, J., Hernández-Lloreda, M. V., Hare, B., & Tomasello, M. (2007). Humans have evolved specialized skills of social cognition: The cultural intelligence hypothesis. *Science*, *317*(5843), 1360–1366.

Hewes, G. W. (1973). Primate communication and gestural origin of language. *Current Anthropology*, *14*(1–2), 5–24.

Heyes, C. M. (1998). Theory of mind in nonhuman primates. *Behavioral and Brain Sciences*, *21*, 101–114.

Heyes, C. M. (in press). False belief in infancy: A fresh look. *Developmental Science*.

Hobaiter, C., & Byrne, R. W. (2011). The gestural repertoire of the wild chimpanzee. *Animal Cognition*, *14*(5), 745–767.

Hockett, C. F. (1960). The origin of speech. *Scientific American*, *203*, 88–111.

Hoefler, S. H., & Smith, A. D. M. (2009). The pre-linguistic basis of grammaticalisation: A unified approach to metaphor and reanalysis. *Studies in Language*, *33*(4), 886–909.

Holekamp, K. E. (2007). Questioning the social intelligence hypothesis. *Trends in Cognitive Sciences*, *11*(2), 65–69.

Hopper, P. J., & Traugott, E. C. (2003). *Grammaticalization*. Cambridge: Cambridge University Press.

Horn, L. (1984). A new taxonomy for pragmatic inference: Q-based and R-based implicature. In: D. Schiffrin (Ed.), *Meaning, Form, and Use in Context* (pp. 11–42). Washington, DC: Georgetown University Press.

Horowitz, A. (2013). *On Looking: Eleven Walks with Expert Eyes*. New York, NY: Simon & Schuster.

Hughes, M. E., & Allen, S. E. (in press). The incremental effect of discourse-pragmatic sensitivity on referential choice in the acquisition of a first language. *Lingua*.

Humphrey, N. K. (1976). The social function of intellect. In: P. P. G. Bateson & R. Hinde (Eds.), *Growing Points in Ethology* (pp. 303–317). Cambridge: Cambridge University Press.

Hurford, J. R. (2003). The language mosaic and its evolution. In: M. H. Christiansen & S. Kirby (Eds.), *Language Evolution* (pp. 38–57). Oxford: Oxford University Press.

Hurford, J. R. (2007). *Origins of Meaning*. Oxford: Oxford University Press.

Hurford, J. R. (2011). *Origins of Grammar*. Oxford: Oxford University Press.

Hutto, D. D., Herschbach, M., & Southgate, V. (Eds.) (2011). *Review of Philosophy and Psychology*, *2*(3) (special issue on 'Social Cognition: Mindreading and Alternatives').

Jackendoff, R. (2002). *Foundations of Language: Brain, Meaning, Grammar, Evolution*. Oxford: Oxford University Press.

Janzen, D. H. (1980). When is it coevolution? *Evolution*, *34*(3), 611–612.

Jolly, A. (1966). Lemur social behavior and primate intelligence. *Science*, *153*(3735), 501–506.

Kaminski, J. (2009). Dogs (*Canis familiaris*) are adapted to receive human communication. In: A. Berthoz & Y. Christen (Eds.), *Neurobiology of 'Umwelt': How Living Beings Perceive the World* (pp. 103–107). Berlin: Springer.

Kaminski, J., Neumann, M., Bräuer, J., Call, J., & Tomasello, M. (2011). Dogs, *Canis familiaris*, communicate with humans to request but not to inform. *Animal Behaviour*, *82*(4), 651–658.

Kaminski, J., Schulz, L., & Tomasello, M. (2012). How dogs know when communication is intended for them. *Developmental Science*, *15*(2), 222–232.

Kay, P., & Regier, T. (2006). Language, thought and color: Recent developments. *Trends in Cognitive Sciences*, *10*(2), 51–54.

Kellogg, W. N., & Kellogg, L. A. (1933). *The Ape and The Child: A Comparative Study of the Environmental Influence Upon Early Behavior*. New York, NY: Hafner Publishing Co.

Kinderman, P., Dunbar, R. I. M., & Bentall, R. P. (1998). Theory-of-mind deficits and causal attributions. *British Journal of Psychology*, *89*, 191–204.

Kirby, S. (2000). Syntax without natural selection: How compositionality emerges from vocabulary in a population of learners. In: C. Knight, M. Studdert-Kennedy, & J. R. Hurford (Eds.), *The Evolutionary Emergence of Language* (pp. 303–323). Cambridge: Cambridge University Press.

Kirby, S. (2002). Natural language from artificial life. *Artificial Life*, *8*(2), 185–215.

Kirby, S. (2007). The evolution of language. In: R. Dunbar & L. Barrett (Eds.), *Oxford Handbook of Evolutionary Psychology* (pp. 669–681). Oxford: Oxford University Press.

Kirby, S., Dowman, M., & Griffiths, T. L. (2007). Innateness and culture in the evolution of language. *Proceedings of the National Academy of Sciences*, *104*(12), 5241–5245.

Kirby, S., Cornish, H., & Smith, K. (2008). Cumulative cultural evolution in the laboratory: An experimental approach to the origins of structure in human language. *Proceedings of the National Academy of Sciences*, *105*(31), 10681–10686.

Knight, C. (1998). Ritual/speech coevolution: A solution to the problem of deception. In: J. R. Hurford, M. Studdert-Kennedy, & C. Knight (Eds.), *Approaches to the Evolution of Language: Social and Cognitive Bases* (pp. 68–91). Cambridge: Cambridge University Press.

Kobayashi, H., & Kohshima, S. (2001). Unique morphology of the human eye and its adaptive meaning: Comparative studies on external morphology of the primate eye. *Journal of Human Evolution*, *40*(5), 419–435.

Kovács, Á. M., Téglás, E., & Endress, A. D. (2010). The social sense: Susceptibility to others' beliefs in human infants and adults. *Science*, *330*(6012), 1830–1834.

Krebs, J. R., & Dawkins, R. (1984). Animal signals: Mind-reading and manipulation. In: J. R. Krebs & N. B. Davies (Eds.), *Behavioural Ecology: An Evolutionary Approach* (2nd ed., pp. 380–402). Oxford: Blackwell.

Lachmann, M., & Bergstrom, C. T. (2004). The disadvantage of combinatorial communication. *Proceedings of the Royal Society of London, B*, *271*, 2337–2343.

Lachmann, M., Szamado, S., & Bergstrom, C. T. (2001). Cost and conflict in animal signals and human language. *Proceedings of the National Academy of Sciences*, *98*(23), 13189–13194.

Laurence, S., & Margolis, E. (2001). The poverty of the stimulus argument. *The British Journal for the Philosophy of Science*, *52*(2), 217–276.

Levinson, S. C. (1983). *Pragmatics*. Cambridge: Cambridge University Press.

Levinson, S. C. (1989). A review of Relevance. *Journal of Linguistics*, *25*, 455–472.

Levinson, S. C. (2000). *Presumptive Meanings: The Theory of Generalized Conversational Implicature*. Cambridge, MA: MIT Press.

Lewandowsky, S., Ecker, U. K. H., Seifert, C. M., Schwarz, N., & Cook, J. (2012). Misinformation and its correction: Continued influence and debiasing. *Psychological Science in the Public Interest*, *13*(3), 106–131.

Lewis, D. (1969). *Convention*. Cambridge, MA: Harvard University Press.

Liebal, K., & Call, J. (2012). The origins of non-human primates' manual gestures. *Philosophical Transactions of the Royal Society, B*, *367*(1585), 118–128.

Liebal, K., Behne, T., Carpenter, M., & Tomasello, M. (2009). Infants use shared experience to interpret pointing gestures. *Developmental Science*, *12*(2), 264–271.

Liebal, K., Waller, B. M., Burrows, A. M., & Slocombe, K. E. (2014). *Primate Communication: A Multimodal Approach*. Cambridge: Cambridge University Press.

Lieberman, P. (2007). The evolution of human speech. *Current Anthropology*, *48*(1), 39–66.

Liszkowski, U., Carpenter, M., & Tomasello, M. (2008). Twelve-month-olds communicate helpfully and appropriately for knowledgeable and ignorant partners. *Cognition*, *108*(3), 732–739.

Locke, J. L. (2008). Cost and complexity: Selection for speech and language. *Journal of Theoretical Biology*, *251*(4), 640–652.

Low, J., & Perner, J. (Eds.) (2012). *British Journal of Developmental Psychology*, *30*(1) (special issue on 'Implicit and Explicit Theory of Mind').

Lupyan, G., & Dale, R. (2010). Language structure is partly determined by social structure. *PLoS One*, *5*(1), e8559.

Lyle, H. F., & Smith, E. A. (2014). The reputational and social network benefits of prosociality in an Andean community. *Proceedings of the National Academy of Sciences*, *111*(13), 4820–4825.

Lyle, H. F., Smith, E. A., & Sullivan, R. J. (2009). Blood donations as costly signals of donor quality. *Journal of Evolutionary Psychology*, *7*(4), 263–286.

Lyn, H., Russell, J. L., & Hopkins, W. D. (2010). The impact of environment on the comprehension of declarative communication in apes. *Psychological Science*, *21*(3), 360–365.

Marticorena, D. C., Ruiz, A. M., Mukerji, C., Goddu, A., & Santos, L. R. (2011). Monkeys represent others' knowledge but not their beliefs. *Developmental Science*, *14*(6), 1406–1416.

Martin, A., & Santos, L. R. (2014). The origins of belief representation: Monkeys fail to automatically represent others' beliefs. *Cognition*, *130*(3), 300–308.

Maynard Smith, J. (1991). Theories of sexual selection. *Trends in Ecology & Evolution*, *6*(5), 146–151.

Maynard Smith, J., & Harper, D. G. C. (2003). *Animal Signals*. Oxford: Oxford University Press.

Maynard Smith, J., & Szathmáry, E. (1995). *The Major Transitions in Evolution*. Oxford: W. H. Freeman.

Mayr, E. (1961). Cause and effect in biology. *Science*, *134*, 1501–1506.

McMahon, A., & McMahon, R. (2013). *Evolutionary Linguistics*. Cambridge: Cambridge University Press.

McNeill, D. (2000). *Language and Gesture*. Cambridge: Cambridge University Press.

Mercier, H., & Sperber, D. (2011). Why do humans reason? Arguments for an argumentative theory. *Behavioral and Brain Sciences*, *34*(2), 57–111.

Miklósi, A., Topál, J., & Csányi, V. (2004). Comparative social cognition: What can dogs teach us? *Animal Behaviour*, *67*(6), 995–1004.

Milinski, M., Semmann, D., & Krambeck, H. J. (2002). Reputation helps solve the 'tragedy of the commons'. *Nature*, *415*(6870), 424–426.

Miller, G. (1951). *Language and Communication*. New York, NY: McGraw-Hill.

Miller, S. A. (2009). Children's understanding of second-order mental states. *Psychological Bulletin*, *135*(5), 749–773.

Millikan, R. (1984). *Language, Thought and Other Biological Categories*. Cambridge, MA: MIT Press.

Mithen, S. J. (2005). *The Singing Neanderthals: The Origins of Music, Language, Mind, and Body*. Cambridge, MA: Harvard University Press.

Moles, A. (1963). Animal language and information theory. In: R. Busnel (Ed.), *Acoustic Behaviour of Animals* (pp. 112–131). Amsterdam: Elsevier Publishing Company.

Moore, R. (2014). Ontogenetic constraints on Paul Grice's theory of communication. In: D. Matthews (Ed.), *Pragmatic Development in First Language Acquisition* (pp. 87–104). Amsterdam: John Benjamins.

Moore, R., Liebal, K., & Tomasello, M. (2013). Three-year-olds understand communicative intentions without language, gestures, or gaze. *Interaction Studies*, *14*(1), 62–80.

Müller, F. M. (1873). Lectures on Mr Darwin's philosophy of language. *Frazer's Magazine*, *7–8*, 147–233.

Neale, S. (1992). Paul Grice and the philosophy of language. *Linguistics and Philosophy*, *15*, 509–559.

Nettle, D. (2012). Social scale and structural complexity in human languages. *Philosophical Transactions of the Royal Society of London, B*, *367*, 1829–1836.

Nettle, D., Cronin, K. A., & Bateson, M. (2013). Responses of chimpanzees to cues of conspecific observation. *Animal Behaviour*, *86*(3), 595–602.

Nevins, A., Pesetsky, D., & Rodrigues, C. (2009). Pirahã exceptionality: A reassessment. *Language*, *85*(2), 355–404.

New, J. J., & Scholl, B. J. (2008). "Perceptual scotomas": A functional account of motion-induced blindness. *Psychological Science*, *19*(7), 653–659.

Ng, W. L., & Bassler, B. L. (2009). Bacterial quorum-sensing network architectures. *Annual Review of Genetics*, *43*, 197–222.

Nickerson, R. S. (1998). Confirmation bias: A ubiquitous phenomena in many guises. *Review of General Psychology*, 2(2), 175–220.

Noveck, I., & Sperber, D. (Eds.) (2006). *Experimental Pragmatics*. London: Palgrave.

Nowak, M. A., & Krakauer, D. C. (1999). The evolution of language. *Proceedings of the National Academy of Sciences*, *96*, 8028–8033.

Nowak, M. A., Krakauer, D. C., & Dress, A. (1999). An error limit for the evolution of language. *Proceedings of the Royal Society of London, B*, *266*, 2131–2136.

Nowak, M. A., Plotkin, J. B., & Jansen, V. A. (2000). The evolution of syntactic communication. *Nature*, *404*, 495–498.

Odling-Smee, J., & Laland, K. N. (2009). Cultural niche construction: Evolution's cradle of language. In: R. Botha & C. Knight (Eds.), *The Prehistory of Language* (pp. 99–121). Oxford: Oxford University Press.

O'Grady, C., Kliesch, C., Smith, K., & Scott-Phillips, T. C. (under review). The ease, extent, and evolution of recursive mindreading.

Ohtsubo, Y., & Watanabe, E. (2009). Do sincere apologies need to be costly? Test of a costly signaling model of apology. *Evolution and Human Behavior*, *30*(2), 114–123.

O'Neill, D. K. (1996). Two-year-old children's sensitivity to a parent's knowledge state when making requests. *Child Development*, *67*(2), 659–677.

Onishi, K. H., & Baillargeon, R. (2005). Do 15-month-old infants understand false beliefs? *Science*, *308*(5719), 255–258.

Origgi, G., & Sperber, D. (2000). Evolution, communication and the proper function of language. In: P. Carruthers & A. Chamberlain (Eds.), *Evolution and the Human Mind: Language, Modularity and Social Cognition* (pp. 140–169). Cambridge: Cambridge University Press.

Ouattara, K., Lemasson, A., & Zuberbühler, K. (2009). Campbell's monkeys concatenate vocalizations into context-specific call sequences. *Proceedings of the National Academy of Sciences*, *106*(51), 22026–22031.

Owren, M. J., & Bachorowski, J.-A. (2003). Reconsidering the evolution of nonlinguistic communication: The case of laughter. *Journal of Nonverbal Behavior*, *27*, 183–200.

Owren, M. J., Amoss, R. T., & Rendall, D. (2011). Two organizing principles of vocal production: Implications for nonhuman and human primates. *American Journal of Primatology*, *73*(6), 530–544.

Payne, R. S., & McVay, S. (1971). Songs of humpback whales. *Science*, *173*, 587–597.

Penn, D. C., & Povinelli, D. J. (2007). On the lack of evidence that non-human animals possess anything remotely resembling a 'theory of mind'. *Philosophical Transactions of the Royal Society B: Biological Sciences*, *362*(1480), 731–744.

Perniss, P., Thompson, R. L., & Vigliocco, G. (2010). Iconicity as a general property of language: Evidence from spoken and signed languages. *Frontiers in Psychology*, *1*, 227.

Phillips, W., Barnes, J. L., Mahajan, N., Yamaguchi, M., & Santos, L. R. (2009). 'Unwilling' versus 'unable': Capuchin monkeys' (*Cebus apella*) understanding of human intentional action. *Developmental Science*, *12*(6), 938–945.

Piantadosi, S. T., Tily, H., & Gibson, E. (2011). Word lengths are optimized for efficient communication. *Proceedings of the National Academy of Sciences*, *108*(9), 3526–3529.

Piantadosi, S. T., Tily, H., & Gibson, E. (2012). The communicative function of ambiguity in language. *Cognition*, *122*(3), 280–291.

Pinker, S. (1994). *The Language Instinct*. London: Penguin.

Pinker, S. (1997). *How the Mind Works*. New York, NY: Norton.

Pinker, S., & Bloom, P. (1990). Natural language and natural selection. *Behavioral and Brain Sciences*, *13*(4), 707–727.

Pollick, A. S., & de Waal, F. B. M. (2007). Ape gestures and language evolution. *Proceedings of the National Academy of Sciences*, *104*, 8184–8189.

Povinelli, D. J., & Vonk, J. (2003). Chimpanzee minds: Suspiciously human? *Trends in Cognitive Sciences*, *7*, 157–160.

Premack, D., & Woodruff, G. (1978). Does the chimpanzee have a theory of mind? *Behavioral and Brain Sciences*, *1*(4), 515–526.

Provine, W. B. (2001). *The Origins of Theoretical Population Genetics*. Chicago, IL: University of Chicago Press.

Pullum, G. K., & Scholz, B. C. (2002). Empirical assessment of stimulus poverty arguments. *The Linguistic Review*, *18*(1–2), 9–50.

Puts, D. A. (2005). Mating context and menstrual phase affect women's preferences for male voice pitch. *Evolution and Human Behavior*, *26*(5), 388–397.

Puts, D. A., Gaulin, S. J. C., & Verdolini, K. (2006). Dominance and the evolution of sexual dimorphism in human voice pitch. *Evolution and Human Behavior*, *27*(4), 283–296.

Queller, D. C. (1997). Cooperators since life began. *The Quarterly Review of Biology*, *72*(2), 184–188.

Queller, D. C. (2000). Relatedness and the fraternal major transitions. *Philosophical Transactions of the Royal Society of London, B*, *355*(1403), 1647–1655.

Radick, G. (2007). *The Simian Tongue: The Long Debate About Animal Language*. Chicago, IL: University of Chicago Press.

Reader, S. M., & Laland, K. (2002). Social intelligence, innovation and advanced brain size in primates. *Proceedings of the National Academy of Sciences*, *99*, 4436–4441.

Reby, D., & McComb, K. (2003). Anatomical constraints generate honesty: Acoustic cues to age and weight in the roars of Red Deer stags. *Animal Behaviour*, *65*, 317–329.

Reby, D., McComb, K., Cargnelutti, B., Darwin, C., Fitch, W. T., & Clutton-Brock, T. (2005). Red deer stags use formants as assessment cues during intrasexual agonistic interactions. *Proceedings of the Royal Society of London, B*, *272*, 941–947.

Reddy, M. J. (1979). The conduit metaphor: A case of frame conflict in our language about language. In: A. Ortony (Ed.), *Metaphor and Thought* (pp. 284–324). Cambridge: Cambridge University Press.

Regier, T., Kay, P., & Khetarpal, N. (2007). Color naming reflects optimal partitions of color space. *Proceedings of the National Academy of Sciences*, *104*(4), 1436–1441.

Rendall, D., Owren, M. J., & Ryan, M. J. (2009). What do animal signals mean? *Animal Behaviour*, *78*, 233–240.

Roberts, A. I., Vick, S.-J., & Buchanan-Smith, H. M. (2012a). Usage and comprehension of manual gestures in wild chimpanzees. *Animal Behavior*, *84*(2), 459–470.

Roberts, A. I., Vick, S.-J., Roberts, S. G. B., Buchanan-Smith, H. M., & Zuberbühler, K. (2012b). A structure-based repertoire of manual gestures in wild chimpanzees: Statistical analyses of a graded communication system. *Evolution and Human Behavior*, *33*, 578–589.

Roberts, G. (2013). Perspectives on language as a source of social markers. *Language and Linguistics Compass*, *7*(12), 619–632.

Rowe, C. (1999). Receiver psychology and the evolution of multicomponent signals. *Animal Behaviour*, *58*(5), 921–931.

Russell, J. L., Lyn, H., Schaeffer, J. A., & Hopkins, W. D. (2011). The role of socio-communicative rearing environments in the development of social and physical cognition in apes. *Developmental Science*, *14*(6), 1459–1470.

Russell, J. L., McIntyre, J. M., Hopkins, W. D., & Taglialatela, J. P. (2013). Vocal learning of a communicative signal in captive chimpanzees, *Pan troglodytes*. *Brain and Language*, *127*(3), 520–525.

Sandler, W., Meir, I., Padden, C., & Aronoff, M. (2005). The emergence of grammar: Systematic structure in a new language. *Proceedings of the National Academy of Sciences*, *102*(7), 2661–2665.

Scarantino, A. (2013). Rethinking functional reference. *Philosophy of Science*, *80*(5), 1006–1018.

Schel, A. M., Townsend, S. W., Machanda, Z., Zuberbühler, K., & Slocombe, K. (2013). Chimpanzee alarm call production meets key criteria for intentionality. *PLoS One*, *8*(10), e76674.

Schiffer, S. R. (1972). *Meaning*. Oxford: Oxford University Press.

Schmidt, K. L., & Cohn, J. F. (2001). Human facial expressions as adaptations: Evolutionary questions in facial expression research. *American Journal of Physical Anthropology*, *116*(S33), 3–24.

Scholl, B. J. (2010). Comment on R. Kurzban's *Evolutionary Psychology* blog, retrieved 8th September 2013 from http://www.epjournal.net/blog/2010/11/whos-afraid-of-the-big-bad-theory-of-evolution/

Schuster, M., Lostroh, C. P., Ogi, T., & Greenberg, E. (2003). Identification, timing, and signal specificity of *Pseudomonas aeruginosa* quorum-controlled genes: A transcriptome analysis. *Journal of Bacteriology*, *185*, 2066–2079.

Scott, R. M., & Baillargeon, R. (in press). How fresh a look? A reply to Heyes. *Developmental Science*.

Scott-Phillips, T. C. (2008a). Defining biological communication. *Journal of Evolutionary Biology*, *21*(2), 387–395.

Scott-Phillips, T. C. (2008b). On the correct application of animal signalling theory to human communication. In: A. D. M. Smith, K. Smith, & R. Ferrer i Cancho (Eds.), *The Evolution of Language: Proceedings of the 7th International Conference* (pp. 275–282). Singapore: World Scientific.

Scott-Phillips, T. C. (2010a). Animal communication: Insights from linguistic pragmatics. *Animal Behaviour*, *79*(1), e1–e4.

Scott-Phillips, T. C. (2010b). The evolution of communication: Humans may be exceptional. *Interaction Studies*, *11*(1), 78–99.

Scott-Phillips, T. C. (2010c). Evolutionary psychology and the origins of language. *Journal of Evolutionary Psychology*, *8*(4), 289–307.

Scott-Phillips, T. C. (2010d). The evolution of relevance. *Cognitive Science*, *34*(4), 583–601.

Scott-Phillips, T. C. (in press). Non-human primate communication, pragmatics, and the origins of language. *Current Anthropology*.

Scott-Phillips, T. C., & Blythe, R. A. (2013). Why is combinatorial communication rare in the natural world, and why is language an exception to this trend? *Journal of the Royal Society Interface*, *10*(88).

Scott-Phillips, T. C., & Kirby, S. (2010). Language evolution in the laboratory. *Trends in Cognitive Sciences*, *14*(9), 411–417.

Scott-Phillips, T. C., & Kirby, S. (2013). Information, influence and inference in language evolution. In: U. E. Stegmann (Ed.), *Animal Communication Theory: Information and Influence* (pp. 421–442). Cambridge: Cambridge University Press.

Scott-Phillips, T. C., Kirby, S., & Ritchie, G. R. S. (2009). Signalling signalhood and the emergence of communication. *Cognition*, *113*(2), 226–233.

Scott-Phillips, T. C., Dickins, T. E., & West, S. A. (2011). Evolutionary theory and the ultimate/proximate distinction in the human behavioural sciences. *Perspectives on Psychological Science*, *6*(1), 38–47.

Scott-Phillips, T. C., Blythe, R. A., Gardner, A., & West, S. A. (2012). How do communication systems emerge? *Proceedings of the Royal Society of London, B*, *279*, 1943–1949.

Scott-Phillips, T. C., Gurney, J., Ivens, A., Diggle, S. P., & Popat, R. (2014). The extent of combinatorial communication in nature. *PLoS One*, *9*(4), e95929.

Searcy, W. A., & Nowicki, S. (2005). *The Evolution of Animal Communication: Reliability and Deception in Signaling Systems*. Princeton, NJ: Princeton University Press.

Searle, J. (1995). *The Construction of Social Reality*. New York, NY: Free Press.

Senghas, A., Kita, S., & Özyürek, A. (2004). Children creating core properties of language: Evidence from an emerging sign language in Nicaragua. *Science*, *305*(5691), 1779–1782.

Seyfarth, R. M., & Cheney, D. L. (2010). Production, usage, and comprehension in animal vocalizations. *Brain and Language*, *115*(1), 92–100.

Seyfarth, R. M., Cheney, D. L., & Marler, P. (1980a). Monkey responses to three different alarm calls: Evidence of predator classification and semantic communication. *Science*, *210*, 801–803.

Seyfarth, R. M., Cheney, D. L., & Marler, P. (1980b). Vervet monkey alarm calls: Semantic communication in a free-ranging primate. *Animal Behaviour*, *28*, 1070–1094.

Seyfarth, R. M., Cheney, D. L., & Bergman, T. J. (2005). Primate social cognition and the origins of language. *Trends in Cognitive Sciences*, *9*(6), 264–266.

Seyfarth, R. M., Cheney, D. L., Bergman, T. J., Fischer, J., Zuberbühler, K., & Hammerschmidt, K. (2010). The central importance of information in studies of animal communication. *Animal Behaviour*, *80*(1), 3–8.

Shannon, C. E. (1948). A mathematical theory of communication. *Bell Systems Technical Journal*, 379–423.

Silk, J. B., Kaldor, E., & Boyd, R. (2000). Cheap talk when interests conflict. *Animal Behaviour*, *59*, 423–432.

Skarabela, B. (2007). Signs of early social cognition in children's syntax: The case of joint attention in argument realization in child Inuktitut. *Lingua*, *117*(11), 1837–1857.

Skarabela, B., Allen, S., & Scott-Phillips, T. C. (2013). Joint attention helps explain why children omit new arguments. *Journal of Pragmatics*, *56*, 5–14.

Skyrms, B. (2010). *Signals: Evolution, Learning, and Information*. Oxford: Oxford University Press.

Slocombe, K. E., Waller, B. M., & Liebal, K. (2011). The language void: The need for multimodality in primate communication research. *Animal Behaviour*, *81*(5), 919–924.

Smith, A. D. M. (2005). The inferential transmission of language. *Adaptive Behavior*, *13*(4), 311–324.

Smith, A. D. M. (2008). Protolanguage reconstructed. *Interaction Studies*, *9*(1), 100–116.

Smith, K., & Kirby, S. (2008). Cultural evolution: Implications for understanding the human language faculty and its evolution. *Philosophical Transactions of the Royal Society, B*, *363*(1509), 3591–3603.

Smith, K., & Wonnacott, E. (2010). Eliminating unpredictable variation through iterated learning. *Cognition*, *116*(3), 444–449.

Smith, K., Tamariz, M., & Kirby, S. (2013). Linguistic structure is an evolutionary trade-off between simplicity and expressivity. In: *Proceedings of the Annual Meeting of the Cognitive Science Society* (pp. 1348–1353).

Southgate, V., Senju, A., & Csibra, G. (2007). Action anticipation through attribution of false belief by 2-year-olds. *Psychological Science*, *18*(7), 587–592.

Southgate, V., Chevallier, C., & Csibra, G. (2009). Sensitivity to communicative relevance tells young children what to imitate. *Developmental Science*, *12*(6), 1013–1019.

Spence, A. M. (1973). Job market signalling. *The Quarterly Journal of Economics*, *87*(3), 355–374.

Sperber, D. (1996). *Explaining Culture: A Naturalistic Approach*. Oxford: Blackwell.

Sperber, D. (2000). Metarepresentations in an evolutionary perspective. In: D. Sperber (Ed.), *Metarepresentations: An Interdisciplinary Perspective* (pp. 117–137). Oxford: Oxford University Press.

Sperber, D., & Baumard, N. (2012). Moral reputation: An evolutionary and cognitive perspective. *Mind & Language*, *27*(5), 495–518.

Sperber, D., & Origgi, G. (2010). A pragmatic perspective on the evolution of language. In: R. K. Larson, V. Déprez, & H. Yamakido (Eds.), *The Evolution of Human Language: Biolinguistic Perspectives* (pp. 124–131). Cambridge: Cambridge University Press.

Sperber, D., & Wilson, D. (1995). *Relevance: Communication and Cognition* (2nd ed.). Oxford: Blackwell.

Sperber, D., & Wilson, D. (2002). Pragmatics, modularity, and mind-reading. *Mind & Language*, *17*, 3–23.

Sperber, D., Clément, F., Heintz, C., Mascaro, O., Mercier, H., Origgi, G., & Wilson, D. (2010). Epistemic vigilance. *Mind & Language*, *25*(4), 359–393.

Stam, J. H. (1976). *Inquiries Into the Origin of Language: The Fate of a Question*. New York, NY: Harper & Row.

Steels, L. (2011). Modeling the cultural evolution of language. *Physics of Life Reviews*, *8*(4), 339–356.

Stegmann, U. E. (Ed.) (2013). *Animal Communication Theory: Information and Influence*. Cambridge: Cambridge University Press.

Stolk, A., Verhagen, L., Schoffelen, J. M., Oostenveld, R., Blokpoel, M., Hagoort, P., van Rooij, I., & Toni, I. (2013). Neural mechanisms of communicative innovation. *Proceedings of the National Academy of Sciences, 110*(36), 14574–14579.

Strawson, P. F. (1964). Intention and convention in speech acts. *Philosophical Review, 73*(4), 439–460.

Sundie, J. M., Kenrick, D. T., Griskevicius, V., Tybur, J. M., Vohs, K. D., & Beal, D. J. (2011). Peacocks, Porsches, and Thorstein Veblen: Conspicuous consumption as a sexual signaling system. *Journal of Personality and Social Psychology, 100*(4), 664–680.

Suppes, P. (1986). The primacy of utterer's meaning. In: R. Grandy & R. Warner (Eds.), *Philosophical Grounds of Rationality: Intentions, Categories, Ends* (pp. 109–129). Oxford: Clarendon Press.

Surian, L., & Siegal, M. (2008). Language and communication disorders in autism and Asperger syndrome. In: B. Stemmer & H. Whitaker (Eds.), *Handbook of the Neuroscience of Language* (pp. 377–385). London: Academic Press.

Surian, L., Caldi, S., & Sperber, D. (2007). Attribution of beliefs by 13-month-old infants. *Psychological Science, 18*(7), 580–586.

Számadó, S. (2011). The cost of honesty and the fallacy of the handicap principle. *Animal Behaviour, 81*(1), 3–10.

Számadó, S. (2012). The rise and fall of handicap principle: A commentary on the 'Modelling and the fall and rise of the handicap principle'. *Biology & Philosophy, 27*(2), 279–286.

Számadó, S., & Szathmáry, E. (2006). Selective scenarios for the emergence of natural language. *Trends in Ecology & Evolution, 21*(10), 555–561.

Tallerman, M. (2007). Did our ancestors speak a holistic protolanguage? *Lingua, 117*(3), 579–604.

Tallerman, M., & Gibson, K. R. (Eds.) (2012). *The Oxford Handbook of Language Evolution*. Oxford: Oxford University Press.

Tamariz, M., Cornish, H., Smith, K., Roberts, S., & Kirby, S. (2012). The effect of generation turnover and interlocutor negotiation on linguistic structure. In: T. Scott-Phillips, M. Tamariz, E. Cartmill, & J. Hurford (Eds.), *The Evolution of Language: Proceedings of the 9th International Conference* (pp. 555–556). Singapore: World Scientific.

Tan, R., & Fay, N. (2011). Cultural transmission in the laboratory: Agent interaction improves the intergenerational transfer of information. *Evolution and Human Behavior, 32*(6), 399–406.

Tennie, C., Frith, U., & Frith, C. D. (2010). Reputation management in the age of the world-wide web. *Trends in Cognitive Sciences, 14*(11), 482–488.

Theisen, C. A., Oberlander, J., & Kirby, S. (2010). Systematicity and arbitrariness in novel communication systems. *Interaction Studies, 11*(1), 14–32.

Thompson, J. N. (1994). *The Coevolutionary Process*. Chicago, IL: University of Chicago Press.

Thornhill, R. (1976). Sexual selection and nuptial feeding in *Bittacus apicalis* (Insecta: Mecoptera). *American Naturalist, 110*, 529–548.

Tomasello, M. (2003). *Constructing a Language: A Usage-based Theory of Language Acquisition*. Cambridge, MA: Harvard University Press.

Tomasello, M. (2008). *Origins of Human Communication*. Cambridge, MA: MIT Press.

Tomasello, M., & Carpenter, M. (2007). Shared intentionality. *Developmental Science*, *10*(1), 121–125.

Tomasello, M., George, B., Kruger, A., Farrar, J., & Evans, E. (1985). The development of gestural communication in young chimpanzees. *Journal of Human Evolution*, *14*, 175–186.

Tomasello, M., Call, J., & Gluckman, A. (1997a). Comprehension of novel communicative signs by apes and human children. *Child Development*, *68*(6), 1067–1080.

Tomasello, M., Call, J., Warren, J., Frost, T., Carpenter, M., & Nagell, K. (1997b). The ontogeny of chimpanzee gestural signals: A comparison across groups and generations. *Evolution of Communication*, *1*, 223–253.

Tomasello, M., Carpenter, M., Call, J., Behne, T., & Moll, H. (2005). Understanding and sharing intentions: The origins of cultural cognition. *Behavioral and Brain Sciences*, *28*(5), 675–735.

Tomasello, M., Carpenter, M., & Liszkowski, U. (2007). A new look at infant pointing. *Child Development*, *78*(3), 705–722.

Tooby, J., & Cosmides, L. (1992). The psychological foundations of culture. In: J. H. Barkow, L. Cosmides, & J. Tooby (Eds.), *The Adapted Mind: Evolutionary Psychology and the Generation of Culture* (pp. 19–136). Oxford: Oxford University Press.

Vahed, K. (1998). The function of nuptial feeding in insects: A review of empirical studies. *Biological Reviews*, *73*, 43–78.

van der Henst, J.-B., & Sperber, D. (2004). Testing the cognitive and the communicative principles of relevance. In: I. Noveck & D. Sperber (Eds.), *Experimental Pragmatics* (pp. 141–171). London: Palgrave.

van der Henst, J.-B., Carles, L., & Sperber, D. (2002a). Truthfulness and relevance in telling the time. *Mind & Language*, *17*(5), 457–466.

van der Henst, J.-B., Sperber, D., & Politzer, G. (2002b). When is a conclusion worth deriving? A relevance-based analysis of indeterminate relational problems. *Thinking and Reasoning*, *8*, 1–20.

van der Wel, R. P. R. D., Sebanz, N., & Knoblich, G. (2014). Do people automatically track others' beliefs? Evidence from a continuous measure. *Cognition*, *130*(1), 128–133.

van Duijn, M. J. (2012). Reading minds: Narrative and multiple-order intentionality. Poster presented at: *2012 EHBEA annual conference*.

van Hooff, J. A. R. A. M. (1972). A comparative approach to the phylogeny of laughter and smiling. In: R. A. Hinde (Ed.), *Non-Verbal Communication* (pp. 209–243). Cambridge: Cambridge University Press.

van Rooij, R. (2003). Being polite is a handicap: Towards a game theoretical analysis of polite linguistic behaviour. In: M. Tennenholtz (Ed.), *Proceedings of the 9th Conference on Theoretical Aspects of Rationality and Knowledge* (pp. 45–58). New York, NY: ACM Press.

van Schaik, C. P., Isler, K., & Burkart, J. M. (2012). Explaining brain size variation: From social to cultural brain. *Trends in Cognitive Sciences*, *16*(5), 277–284.

Veblen, T. (1899). *The Theory of the Leisure Class*. London: Macmillan.

Verhoef, T., Kirby, S., & de Boer, B. (2014). Emergence of combinatorial structure and economy through iterated learning with continuous acoustic signals. *Journal of Phonetics*, *43*, 57–68.

Vogt, P. (2002). The physical symbol grounding problem. *Cognitive Systems Research Journal*, *3*(3), 429–457.

Wagner, V. E., Bushnell, D., Passador, L., Brooks, A. I., & Iglewski, B. H. (2003). Microarray analysis of *Pseudomonas aeruginosa* quorum-sensing regulons: Effects of growth phase and environment. *Journal of Bacteriology*, *185*, 2080–2095.

Wason, P. C. (1960). On the failure to eliminate hypotheses in a conceptual task. *Quarterly Journal of Experimental Psychology, Section A: Human Experimental Psychology*, *12*(3), 129–137.

Wellman, H. M., Cross, D., & Watson, J. (2001). Meta-analysis of theory-of-mind development: The truth about false belief. *Child Development*, *72*(3), 655–684.

Wharton, T. (2003a). Natural pragmatics and natural codes. *Mind & Language*, *18*(5), 447–477.

Wharton, T. (2003b). Interjections, language and the 'showing-saying' continuum. *Pragmatics and Cognition*, *11*, 39–91.

Wharton, T. (2006). The evolution of pragmatics. In: K. Brown (Ed.), *The Elsevier Encyclopaedia of Language and Linguistics* (2nd ed., pp. 338–345). Amsterdam: Elsevier.

Wharton, T. (2009). *Pragmatics and Non-Verbal Communication*. Cambridge: Cambridge University Press.

Wheeler, B. C., & Fischer, J. (2012). Functionally referential signals: A promising paradigm whose time has passed. *Evolutionary Anthropology*, *21*(5), 195–205.

Whiten, A. (2005). The second inheritance system of chimpanzees and humans. *Nature*, *437*(7055), 52–55.

Whiten, A., & Erdal, D. (2012). The human socio-cognitive niche and its evolutionary origins. *Philosophical Transactions of the Royal Society, B: Biological Sciences*, *367*(1599), 2119–2129.

Williams, G. C. (1966). *Adaptation and Natural Selection: A Critique of Some Current Evolutionary Thought*. Princeton, NJ: Princeton University Press.

Williams, P., Winzer, K., Chan, W. C., & Cámara, M. (2007). Look who's talking: Communication and quorum sensing in the bacterial world. *Philosophical Transactions of the Royal Society of London, B*, *362*, 1119–1134.

Wilson, D. (2000). Metarepresentation in linguistic communication. In: D. Sperber (Ed.), *Metarepresentations: A Multidisciplinary Perspective* (pp. 411–448). Oxford: Oxford University Press.

Wilson, D., & Sperber, D. (1981). On Grice's theory of conversation. In: P. Werth (Ed.), *Conversation and Discourse* (pp. 155–178). London: Croom Helm.

Wilson, D., & Sperber, D. (2004). Relevance Theory. In: L. R. Horn & G. Ward (Eds.), *The Handbook of Pragmatics* (pp. 607–632). Oxford: Blackwell.

Wilson, D., & Sperber, D. (2012). *Meaning and Relevance*. Cambridge: Cambridge University Press.

Wimmer, H., & Perner, J. (1983). Beliefs about beliefs: Representation and constraining function of wrong beliefs in young children's understanding of deception. *Cognition*, *13*(1), 103–128.

Wittgenstein, L. (1953). *Philosophical Investigations*. Oxford: Basil Blackwell.

Wray, A. (1998). Protolanguage as a holistic system for social interaction. *Language and Communication*, *18*, 47–68.

Wray, A. (2000). Holistic utterances in protolanguage. In: C. Knight, M. Studdert-Kennedy, & J. R. Hurford (Eds.), *The Evolutionary Emergence of Language: Social Function and the Origins of Linguistic Form* (pp. 285–302). Cambridge: Cambridge University Press.

Wray, A., & Grace, G. W. (2007). The consequences of talking to strangers: Evolutionary corollaries of socio-cultural influences on linguistic form. *Lingua, 117*(3), 543–578.

Wright, S. (1931). Evolution in Mendelian populations. *Genetics, 16*, 97–159.

Xu, J., Dowman, M., & Griffiths, T. L. (2013). Cultural transmission results in convergence towards colour term universals. *Proceedings of the Royal Society of London, B, 280*(1758), 20123078.

Zahavi, A. (1975). Mate selection: A selection for a handicap. *Journal of Theoretical Biology, 53*(1), 205–214.

Zahavi, A., & Zahavi, A. (1997). *The Handicap Principle: A Missing Piece of Darwin's Puzzle*. Oxford: Oxford University Press.

Zuberbühler, K. (2002). A syntactic rule in forest monkey communication. *Animal Behaviour, 63*(2), 293–299.

Zuberbühler, K. (2005). The phylogenetic roots of language: Evidence from primate communication and cognition. *Current Directions in Psychological Science, 14*, 126–130.

Index of Names

Subject Index

Note: Numbers in **bold** refer to entries in the Glossary.